KU-755-962

Aberdeenshire Library and Information Service
www.aberdeenshire.gov.uk/libraries
Renewals Hotline 01224 661511

After finishing university Oenone Crossley-Holland wanted a job she could really care about. She became a teacher with the Teach First scheme, a charity founded to encourage graduates to work for at least two years in challenging secondary schools. She has written a column for the *Guardian* on her teaching experiences.

HANDS UP!

When Oenone Crossley-Holland started teaching at an inner-city school in London, she had no idea what to expect. She just knew that there was no going back. She would have one of the most challenging years of her life, in which she would get involved in the lives of some wonderfully (and sometimes horrifyingly) exuberant students, and find herself tested to the limit. In this colourful and moving account, Oenone tells of the lows and unexpected highs of the sharper end of teaching. Will she make it through the year? Will she make it through another day?

OENONE CROSSLEY-HOLLAND

HANDS UP!

Complete and Unabridged

ULVERSCROFT
Leicester

First published in Great Britain in 2009 by
John Murray (Publishers)
London

First Large Print Edition
published 2010
by arrangement with
John Murray (Publishers)
An Hachette UK Company
London

British Library CIP Data

Crossley-Holland, Oenone.
  Hands up!.
  1. Crossley-Holland, Oenone. 2. Teachers- -England
  - -London. 3. Schools- -England- -London. 4. London
  (England)- -Social conditions- -21st century.
  5. Large type books.
  I. Title
  371.1'0092–dc22

  ISBN 978–1–44480–480–5

Published by
F. A. Thorpe (Publishing)
Anstey, Leicestershire

Set by Words & Graphics Ltd.
Anstey, Leicestershire
Printed and bound in Great Britain by
T. J. International Ltd., Padstow, Cornwall

This book is printed on acid-free paper

To Robin and Jo

A (FAIRLY) NORMAL WEEK

MONDAY
'Miss.'
'Yes.'
'Miss, you know double-glazing?'
'Yes.'
'Yeah, well would it stop a bullet?'
'No.'
'Well then, what's the point of it being double-glazing, Miss?'

TUESDAY
A proud Year 7 student holds up a piece of paper — A4 lined. While I have been helping other students, she has grabbed hold of my hole puncher. 'Miss, look. It's cheese paper.' And indeed the paper does look like Emmental. 'Oh my,' I say, 'you're mad!' 'But, Miss,' she says, 'it's the best kind of paper.'

WEDNESDAY
'So the salesman went to the house,' I tell the Year 7 class, 'and he knocked and knocked but nobody answered. But when he looked

1

back, he saw the faces of little children in the windows . . . ' I'm standing at the front of the classroom telling a story about a haunted house. I'm coming to the end of the story, and suddenly all the girls start screaming and pointing at the interactive whiteboard, which has taken on a life of its own. The mouse cursor is veering from side to side, and images of creepy-looking houses (that I'd prepared) are flashing up independently. No one is at the computer.

THURSDAY
At the bus stop, a pipsqueak of a girl comes up to me. This particular girl is always talking in class and predominantly off-task. Outside the classroom she can't wait to show me pictures of her dog and interrogate me. Do I like eggs? Am I allergic to cats? She keeps relaying my answers to her friends standing nearby, who call her a teacher's pet. 'Miss, am I a teacher's pet?' she asks. 'No. You are a complete terror in class.' She scrunchs up her nose, uncertain what being a 'terror' might mean. 'Wot, Miss?' 'You're a little monster in class.' Squealing with delight, she relays this reassuring information to her friends.

FRIDAY

The student council are hosting a Red Nose Day fund-raiser. A few of the students have been very inventive with red icing sugar and cream crackers and a group of older pupils have organized a game for the teachers. A panel of pupils have dressed up as teachers, and we have to guess who they are. For an extra ten pence the models come to life and give an impersonation. I can spot myself a mile off. For the extra donation she stands with her hands on her hips staring with huge eyes: 'We're wasting time here. We're not going to get As if we waste time.' Very funny.

AUTUMN TERM
FIRST HALF

The alarm didn't need to go off: I had been half awake for hours, waiting for the moment.

'What time is it?'

'Six.'

'Oh God.'

'Can I make you some breakfast?'

'No. I feel sick. I've got to go. I feel shocking.'

'Me too. I think I'm still drunk.'

I dressed in yesterday's clothes and left, accidentally leaving the front door open.

This had not been the plan. The vodka, the lack of sleep, some guy I'd met on Friday, the prospect of the first day back at school: all along the Central and Jubilee lines I concentrated very hard on not being sick. *Just wait till you get home. You can make it.* Half an hour later, arriving back at my tiny flat, I threw up. I brushed my teeth, had a shower, dressed again, applied make-up around bloodshot eyes, could not contemplate breakfast, then headed out for school.

The bus picked me up from the end of my street and dropped me at the school gates. It is a fifteen minute commute. I sipped at a

7

bottle of Coke. Normally when I take the bus there are a handful of students also heading to my school. The later I am, the more the bus is crammed with them. Mercifully, the arrival of the students in our first week back was to be staggered. Today only the new Year 7s — the students in their first year at the school — would arrive, and they'd been given a later start time, to be inducted rather than taught.

The last few days of the summer holiday are filled with the knowledge that you're enjoying the last moments of freedom before the academic year that stretches ahead of you. The previous year I'd spent the week up until the beginning of school in the South of France with twenty friends. As a pale-skinned redhead, I had a spattering of freckles from hours spent doing very little by the poolside. One of my companions for the train journey back to England was another English teacher, and the two of us spent much of the journey devising what we imagined would be the worst possible way to prepare for the imminent return to school.

'A heavy weekend . . . '

'Booze.'

'Karaoke.'

'Anything to wreck your voice.'

'A pack of cigarettes.'

'Cigars.'

How we laughed.

I measured the distance between my first year of teaching and this, my second. In the classroom next to mine, in my first year, was an English teacher called Sophie. I had watched her very carefully. Sophie had already taught for a year as I began my first one.

'Do you promise?' I would ask her. 'Promise that the second year is not as bad as the first?'

'It'll never be as bad as the first year.'

Every teacher had told me that.

I knew what I was returning to, pretty much, though there would be small changes. Rather than not having the vaguest sense of what I was doing, I'd be qualified and marginally more competent. Sophie had left to teach at another school a stone's throw away, and there would be new members in the department, and new students. But by the time that I was on the bus I was no longer dreading the return. I felt buoyed up in the way one does just before entering an exam, when the sense that there's no turning back overtakes you: I was a bit hyper, spaced from the hangover — but, even so, ready for the new year.

I teach at an inner-city secondary school. I hear they are beginning to be called urban-complex schools. What are the stereo-types it fits? There are a concrete yard, scraps of grass, walls, fences and high gates. There are a few picnic benches and, almost incongruously, a large pagoda in which groups of girls — it is an all-girls school — sit at break time braiding each other's hair. The picnic benches are also turned into ad hoc beauty stations. At one you might see hair extensions being viciously cut out and ripped from a braided scalp, at another, strips of hair about to be sewn in.

The school itself is split across two buildings, divided by a playground just bigger than a basketball court. There is a Victorian block that's four storeys high, and a 1960s tower block with eight floors. Pretty it is not, nor all that functional really. The playground seems always to be at the mercy of the elements. On the last day of summer term, the staff barbecue had to be delayed as torrential rain fell and the playground became a shallow pool. The wind blows across it, driving the break-time crisp packets into small twisters. When the winds are stronger, various doors have to be locked to stop them slamming open and shut of their own accord. On the windiest of days last year I received a text from a fellow teacher at a nearby school: 'The roof just blew off our school! All safe. Three day weekend! Yes!' My own colleagues reported at lunch that some of the smaller children in the school had been picked up by winds and flown across the playground. As a consequence, no one was allowed out at break.

'If you want some fresh air,' one deputy announced over the loudspeaker, 'stick your head out of the window when you get home.'

Snow fell in the winter of last year. I happened to be standing behind our principal as we both picked our way across the lightly covered playground. I heard her ask the men in charge of the premises to make sure the snow was cleared by break time. I made a sad face at the prospect.

'Yes, I know, it seems a bit cruel.'

'Is it because of snowball fights?'

'Yes, and I've known students who've just arrived from hotter countries to fill their blazer pockets with snow — hoping to keep it for later.'

On the first morning back it suddenly seemed quite exciting to be reunited with all the other staff. Julia came up behind me and pinched my waist, I swung round confused for a second as to which teacher knows me well enough to do this. Julia wears perfectly ironed clothes and is intimidatingly good at discipline.

'Did someone tell you to sit down here on these steps outside my classroom?'

'Wot? No . . . '

'No, no, no. That was a *rhetorical* question. That means I wasn't *expecting* an answer. Now stand up.'

I don't know how many times, in my first year, infuriated beyond words, I dragged luckless students into Julia's room after the lesson. With the youngest offenders she'd have them nodding along, and answering her questions in a matter of seconds before she ended the grilling by slipping in a little joke — making them good-natured and repentant. Students whom I felt I could do nothing to get through to would emerge respectful, clear about the rules, and positive about behaving a whole lot better in the following lesson. I always felt thankful towards Julia for straightening out my wayward students, but also a little despondent.

'I think it's because I'm a mum,' she'd tell me. 'You know, I know how to press their buttons.'

Julia doesn't have naughty students in her class. It took me more than a year of teaching to realize that this was a decision she made a long time ago. All through my first year I had a chart on the whiteboard in my classroom. On the right side, beneath a smiley face framed by a halo, I recorded the names of the pupils who were behaving, working, and answering questions in the lesson. And on the left side, beneath a demonic sad face with devil horns, I wrote down the names of bad students. No, not bad students: students whose behaviour was bad. I remember running into Julia's classroom and telling her that I'd had an epiphany. I was going to wipe off the 'bad' side on the board because, like her, 'I don't have naughty students in my class.'

'Nice one, Nony.'

'Yeah. I *do not* have naughty students in my classroom.'

'Yeah.'

But I do have naughty students in my classes, and now there is nowhere to write their names.

My first year was a catalogue of failed attempts. Having had a good track record of success in my life (passed the driving test first time, As at A-level etc.), I now got things wrong lesson after lesson. I took over a class about to sit their GCSEs. For their first lesson I photocopied the first chapter of *Great Expectations* for us to study — I imagined we could read the pages together and discuss them. We didn't even make it through the first paragraph before a fight

13

broke out between two students. They went for each other's hair and throats. I hesitated, not knowing what I should do. Sophie heard shouting and came in to see the whole class out of their seats crowding around the two girls. She sent a student for senior management, and the two girls were taken away.

A little shaken after the fight, I tried to read to the class.

'Wot?'

'Wot, is this in English?' Every other word was foreign to them.

One of the girls caught in the fight went to Sophie's classroom at the end of school every day for several weeks to beg her tearfully to switch her from my class to Sophie's. Sophie didn't tell me till the end of the year.

Learning from my first mistake, for their second lesson I tried to prepare them more digestible extracts of text.

'Miss, wot are brambles?' one girl asked. Sophie had told me one of her students had asked her, perfectly innocently, what the word 'garden' meant.

'Um . . . they're like nature's barbed wire — like on a rose.'

We made slow progress, but at least no fights broke out.

A few lessons later we tried to watch a clip from a DVD of the novel. When Magwitch turned up unexpectedly on the marshes, a few girls genuinely gasped. Others felt a scary moment required full-scale shrieking, and there was a domino effect round the classroom until the whole lot were hysterically screaming and then out of their seats. Teachers from adjacent classrooms ran to silence the class that I could not.

I like school: the hallway; the staff whom I've got to know; the men who look after the premises, who, when they see me, straighten their legs, point at their kneecaps, and shout, 'No knees!' (I do have knees, but people always call me Nony.) It was still gently warm in early September, and I felt the expectation of a new school year. I was as brown as it is possible for me to be — a darker shade of off-white — from two weeks' yachting, and I felt I knew what I was doing, what I was going to be doing, in my classroom.

All through my first year I'd waited for the moment when it would all get better. Other teachers promised each next landmark — Christmas, Easter — as a new start. I kept waiting for a sudden noticeable shift, but it wasn't until the end of the summer term that I realized that I was standing and talking calmly, rather than squeaking out words as fast as I could in the hope of whipping classes into enthusiasm.

The first morning back was a series of quick meetings. All eighty or so teachers gathered in the echoing dining hall, where Cecelia, the principal, welcomed us, announced the GCSE results, and congratulated us on the rise in attainment. Fifty-eight per cent of students had got five or more GCSEs at grades between C and A*. This doesn't sound so bad — the national average for that year was 64 per cent — but when you looked at English and maths there was a dramatic drop. Only 32 per cent — in practice, about 60 students out of just under 200 achieved a C or above in the two subjects that colleges and future employers look for.

Another set of data shows another side of the story. The CVA (contextual value added) score tells you how much a student has gained from the moment they arrive at secondary school, aged eleven, to the point when they leave, aged sixteen. This measurement takes into account what the student's attainment is on joining the school, but also levels of deprivation and special (or additional) educational needs.

Whether a child is entitled to free school meals is an indicator of deprivation — lunch is provided if a parent receives income support or jobseeker's allowance, or if the parent is an asylum-seeker. Twenty-one per

16

cent of all students in England are entitled to free school meals, but just over 60 per cent of the students at my school receive them. Partly because of our intake and partly because of the results we do achieve, the school's CVA is among the highest in the country.

Cecelia also filled us in on the progress of the building works. Just after Christmas, half the staff — myself included — had moved out to Portakabins while the Victorian block was renovated. For the first few months of the autumn term I would still be teaching in the Portakabins. The grey prefabs sit beside a brown sports pitch. The pupils spend their day yo-yoing back and forth between them and the tower block — losing as many minutes on their journeys as possible. When I became infuriated last year with two students who were always late to my lessons, another teacher offered to keep them in at break time for me. A letter was delivered at the end of their short detention:

Dear Ms O. Crossley-Holland

Me and Becky are sorry we are consistantly late to your english lessons, and also for being 15 mintues late to the last lesson on friday.

This will not happen again, but we was on the 7th floor in the other building and it was heavily raining so we waited till it held off a bit, then went to the bathroom.

    Sorry again miss! ☺

    Adalia casas

    ---------X---------

We are one of the new (or maybe not so new now) city academies. Last year, with our new status came a huge injection of money: a massive wad from the government and a smaller amount from our private benefactor. Our private benefactor is a single philanthropist rather than a private business: a local who made good in manufacturing, and has returned to support local education.

★ ★ ★

The second meeting of the day was for the Year 7 tutors. Aged eleven and twelve, Year 7 students are still children. There is no sixth form at the school yet, and so students leave in Year 11 after completing their GCSEs, having turned, or being about to turn, sixteen.

Every day from 8.35 to 8.50 the students are collected and registered in their form groups. Claire leads our team of tutors as the head of Year 7. We ambled up to our first meeting on the sixth floor of the tower block. There were a few grumbles about the fact that, as Year 7 tutors, we would all be tied up with the pupils on the first day, while those attached to other year groups, although technically at work, could savour a few more hours of peace and solitude.

I joined a pastoral team who had worked together for five years. In July the tutors had said goodbye to the Year II students whom they had seen grow from children to young adults, and now they were returning to the beginning with a new set of twenty-five children to oversee. We went around the table introducing ourselves.

'Hello, my name is Oenone and I am really excited about being a Year 7 tutor.'

'Hello, my name is John and I am not looking forward to being a Year 7 tutor.'

'Why not?' I asked.

'Because Year 7s are so little and needy.'

'The thing we have to remember about Year 7s is that they cry,' Claire interjects in the gravest of tones. Everyone groans. Everyone except me. Claire is firm and matter-of-fact, and has a tone I can't put my finger on. I've watched her teach. She is fast but clear. In her never-faltering, serious voice she gives her sixteen-year-olds step-by-step instructions for drawing various mathematical shapes.

'The first step of this exercise will be to take the plastic off the compass. Yes, that's right, take the plastic cover off.'

She's not patronizing the class: this is the first step of the exercise. It's not a joke for the benefit of the other adults in the room — or is it?

After the meeting, the Year 7 pupils gathered in the hall. Some parents accompanied them all the way to their seats, lingering a little, as worried as their daughters. The girls showed varying degrees of discomfort. They were seated alone, or with a group they knew from primary school, or with someone they didn't know and were too scared to strike up a conversation with. There were just under two hundred of them, and they were making less noise than a class of thirty Year 8s.

Waiting for Claire to take over the proceedings, I prowled around the edges and looked for students I'd already met at the induction day last year, or at the interviews that the parents attend to register their children. The school is nonselective: priority is given to parents who already have a child at the school, and after that it is first come, first served. The interviews at the end of the summer term give you a chance to learn a small amount about the child and her parents.

Looking at the rows of girls in navy blazers,

I remembered the students I'd interviewed. One girl had been so sparky. She had dark eyes and a head full of dark curls. She had come to the interview with her mother; she told me her father had died. They were refugees from Afghanistan, and, because the daughter was fluent in English and the mother spoke only Farsi, it was the daughter who confidently supplied me with all the details I needed. I remember feeling quite moved by this small girl who seemed so feisty, and who seemed so eager to make a strong first impression.

Another interview had been more disturbing. The student had left one primary school to attend another. I asked why this was, and the White British mother leaned towards me to take me into her confidence. 'Well, there was some disagreement between the headmistress and me. She was Bangladeshi, you know?' I recorded her words on the form. Among the students seated in the hall I couldn't see the daughter: I don't know why, but she had not taken up a place at the school.

I'm lucky that, though working in a school where 80 per cent of students are not White British, I very rarely come across incidents of racism. Friends teaching at predominantly white schools have told me that racism there

21

is rife. The area surrounding the school has a reputation for antagonism between the indigenous white working-class community and the African and Afro-Caribbean immigrants, but within the school gates the pervading atmosphere is one of respect for diversity — if not respect for authority.

In among the frightened girls taking their seats in the hall, I noticed one who seemed more confident. She had collected a small group, and was busy inviting other lone girls to join. She is called Stella. She's tiny, with a mass of thin braids woven into her scalp and gathered in a small bunch at the crown of her head — and, though only eleven, she circles her eyes in smudged eyeliner and mascara. The school registers her ethnicity as Black Nigerian. As she was arranging and introducing girls, she noticed me.

'Miss,' she said excitedly, 'I told my mum that story.'

'The urban myth about the hook?'

'Yeah, and she told me another one.'

I looked at her eagerly, delighted that my storytelling had made such an impression.

Towards the end of summer term, the girls who were to join the school in September came for the day to get a taste of what the big school would be like. I had been assigned a group to teach a lesson to, and then at the last moment was asked to occupy another group in the library for forty minutes. I grew up listening to my father tell me tales of the Norse trickster god Loki or local folk tales, and so I always know I can tell stories if I can't think up activities out of thin air. And so I had told a few short stories to the girls left in the library, punctuating the telling with small questions to the audience to check they were following. It had been Stella's hand that had shot up first to answer every question. I remember thinking she must be among the brightest of the new intake.

I had hoped Stella would be one of my students, and I warmed to her even more seeing how kind she was being to all the lost sheep.

After a brusque welcome, Claire asked the students to turn to their neighbours and discuss where they'd like to be in ten years. They murmured to each other for a moment, then Claire asked for a few brave volunteers to come to the front to share their ambitions. A few confident hands shot up, and Claire drew them to the front of the hall.

'And what would you like to be doing in ten years' time?' Claire asked the tallest girl in the row.

'I'd like to be a geisha.'

No one heard her clearly or could make

sense of the word. 'Am I the only one who didn't hear that?' Claire asked the rest of the Year 7s.

'I'd like to be a geisha,' the girl repeated.

Emily, another English teacher, standing a few feet away, wheeled her head round and caught my eyes with a worried expression. Claire looked towards other staff in the room, still unsure what this girl was saying. 'Pro-sti-tute.' Emily silently mouthed the word at Claire.

'Ah, yes,' Claire said, recovering the situation — 'this student wants to be a type of Japanese artist.'

After a reminder that whatever they wanted to be in ten years would require hard work now, Claire sent each group of obedient students off with their tutor.

★ ★ ★

The flawless behaviour of the Year 7s for the first few days is unsettling. I like to know who is likely to play up, and I definitely like to know how challenging they will be. Back in my classroom, my tutor group listened to me silently. One timid girl, swathed in a black headscarf, was daunted by the proceedings and wept quietly. I took her outside, and she continued to cry as she tried to tell me all the

24

things that were worrying her. Between sobs, she listed all her uncertainties about what classroom she was meant to be in and when.

The Year 7s had a tour of the school, stemmed their weeping, clutched their new school diaries, saw the classrooms they would go to to be registered each morning, and left for home again with the instruction to return for 8.30 the next day.

My classroom was not as tidy as it might have been. It was sparsely decorated with brightly coloured laminated A4 sheets on which I'd printed out literary terms and grammar tips. '*Ain't* is not a word.' '*Gonna* is not a word.' 'Commas, which are very useful, separate different parts of the sentence.' I'd been in the Portakabins for a whole term while the school buildings were renovated, and, knowing my room was only temporary, I'd done little to it.

I was thankful for the gentle end to summer, as the classroom had boiled in the heat of late spring. The premises staff had installed air-conditioning units, but, as they seemed to add to the noise and chaos of the classroom, I'd decided not to use them. The windows of the room looked down on to a road, traffic lights and the school gate. With all the windows open, the traffic made the quieter voices hard to hear. Sirens would break the calm, and I would pause and wait mid-instruction for them to pass. Outside, city life continued.

The school is flanked by newsagents selling pupils their breakfasts of confectionery. On the streets behind this central road are rows of council blocks. Some students walk to school, but others travel from the neighbouring areas: Elephant and Castle, Peckham, some from edgy Brixton.

' 'Edgy'? What does that mean, Miss?'

'Well, um, Brixton is edgy, trendy . . . slightly dangerous, but also very cool.'

'Brixton? Brixton's cool? According to who?'

I sometimes forget that middle-class perspectives are not universal.

Towards the afternoon I could feel the previous night's lack of sleep slowing me down. I managed to be coolly detached with my tutor group — impressing on them that they could come to me with any questions or worries, but trying my hardest to give the impression that Miss Crossley-Holland is the kind of teacher you don't mess around with.

Once they were gone, I swung into Julia's classroom to confess my night's antics and show her the spattering of text messages that had arrived during the day from the new guy. Julia laughed at me, and, grinning, I reeled back into my classroom.

The last event of the day was a department meeting. There are eleven of us in the department, three of whom were new this September: a new head of department, an NQT (a newly qualified teacher) and another new teacher. The head of department is called Steph, and my first impression of her, as she swept around the classrooms introducing herself at the end of the summer term last year, was that she dressed in natural fibres. I remember that this filled me with confidence, and it was what I reported back to Julia when she asked me what I'd thought about the new leader she had not yet seen.

I was curious to see how Steph would come in and take over a department. Not an easy job.

'Natural fibres in what kind of colours?' Julia had asked me.

'Neutrals, and stripes.'

'Good.'

Julia had spent my first year at the school training me up. As a lead practitioner, she had been given charge of me and set about shaping me in her own mould. We met formally once every week. She would bring me a cup of tea and sit and listen as I relayed how badly recent lessons had gone. She'd laugh and tell me stories of the school she'd previously taught in — how once, driven beyond her breaking point by the students throwing chairs across the room, she'd flipped a few tables to get their attention. It put things in perspective.

One year in, though only an NQT, I had been at the school a whole year more than three of the eleven in the department. I have highly specialized knowledge of how to unblock the photocopier, and where to find essential documents on the shared area of the computer. But I also know that the pupils will behave only as badly as I allow them to, and that if they are shouting at each other, it's because they don't understand the work I'm trying to get them to do. This realization came a good way into my first year of teaching. I remember relaying it to another mentor who was guiding me. He was impressed by how quickly I'd picked this up. What surprises me is how often, after a bad lesson, or a bad day, I forget it.

I remember sitting at my first department meeting last year clueless. I had no idea what I would be doing in the following weeks, and what's more I had no idea what anyone was saying at this meeting I was sitting in. Teachers speak a simplified, clear language for students and a code language with other staff. 'Where are the APP documents for KS3?' Who knows?

As the department sat around the table, we discussed what we would be teaching in the following seven weeks leading up to half-term. Kitty, one of the new teachers, looked as bemused as I had been a year ago.

'You'll pick it all up quickly,' I tried to reassure her.

'Yeah, I'd just like to know what I'm going to be teaching.'

★　★　★

Alone at last, I sat down at my desk. I took out my new timetable and studied it closely. I would be teaching four classes. Two of the classes were Year 7s — the eleven — and twelve-year-olds. The students are streamed by ability, and I had the top-ability Year 7 set and a low-ability set, the seventh group of eight. I had a Year 10 class which also fell under the classification of lower ability, mostly predicted Ds at GCSE, with the odd one predicted an E and one C, and these would be my biggest challenge, I thought. I felt hopeful, though. Julia had achieved the seemingly impossible in the past academic year: she'd taken a very low-ability set, predicted predominantly Es, and in one year enabled them to all achieve Cs and Bs in the English literature and language exams. So I know it is possible. I know that Julia would get up at four in the morning to mark work to return to her class quickly. And she worked as hard at raising self-esteem — blasting them with quotations from Oprah Winfrey — as she did at enabling her students to write essays. Her hold on discipline is unflinching. The last set I'd be teaching was a group of Year 11s — the second-from-top Year 10 set I had had last year. I would be taking them for their final year at the school, preparing them in the run-up to their GCSE exams.

After noting the lessons I would be teaching in my planner, I sketched out the shapes of the tables on a blank piece of paper. A seating plan for the Year 11s. Without looking at a register, I arranged the thirty names across seven tables. Abimbola cannot sit next to Becky, and Becky and Adalia need to be on separate sides of the room. Aysha is on my side, so she can be responsible at the back of the room. Adalia needs to be at the front, but at the side. Putting less able with more able, loud with quiet, criss-crossing the page with my pen I mapped out something which I hoped would work. With the Year 7 classes and the Year 10 class I could do no more than arrange the names alphabetically. I grimaced as I read through the Year 10 register — I didn't know any of the students, but I'd heard far too many of the names mentioned across the staff dining table at lunch. As a precautionary measure, I logged on to the school computer system and painstakingly looked up each child's details. I copied out the list of phone numbers and the names of the parents or guardians. Some of these numbers would graduate to being stored in my mobile.

Ella was waiting for me at home. Last December, after returning from a company Christmas trip to Dubai, my ever-enthusiastic flatmate announced that she was throwing in her glamorous marketing job to teach. After a few months of watching me vacillate between highs and lows, she wanted something similarly exhausting. She'd been placed in a school way out in north London, and today had been her first day too — but a day of staff training, no kids.

It was still light when I got into bed. After my first day last year I had had to go for a long run to use up some of the energy I was buzzing with. Today I'd had just enough adrenalin to make it home. I'd returned Will's extravagantly flattering text messages with more cautious ones mimicking the voices of his students — he had also had his first day at school, a prep school in north London, worlds apart from my own academy.

'Sir, why do you smell of vodka?'

'Because vodka is my cologne of choice thanks to teaching you treasures . . . ' Like Ella, he had in fact had a staff training day — no students to breathe over.

I was drifting off when I received an unexpected expected phone call. He suggested supper on Friday.

★ ★ ★

Tuesday felt like the real beginning.

Come into my classroom silently. Sit down. Take out your school diary. Copy down the date and the learning objective from the board. Start the first task — there will be instructions on the board. In this classroom, nobody speaks over anybody else. When I speak, you listen. No gum, no litter on the floor, no drawing on the desks. Are we all clear?

The new Year 7s are no less lost than they had been on Monday. They are wide-eyed and terrified. Not just of me, but of the long corridors, the big buildings, the bigger students. They are perfect in this state. They fly through the lesson I've prepared, listening intently to each other, crisply falling silent whenever I tap three times on my desk — something we've practised first. Some hover near me at the end of the lesson holding out their diaries, tears in their eyes, asking where they are meant to go next. Half of me wants to be the very picture of reassurance, but I know it's suicidal to start off warmly.

My Year 7s are at the tables where I've placed them. They sit in groups of four next to someone who has either the place in front or the place behind on the register. I know that in a week or two I'll need to shift students around: carefully place the fidgeters and talkers away from each other, keep one or two in hot spots, always directly in my line of vision. But for the first days I don't need to worry about bad behaviour, just make sure that I set routines in place using a voice which says, *I mean it, I'm one step ahead of you*.

The girls have been students for far longer than I have been a teacher. And by the second time we meet, knowing what to expect, they are poised and waiting, observing everything. They automatically do the tasks I've told them about in the previous lesson. Diaries go on to tables; some place well-stocked pencil cases beside them, others just have a pen — but at least, at this point in the year, they do have a pen. My voice rings out, and only I can hear its slight uncertainty.

I am still relatively new to this teacher game, and in front of a class I don't know I feel to begin with that I'm still trying on the role for size, still growing into it.

In my top Year 7 set (the top stream), I notice a girl with unusual poise — Camilla. Her movements are very slow and graceful, she has an air of maturity and gentleness, and I suspect that she, if anyone, knows that I am still learning. And indeed, when she writes later in the term of her first impressions of the school, she remarks, 'The English teacher didn't even look like she chose the right profession. She barely looks a day over twenty-one.' In her first letter to me, set as a homework task to help me get to know the students and to give me a first chance to assess their ability, she tells me her thoughts for the future: 'I've thought about being a model to put my legs to good use, but also considered being a lawyer to make use of my brain.'

The students are dressed in green. Bright-green shirts, navy-blue blazers, and navy pleated skirts. In any classroom, only a handful are White British: the others have their roots in distant countries — many are Nigerian and Turkish, but others are from Sierra Leone, Eritrea, Afghanistan, Pakistan, India or Colombia. A large handful wear a hijab; others have complex patterns of braids and cornrows. The white students, by and large, have pale complexions, hair blonde or light red.

I have a treat in store for my two Year 7 sets. We are going to be studying, over the course of the first half-term, Robert Browning's poem 'My Last Duchess.' Crimes of passion, adultery, jealousy, a victim, a villain: I'll spin the poem out, so each lesson they'll get a tiny piece of evidence to add to their investigation, a line from the poem which is its own riddle.

'I want everyone in the class to show me in a freeze frame what you think the word 'crime' means. You need to get into a position, staying in your chairs, and show me the meaning of the word.'

Twenty-five girls silently grab knives and point guns; some look mischievous, and a few are very uncomfortable about having to perform.

'Good — hold those positions.'

My eyes scan each actor approvingly, picking out particularly dramatic poses, eyes that are popping out of heads, hands that grab imaginary necks.

'Right. And now I want you to show me what you think the word 'passion' means.'

More students are uncertain this time, but

most hug imaginary figures and pout their lips. One girl holds the expression of a distressed opera singer.

'Good. Now you have two minutes on your table to discuss what you think a 'crime of passion' might be. Go!'

At eleven I went down to the staffroom.

'Hello, love,' Jan poured tea into a styrofoam cup. She presides over a tray of pastries at break time, and at lunch doles out generous portions as long as her boss isn't watching. I sit down with the few English teachers in the room and sip scalding-hot tea.

'My 7s are a-m-a-z-i-n-g,' I said.

'I've already had to talk to one of mine,' said Steph. 'She couldn't sit still. Amber.'

'Oh yeah, she's in my tutor group. I had to move her to a seat away from the others this morning.'

We gave each other the obligatory round up of our respective summer holidays and then the fifteen minutes were up — how could it be lesson time already? — and we traipsed back to our rooms.

* * *

I see each of my classes four times a week, and because the Year 7s had Monday to find their way around the academy before the

36

older students returned, we had two school days before I was reunited with the students I taught last year, now in their final GCSE year. A few came to see me in my classroom to say excited hellos, and a couple rushed to hug me awkwardly.

'Miss!' Adalia screamed my name in the corridor. I was standing with Kitty, who flinched at the sound and looked bemused and a little horrified as Adalia threw her arms round me.

'Miss, I got an A★ in my Spanish.'

'That's amazing!' She'd taken the GCSE in her mother tongue a year early to get it out of the way. Adalia spent most of last year either with her head on the desk or wildly chatting with whoever she was sitting next to, if I was lucky, or someone across the room if I was not. She is Argentinian, tall and curvy, and clearly spent much time making herself up for school every day.

I try to be clear in my mind that this term is a fresh start with the Year 11s. Last year, they were a class I always looked forward to seeing, but at the end of the hour more often than not I felt very frustrated. They are bright and perceptive, but I regularly felt like a sea wall unable to hold the surge of thirty fifteen-year-old girls vying for help or boisterously disrupting the waters. Actually, that was towards the end of the year. At the very beginning, they were downright riotous. And after that, as payback for my phone calls and letters home, they held a silent protest and refused to speak a word. It was Becky — a Jamaican girl — who eventually broke the protest: though no angel herself, she spat out that she thought it was stupid and she wasn't going to play along. Becky is rather beautiful when she isn't scowling; she has quite a pale round face, with a spattering of freckles across her nose. She's a strange combination of anger and embarrassment.

Within about five minutes of our first lesson I know I have not created a fresh start, and my familiar manner undermines my attempts to run through the rules I expect them to follow. Having known them for so long, and liking them so much, I find myself very weak at re-establishing better behaviour. Rather than firmly instilling a sense that we are at the beginning of a new year — their all-important GCSE year — I feel as if we're only picking up from where we left off: not so much chaos, but uncertain order.

'Adalia, listening.'

I touch my earlobe automatically as I give the instruction.

'Sorry, Miss,' she chimes. Always politely apologetic, but always talking.

'Becky, facing the front.' Following her moment of glory, drawing an end to the silent protest, Becky had a chequered time. I hoped it would be a good year for her, though I knew the odds weren't strongly in her favour. With my previous Year 11 set, the changes that I'd always hoped would happen as the exams drew close never materialized. I was now under the impression that students didn't change their spots.

'Thank you, Adalia.'

'Girls, *listening* . . . ' I'm not impressed that I haven't managed to get silence.

I tell them I've thought about them a lot over the summer: 'I went sailing round the Greek islands, but as I was sunbathing on the boat I was thinking about what we need to do this year.' A few giggle at me as I describe the scene. If I perform stories for them, or play up to any role, they quickly become malleable.

My role of geeky English teacher appeals to their indulgent sides. 'I've written three aims for us to have in our minds over the year — things I really want us to concentrate on. I was thinking, as I was putting on suncream, Is there one thing that might stop you all from getting the best grade possible come the exams? I think you are all really bright, you have fantastic ideas . . . but most of you write

39

very slowly. We need to concentrate on developing our ability to write good quality and sufficient quantity under timed conditions. I also want us to take pride in our work, and to develop our thinking about what literature teaches us for life, not exams.'

There was one new girl in the class, used to being the only black girl in her school, and I wondered what she was making of all the commotion and the young teacher at the front trying to focus the class on the year ahead.

Three classes down, only one more to meet. I went down to lunch. Julia interrogated me on whether I'd received any more text messages.

'Yeah. He rang. We're seeing each other on Friday. I'm not sure — he seems quite intense,' I said, pulling an uncertain face.

'Oh, you make me laugh,' she said giggling.

★   ★   ★

I knew the Year 10s were going to be a difficult group. Unlike the Year 7s, they have been at this school longer than I have. It makes me think that they know things I don't. And, rather than being children, they are intimidating teenagers. They have just sat their SATs exams, and based on their results

40

in these they are predicted Es and Ds in their GCSEs.

I hold my seating plan and stand in the doorway, blocking the entrance. They arrive in dribs and drabs.

'Good morning. You are . . . ?'

'Coleen.' Not smiling, wary, looking out from under a heavy, straightened fringe which is surrounded by masses of dark curls, looking at me as if she is severely displeased to be here.

'Right, can I have you on this table here?'

'And you are?' I ask, turning to the next girl bustling to get past me and through the door.

'Siobhan,' she says, as if it's strange I'm asking her name. She's white and quite tall, with a blonde ponytail gelled to her head. Around the hairline she's carefully sculpted any loose wisps of hair into small curls which are also glued down. She is clutching a large, green mock-croc handbag that serves as her school bag. Completely uninterested in what I am about to say, she switches her attention to Coleen, who shouts across me, 'She's done a seating plan.'

'Hello, Siobhan, I'd like you to sit on that seat underneath the window,' I tell her. Siobhan throws her handbag down on to a table on the other side of the room.

I place a few more students, then realize that the seating plan has, for some reason, fallen apart.

'Siobhan, please can you sit in the place where I asked you to sit.'

'Oh but, Miss, I don't want to sit there. I can't sit with her.' Adamant, forceful.

I cajole her back into her seat, and turn to deal with others who are struggling to follow my first instructions. Siobhan, without my noticing, has again slipped to the other side of the room.

Several students have entered the classroom with blank faces; they eye me up slowly with a look of outright disdain. This is not where they want to be they seem to say as they stretch back in their chairs, bags on their backs, arms folded. Others clearly don't trust me but are reserving final judgement till later on. Folashade enters last. She comes in, eyes me up and down, and makes it perfectly clear in her first thirty seconds in the room that she is not lacking in loud confidence. Lakeisha alone is self-assured and kind enough to give me the benefit of the doubt from the beginning. She smiles exposing rows of braces. She is small and pretty, and has a black headscarf covering her hair. She sits looking me in the eye and listens carefully.

By the time I get around to finally stating

my rules and routines, they have flouted most of them. I know I will keep several girls back at the end to speak to them.

'We're going to start your GCSE course-work with the creative-writing piece,' I tell them. 'And the way we are going to start is by looking at a poem. This poem is one of the poems you will need to know for your exams in two years' time. But we're going to start by answering some questions in groups about each stanza of the poem. Who can tell me, raising your hand, what a stanza is?'

No hands go up, but lots of voices shout out various answers.

'OK, I need you to put up your hands, because we can't hear each other if we all talk at once.'

Silence.

I distribute Carol Ann Duffy's poem 'Education for Leisure' — a stanza to each table, with a small list of questions. Who is speaking? What do they think of themselves? What do they think of the outside world? 'Try to find evidence in your stanza to back up your answers. You're going to feed back to the class in eight minutes.'

Chaos descends. I go to one table, crouch down, and ask who is going to read the words to the rest of the table. One student starts quietly:

43

Today I am going to kill something. Anything.

'Sounds like a psychopath,' Coleen grumbles, her face almost hidden by her hair. 'Good,' I say fiercely, wanting to shock her into sitting up and paying attention. 'Can you tell me *why* you think he sounds like a psychopath?' Coleen shifts forward in her seat, encouraged by my frighteningly positive response, though maintaining a look of bored uninterest on her face.

I work my way around each table, asking them the questions on the sheet and trying to get them to link their answers to the text. It is difficult to work like this, as all the five groups I am not with raise their voices in pandemonium. A few quieter students are attempting the task, but the loud majority make it difficult to hear anything. Every few minutes I strain to raise my voice above theirs and tell them to settle and quieten down, which they do, for a few seconds.

Before the students share their findings with the rest of the class, I read the whole poem out:

Today I am going to kill something.
Anything.

The line has the effect I want. It is startling, and the students pay attention. I try to sound rather manic while I read the poem. I rather fancy the idea that the class think I am as mad as the speaker.

The students have listened to the poem, but when it comes to listening to each other the proceedings fall apart. Several separate conversations are going on while groups are trying to share their small observations. We go through a pattern. I stop the proceedings, apologizing to the person who is speaking. I turn to the girls talking to each other and ask them to stop, explaining that it is rude to speak over other people. They stop while I am speaking to them, before turning back to each other to finish the last words of their conversation. I wait impatiently for them to shut up so that I can ask the original speaker to resume sharing her thoughts.

While things were not working out as one would hope, I thought about the lesson. Group work had been an unmitigated disaster. No freedom for this class. No chance to waste away the hour. I would need to guide them much more from the front of the classroom, giving them much smaller tasks. The one concrete thing I felt I had learned from my first year teaching was that students need to be given a task, given minimal guidance, and left to their own devices to actively rather than passively learn. How was

I going to pull that off here?

Somehow, with all the stopping and starting, the lesson is quickly over. I summarize my thoughts about the lesson and share them with the class. 'Well done to those of you who participated today and who were not disruptive. To those of you who were disruptive I would like to say this: my job is to enable you to achieve. I am not interested in anybody stopping anybody else learning. Could I speak to Folashade, Erez, Coleen, and Siobhan now please. Everyone else may go to break. Please tuck your chairs under.'

Again I stand at the door, to make sure that those asked to stay behind don't make a quick exit. The selected few take a defensive stance, arms folded, heads turned away from me. I take out my planner and turn to the page where I had copied down the telephone numbers of the parents and carers for each of the students in this class. How satisfying to be so well armed.

I sit down and address the lesser offenders, Siobhan and Coleen.

'I want you to take this as a very serious verbal warning.' Their heads are down, chins pushed forward. 'Your behaviour today was unacceptable. I want to see a big improvement tomorrow. Do you understand what I'm saying?'

Siobhan flashes a smile, 'Yes, Miss.'

'You may go, Siobhan.'

Coleen flashes her eyes up at me and tilts her head to acknowledge what I've said.

'Right, Coleen, you may go.'

The two who've been allowed to leave burst into loud protestations and laughter as the door closes behind them.

Folashade and Erez remain. I pull my planner towards me and scan down to Folashade's mother's number. When they see what I am going to do, both students' defiant expressions were noticeably softened by a hint of surprise.

Folashade's mother answers, and I explained that her daughter's behaviour had been unacceptable today, that I expected she would arrive at the next lesson as a well-behaved student, and that other staff had in fact told me that Folashade was polite.

The mother asks to speak with her daughter, and I hand over the phone. Folashade takes it delicately, struggling to grip it between fake nails which are intricately painted with small swirls of colour and embedded with diamante studs. She breaks the scowl she'd been fixing me with and smiles as she lies through her teeth about how she had not been talking, not been rude. I can hear her mother shouting irately at the other end of the phone. Folashade moves the phone several centimetres away from her head and looks at it with distaste as it vibrates with her mother's anger. She shows no remorse.

* * *

Aside from the errant behaviour of my Year 10s, the first days and week went ridiculously well. I was back in the swing of term time. A year previously everything was hit and miss — whether students learned anything in my lessons was pot luck. Now I was covering material I was familiar with. Even when I'd had no idea what I was doing in my first year, I'd still felt I'd found a job I'd be happy to stay in — it was so endlessly challenging and exhausting in the kind of way that means you felt excited rather than depressed. By October of my first year I was reading articles about fast-track leadership programmes and fancying myself as a head of an inner-city school. A year on, I still felt confident that I wanted a career in education.

The first few dates with Will had also gone rather well. He'd arranged supper at his house for Friday. He'd sent messages checking that it would be OK to watch at least the first half of some rugby match on Friday evening. I dropped in to see a male member of the English department, John, an Antipodean sports enthusiast, to find out his thoughts on a guy who was proposing an evening watching rugby for a first date.

'Well, it is the opening match of the World Cup . . . ' he said in the most sympathetic of tones.

'Yes, but for a first date? Would you suggest that?'

'No . . . '

'Does it suggest he's not really that bothered?'

'Look, did you suggest going for a drink?'

'No, I said I didn't want to sit opposite him in a restaurant and feel like I was getting the Spanish Inquisition.'

'Well then. Rugby sounds good to me.'

'Hm. We'll see.'

During the first weeks of school, lessons were meticulously planned, the first pieces of writing were marked, and yet I still left well before five to go home and meticulously plan what to wear to meet Will. For the Friday supper at his house I had chanced it and turned up with an overnight bag. He prepared a meal of raw sliced aubergine, sliced tomatoes and fried chicken.

'Look at the colours of the aubergine . . . Cutting them with this knife is heaven — this is my favourite knife.' We sat eating in front of the match. I feigned a small amount of interest in the rugby, and sat quietly as he stood up to sing the French national anthem at the top of his voice.

We'd first met each other a few days before the fateful ten hours of Sunday vodka-drinking. Ella had found him out in Ireland, in a small village they had both spent many summers holidaying in. She had thought the two of us might like each other, and so invited him round for supper.

'He's thirty-seven.'

'That's definitely too old.'

'He's very good-looking in a kind of striking way. He sort of looks like a pirate.'

'Tall?'

'Yes, very.'

'How tall?'

'Well over six foot.'

'And he's a teacher?'

'Yes, a prep-school teacher — but he used to do some kind of travel journalism.'

'Hm. I don't think I want to go out with a teacher.'

Ella had shown me his picture on Facebook.

'No, I don't think so . . . He looks like Bob Geldof . . .'

Both being teachers gave us tremendous ground to cover for the first month of suppers. He listened as I described the graduate teaching scheme I was on.

'The idea with Teach First is that you dedicate two years to addressing educational disadvantage in inner-city schools. And then, after two years, you can either leave, and get a job in the City or doing whatever, or you stay on in teaching. But if you leave, you're still part of the mission to address educational disadvantage.'

'Oh my God, you're part of a cult,' said Will.

'No . . . well . . . they did make us chant the mission statement.'

'Oh my God. You've been had. It's a con. No training, and then into schools where you'd have to be fucking insane to work.'

'Yes, in at the deep end — no life raft, no bulletproof vest.'

This was not quite the case. I'd had six weeks down in Canterbury at Christ Church University during the summer to prepare me for my first year — and then at school I'd been assigned to Julia, who was willing to work as hard to make me a good teacher as she was to make her F-grade students, who other teachers said were unteachable, get solid Bs in both their English exams. Every time she made her students a certificate decorated with pictures of SpongeBob and proclaiming 'Miss Miller is proud of you,' she'd make me one too.

Julia would sit at the back of my class for one lesson each half-term. Her pen barely stopped moving, writing down what the students were saying, writing down what I was saying. The feed-back was not for the faint-hearted. When you don't know much about teaching, there's a long way to go to get good. After a few perfunctory comments about what I had done right — books on the table before the lesson; stayed calm; good preparation — she'd get down to the point.

'I think the behaviour is really stopping you from teaching.'

'Yes . . . I know . . . I don't know what to do.'

'Did you see Jamie was eating crisps?'

'No.'

'And who's that girl who was sitting there,' Julia pointed to the spot where Tracey sits. 'She was being very undermining. Use the behaviour system to get people out of the room who are undermining your authority.'

The problem was that, in the first year, I didn't really feel I had any authority, and so sort of saw it as perfectly natural, and to be expected, that the students sabotaged the lessons.

Julia would go through behaviour techniques again and again with me.

'Tone of voice. You've naturally got quite a soft voice. You need to work on an 'I mean it' voice. And I sometimes walk around a class with a book in my hand, just looking at them and writing down any old thing, and it really freaks them out — they get all scared and are like 'Miss, Miss, what are you writing down about me?' You've just got to pick them off one by one and find their weak spot. Find a way of getting to them. It's psychological warfare.'

During the evenings when we weren't having to watch another important rugby match, Will and I sat relaying details from lessons.

'I've had them practising indenting the beginning of their paragraphs today and using commas,' Will told me.

'Gripping,' I said.

'Yes. I made one of them the tsar of commas, and then they all wanted to be tsars so they made up their own titles.'

'Tsars?'

'Yes, so one boy wrote . . . ' Will laughed so hard he couldn't finish his sentence. 'He wrote, 'My name is Adam and I am the monkey tsar, and my job is to feed the monkeys like Mr Davis.'

'He wrote that? That's so cheeky.'

'I've told my Year 7s that I'm going to

throw them out of the window if they forget to write in paragraphs,' I said to Will.

'Defenestration — fantastic punishment. You should also threaten keelhauling.'

'I don't know what that is.'

'On boats, a sailor was thrown over the edge with a rope tied around his feet. His friends stood on the other side of the boat and had to pull him up before he drowned.'

'Oh my God.'

'But of course if he didn't drown, what else might happen to him?'

I gasped. 'He could be knocked out by the rudder?'

'Or, what do you get on the underside of boats that have been in the water for a long time?'

'Oh my God, barnacles.'

'Yeah, you'd be ripped to shreds by barnacles.'

'That's a fantastic punishment to threaten them with. Thank you, Will.'

And of course we debated the ins and outs of the education systems in which we worked until we had said everything there was to be said.

'You're wasting your energy trying to teach kids who don't want to learn.'

'Why should where you're born decide your future?'

'That's the way it is.'

Will always took a staunch Conservative line for the sake of a good argument: private education for those who can afford it; grammar schools to cream off the brightest; forget the rest.

'You can't do that.'

'OK, throw resources at the schools for the remaining students.'

Indoctrinated by Teach First, I argued a marginally less Conservative line: private schools should set the bar high, and then non-selective state schools with phenomenal teaching and strict rules should provide everyone with a good education regardless of parents' financial or social circumstances.

'It can't be done.'

'It can be.'

★　★　★

Back in the classroom, my new Year 10s had a lesson on how to use alliteration, a lesson on varying sentence length, a lesson on how to use repetition for effect, and a lesson on how to suggest something rather than explain it. Only a couple of weeks after the first disastrous lesson with them, they began to lull me into a false sense of expectation that we might actually achieve something this year. Each lesson Folashade, Coleen, Erez or Siobhan would be sent to another classroom, having run out of warnings; the next lesson they'd find a new English-department report on their desks with three personalized targets for them to try to achieve in the following lessons. But those girls who had been reticent and untrusting at first slowly began to quieten for me when I asked and to listen carefully to what I was saying. I gradually began to see each character: the more confident Chamel, who is happy to be called upon for answers and completely unbothered if she gets them wrong; quiet, anxious Cally, who does not speak in front of the class; and Ummi, who I thought would be better cast as a mythic benign faun in a forest rather than a student in a navy blazer.

By mid-September the 10s had a new seating plan, and were being bribed in each lesson with thank you slips to be cashed in for prizes at the end of the week. The slips were dished out any time a student was seen doing what she was supposed to be doing.

'Well done for putting up your hand.'

'Well done for listening carefully.'

'Well done for attempting the work.'

I marvelled to see how the fifteen-year-olds waited with bated breath for a piece of paper. The lesson came when they were ready to write their first piece of GCSE coursework — a piece of creative writing.

Before the class I line them up outside the room and stand with my arms folded, waiting for silence. They don't fall silent, and so Julia, who is also standing at her door (her own students were already sitting silently in her room), came to assist.

'Listen up, girls . . . ' For some reason they immediately fall almost completely silent. 'Now, I'm already teaching and Miss here is *trying*' — her voice has been very calm, but now she is clearly showing them she is not pleased, 'to get you lined up quietly so that you can go into the class and do the lesson she has *planned* for you to do.'

Complete silence — except that Siobhan and Erez, who are lounging against the wall at the back of the line, slightly round the corner, are giggling and talking to each other.

'Right, Miss, you take the rest in — I need to speak to those two girls at the back.'

I'm about to take them in, feeling thankful but somehow as though I've also had a bit of a talking-to myself, when the deputy head walks by.

'Right, girls, what's going on here?'

They shuffle towards my door quietly.

'Coleen, earrings please . . . '

The rest of the class are settled and

sobered by Julia's efforts and the presence of the deputy, and wait quietly. Coleen enters, eyes red, tears streaming down her face. She sits down and lays her head on the desk. The two fifty-pence-sized non-regulation diamante earrings have been confiscated.

'Right,' deep breath, fresh start, 'you've all got a booklet in front of you with lots of pictures in it — Coleen, listening.' (She is angrily discussing jewellery with those surrounding her.) 'I want you all to imagine you are in the picture, and I'm going to ask you some questions. Without talking to anyone, just write down your thoughts about the picture on the page and your answers to any of the questions I ask.'

All good so far. At Julia's suggestion, the class are set to write creatively about being in a cell in a prison. Julia is keen on macabre subject matter: war, death, witches, murder — it tends to produce better results.

'OK, everyone listening, I want you to look at the first picture.'

Julia pops her head around the door.

'Miss, those two students I was speaking to won't be coming to your lesson today.'

'Thank you,' I mouth without speaking, and in her eyes I can see she's telling me that she *tried* to explain to them *politely* what the appropriate way to behave was, but that they

58

chose not to listen sensibly to her and so will suffer the consequences.

'Right . . . looking at the first picture, what does that bed feel like to lie on . . . what does the blanket feel like?'

'Wait, Miss, what are we meant to do?'

'Miss, you're going too fast.'

'Wot?'

'What are we doing?'

Coleen has taken the opportunity of the break in the silence to continue the earlier conversation.

'OK.' I am patient. I am a patient, calm person. 'Let's do the first one together.'

We work through the booklet, and the girls record the sounds they can hear at night when they're supposed to be sleeping, the temperature of the steel bars when they wake in the morning. They journey through the long, fluorescent lit, polished-concrete corridors writing down their impressions.

At the end of their note-making, I read them an example of a descriptive piece that I have written. They go through it highlighting examples of short sentences, repetition, alliteration. They identify that each paragraph tends to concentrate on one sense — what can be heard, or what is felt.

Finally it is their turn to write the first section of the piece of creative writing. I've prepared them to write in as many ways as I can think of, and, by what seems like some miracle, I set the task and for forty minutes there is only the sound of thank-you slips drifting down on to tables.

There is one student, though, who I'm clearly not getting very far with. Her mother's number is saved on my phone.

'Hello, Mrs Randel, it's Oenone Crossley-Holland, Coleen's English teacher.'

'Yes, hello.'

'I was wondering if you'd be able to come in for a meeting with me — and Coleen. I think it might be helpful if we all sat down and discussed how we're going to move forward.'

'Yes, I can come in.'

'Could you come in tomorrow after school? At 3.15?'

★ ★ ★

In the moments before her mother arrived at reception downstairs, Coleen sat across a table from me. The windows and wall were behind her, my own desk to her left and my right. She is Turkish, and looks rather like a Persian cat. As with many of the students, I think she would be very beautiful if she smiled more and grimaced less. As she's no more than five foot, I tower above her, but she's not intimidated. Her eyes were lidded with metallic turquoise eyeshadow, the diamante earrings returned and ensconced.

With just the two of us in the room, she is not hostile.

'Have you thought about what you'd like to do after you leave here?' I ask.

Without looking at me, she shakes her head.

'Like, for sixth-form college? Are there any courses you've thought about?'

These are questions with a specific purpose. After she's told me what she would like to do, I will work my way back round to English and how, considering she's got to be in the class anyway, she might as well give the subject her best shot.

'Art maybe.'

'Art . . . wow, that's brilliant. What kind of art do you like making?'

And now everything changes. In an instant she is bashful and animated, smiling in between her answers.

'Lots of kinds. Painting and drawing.'

'Wow, so you must be doing art GCSE?'

'Yeah, an' I was chosen to do classes in the summer and we went down to that place on the river.'

'Um, the Tate?'

61

'Yeah, there I think. Yeah.'

'That's great.' This is wonderful — a normal conversation between the two of us.

'Do you want to call your mum to ask how she's getting along?' I ask, and pass her my phone. Coleen rings, grumbles at her mum, then tells me, 'She's downstairs.'

I go and collect her, and by the time we return Coleen's body language has reverted to pre-art conversation.

'So,' I start, 'as you know, I've asked your mum to come in because I'm concerned about your behaviour in class.' I look towards Coleen's mother as I'm saying this, and she nods her head in agreement.

'Coleen was just telling me how she really enjoys art, and that's fantastic. And I can see she probably doesn't think English will be of much use to her in the future, but I know that if she gets a C grade in English then any college that she wants to go to will open its doors for her. And . . . ' I'm in full fully-rehearsed mode, 'and, aside from the qualification, Coleen, you're always going to be using English. If you were talking about your painting, you'd need to be good at explaining your thoughts. Your English GCSEs are all about helping you to do whatever it is you want to do in the future.'

Coleen's mother explains that she has

already told her daughter all the above, and that she's also already extracted a promise that Coleen is going to try her hardest this year.

'Coleen, what I want to know is what can I do, as your teacher, to make you more able to do the work in English.' I don't know if compromise is the right way forward — she agrees to do this and this, and I'll agree to do that — but it is a formula that occurs to me, and I want her to see that I am willing to work with her.

'Is there anything you can think of that would help you?'

'Come on, Coleen,' her mother interjects. 'Your teacher is asking you a question.'

'Music. More music. And I don't like putting my hand up.'

'Right. OK. So you're saying you'd like maybe, um, more varied lessons? And bits of music at points during the lessons?'

'Yeah.' Eyes towards the table.

'Right, I can do that. So, I'm going to write down on the notes for this meeting that the teacher is to try to plan, where possible, for there to be music in the lesson.' I record the point. 'And in return I want you to do two things. When I'm talking, I want you to listen in silence — that's the first one. And the second thing is that I want you to complete

63

the tasks set in the lesson. Can you agree to those two things?' I record the last two targets. They'll go on to a new report, and I'll tick them off if she achieves them each day. If she doesn't, I'll try the somehow near-impossible task of getting a student to come back for detention.

A tilt of the head and a shrug of the shoulder.

'Come on, Coleen, answer your teacher.'

'Yes, I said yes, all right?'

'Good. Thank you for coming in, Mrs Randel. We'll be in touch.'

★ ★ ★

In my first year after Oxford I worked as a theatre usher and as a temp at Condé Nast — fancying myself for a while as destined to work on the pages of *Vogue*. Permanent jobs kept appearing on the noticeboards, but I didn't apply for them. Ella and I moved into our tiny flat and bought a table from Ikea big enough to comfortably sit twelve. We threw impromptu fancy-dress dinner parties with people we'd just met; food would be served at midnight after drinking a fridgeful of the cheapest cava that Tesco deliver. On Mondays I'd be sitting bleary-eyed in the offices of *Easy Living* or *Glamour* trying to fight the desire to crawl under the desk and take a nap. On Tuesdays there'd be no sense that the week needed to be salvaged and an early night was needed: having flagged all day, I'd pick up for another evening.

At a party in the country one weekend, Alex, the boyfriend of a close friend from my college at university, had entertained everyone with stories about the tough inner-city school he was teaching at. The knives, the metal detectors, the students whose authority ranked several places higher than his in the pecking order: it sounded as if a job like that would provide an endless source of amusing dinner party stories.

'You should do it, Nony,' Alex said to me on the train coming back to London.

'Yeah.'

At first it seemed like a truly awful idea, but the allure of having witty little stories to tell at dinner parties slowly began to make the two-year Teach First programme seem rather appealing.

And so in my first year of teaching I gave up late-night suppers and was happy to forgo a life during term time. The huge table became a desk, and I sat up till ten marking students' work and planning the following day's lessons.

In my second year I thought I'd make a

concerted effort to strike a healthy balance — but somehow spending evenings kissing Will made me care less about school. The weekday evenings not occupied by Will were spent with friends for quiet drinks. But I always kept an eye on the clock. Jen, a friend from my schooldays, had a birthday party at a pub on the evening after the interview with Coleen's mum. And another friend had a gig starting at 9.30 that everyone from the party was going along to. I arrived early and sat waiting for the rest of the guests, who came after their day's work had finished. By nine my evening was over.

'You're not going already.'

'Yeah . . . school tomorrow.'

'But it's only nine . . . Stay for another hour.'

★ ★ ★

While senior management dropping by with my Year 10 class resulted in confiscation of jewellery and removal of certain students to the referral base (think Roald Dahl's chokey without the shards of glass sticking out from the walls), with my two Year 7 sets to have senior management stopping by was like having a state visit.

Harriet Curtis, the deputy head, often

opened the door while I was teaching the Year 7s in the first weeks. Each time I ushered her in.

'Who would like to tell Miss Curtis what we are doing today?'

A few hands shoot up.

'What?' I say, eyes bulging at the class. 'Do only five people in this class know what we are doing?'

The rest of the hands go up more slowly, and I turn to Harriet to signal that she should choose a student. She chooses Angela, who is sitting beside Stella — who, as luck would have it, had been placed in my class, though surprisingly in the lower-ability set. Though Stella's answers are always sparky, she struggles to write, each word being an assortment of spider's legs floating above the line.

Angela is from Jamaica. She smiles broadly, and speaks with a Jamaican lilt — a different intonation from that of the students who've always lived round here, each sentence rising up at the end.

'What have you been *learning* today?' Harriet looks towards Angela and emphasizes the word 'learning'. She is in charge of the curriculum across the school, and well versed in Ofsted criteria; she knows that one of the measures of a good lesson is that a student can explain what skills they are developing. I know this too, but with such a charming, well-behaved class before me, so obviously engaged, I'm not too worried about what Angela's answer will be. The learning objective for the lesson was to understand what ambiguity is and to develop the ability to understand implied meanings — to understand what Browning's Duke might mean when he hints at how inappropriate the Duchess's smiles are; to understand that we should think very carefully about what he means when he says he 'gave commands; / Then all smiles stopped together'.

'Um, well, what we're doing is like, um, learning that you, um . . . ' Each word is deliberated over, Angela's brow drawn together in concentration. The class are waiting — some patiently, relieved that they have not been chosen, some trying to tell me with their eyes that they have an answer to this question. At this point of the year all are still respectfully silent in front of senior management, and also listening to each other speak in the class. They have all the skills they've learned at primary school, and haven't unlearned them yet.

'That . . . um, Miss has taught us that you can look at something one way and understand something, and, um, look at it another way and understand something else.

Like with a picture, you can see different things in it if you look at it in different ways.' Angela flashes a grin, having finished her point.

Harriet turns towards me, impressed.

'How *very* interesting,' she says to Angela. I am burning with pride, and feel like falling over sideways at Angela's perfectly eloquent explanation.

By the third Friday of term we are ready to look at the last few lines of the poem, where the Duke, showing off to the Count's envoy, asks him to pause before they go downstairs and 'Notice Neptune, though, / Taming a sea-horse, thought a rarity, / Which Claus of Innsbruck cast in bronze for me.'

'Hands up,' I preface the question, 'who's seen *The Little Mermaid*?' About a third of the class have.

'Can anyone remember who the Little Mermaid's dad is?' All hands go down, though Genesis's goes up.

'Yes?'

'Um . . . ' her eyes roll from corner to corner, her mind blank.

Not wanting to lose momentum, I proceed. 'He's Triton, do you remember? He's a merman, and god of the seas. Well' — this isn't a perfect explanation but I haven't prepared it — 'Neptune is also a sea god . . . I

69

need a volunteer . . . Chantelle, fantastic, come up here.'

I pull out a tall stool and tell her to stand on it.

'Do not fall off,' I instruct her as her legs wobble standing first up on to the table, then on to the stool. She is my tallest Year 7: nearing six foot, she is the same height as me. I turn to the rest of the class as I give her a hand to steady her.

'What is my most important rule?'

A few giggles, and Stella puts up her hand.

'No blood on the carpet.'

'Exactly.' We had covered this rule when, earlier in the week, a finger that had sprung a leak after being trapped in a laptop was held up and I feigned more interest in whether there was any blood on the laptop or the carpet — a trick I'd learned from my mother.

'She doesn't care,' the whisper had rippled around the room. I don't care. I find the endless whimpers of ill students a real pain.

A fair few students have thrown up in my classroom; one even ran in from the hall to vomit into my bin. And every single lesson starts with one or two students coming up to tell me, 'Miss, my belly . . .'

'Oh dear. Make sure you rub it, and tell me if it gets worse.'

'Miss, I've got a headache.'

'Poor you. Make sure you drink some water, and tell me if it gets worse.'

Some are so caught up in the drama of malaise that they have another student explain, 'Miss, she says she can't see straight.' It is always the writing hand that is sprained and wrapped by an amateur in bandages — 'Do your best with your other hand' — and occasionally I receive a scrawled note, held out by a sincere-looking student, 'Miss, I can't talk, I've got a sore throat.' The mute student sits beside her friend writing notes until there is something she really wants to say.

I haven't had a more serious medical drama since teaching at a school in North India during my gap year. It was where Ella and I had first met each other — we were placed at the same school in the foothills of the Himalayas. In one of my classes a student had an epileptic fit, and I sent someone to run for help. The fit soon passed, but rumours that the child was possessed by the devil continue to circulate. They were confirmed by the principal's Christian wife, who informed me of the need for an exorcism. Raj was, like many misbehaving students, a joy to spend time with outside the classroom, though fairly exasperating once required to sit silently in a chair — but

71

possessed by the Devil he was not.

There were no gaping wounds in my classroom in the Portakabin thus far, but everyone was fantastically engaged because Chantelle's head was almost touching the ceiling and this was clearly a little dangerous.

'Right, now I need another volunteer.' Everyone wanted to be part of this. I picked Stella, partly because she is one of the smallest in the class and partly because she always has her hand up first. Though she is, in a small way, definitely one of my favourites, I'm very careful not to show it.

While I tell Stella to come up to the front, I rummage around in tubs behind my desk, searching for a rope, string, or — perfect, a spare computer cable.

'Now, Chantelle,' I hand one end of the cable to her and loop the other around Stella, who is standing in front of Chantelle on the floor. 'I want you to hold on to this harness. You are Neptune, and Stella is a sea horse and you are riding her.' Chantelle and Stella laugh a little as Chantelle tightens the cord and Stella holds it in front of her with her hands to avoid being garrotted.

I'm just about to start asking questions about who is in charge here in this little scenario, who (using all the key words for the lesson) is *dominating*, who is *controlling*, who *inferior*, when I catch sight of the head, Cecelia, through the glass panel of my door. She comes in, and my heart rate rises.

'Hello,' I say. I feel the situation needs a quicker explanation than a student would give, so I fill her in myself. 'We're just looking at the statue in the poem 'My Last Duchess'.' I add cautiously, 'I hope we are not breaking any rules.'

'Well, you might be,' Cecelia replies, 'but as long as she knows to be careful . . . '

'Oh yes,' I affirm, 'she definitely does: she knows the class rules.'

Cecelia seems content enough, and so I turn to the rest of the class and start asking questions.

With a nod towards me Cecelia leaves, and without the pressure of being watched I ask the class the most important question we've been building up to. They've already identified that Neptune is clearly *controlling* the poor sea horse. 'Can anyone think of another relationship in the poem that is like the relationship between Neptune and the sea horse?'

The penny drops for a large handful, and they gasp and strain out of their seats, hands raised, in the moment that photos on posters catch when advertising teaching as a career.

★　★　★

In my first year, Thursdays were my worst day of the week. A full-timetable day. By the end of September I felt I had acquired a new understanding of Edvard Munch's *The Scream:* the piece is not a representation of the human species gripped by existential angst, but a depiction of a teacher at the end of a full-timetable day. I remember that as I made it to the end of another Thursday I would actually think to myself, 'Good, I'm alive. I have survived another Thursday.'

My timetable this year is an easier obstacle course. Fridays are the worst, with four hour-long lessons in a row and only one twenty-minute break, between the second and third. As the first half-term drew to a close, my birthday fell on a Friday. I'd arranged to have drinks at a bar with one hundred and twenty of my absolutely closest friends on the Saturday night, and so Will offered to take me out for a birthday supper on Friday. All I had to do was get through the last four lessons of the week.

I taught two lessons to the Year 7s, and gave the Year 10s laptops to type up their coursework. Coleen set to work, typed up the block of writing she had in her book, and declared that she had finished twenty minutes into the lesson. I printed her work and sat with her penning suggestions in the margin and indicating where new paragraphs should start.

'Wot?'

'You need to use paragraphs to shape your writing . . . make it easier for the reader . . . '

'Wot? No, I've finished.'

'Yes, just have a look at the few questions I've written you and put in the paragraph breaks.'

I moved away before Coleen could answer back. I left her to work on the piece and glanced at her screen ten minutes later. She deftly switched from internet chat site back to her English work. No changes had been made. At the end of the lesson she printed out a fresh copy of the work I'd already marked and handed it in.

After the Year 10s, the Year 11s traipsed in for their penultimate lesson of the week. I wanted them to rewrite their piece of creative-writing coursework. For most of them it was the weakest piece of work in their coursework folders, which were meant to be completed in the first year of the two-year GCSE course. I wanted to make one last attempt to ensure they had the most marks possible before going into their GCSE exams. As the piece of creative writing with the 10s

75

had gone quite well, I'd been working on the same exercise with the 11s.

All thirty came in as keen for the lesson to be over as I was. I make my Year 7s enter in silence, but — perhaps mistakenly — think the Year 11s, who are all fifteen or sixteen, are old enough to be treated a little more like adults. They wander around, playfully laying the odd thump on each other's shoulders, and my voice strains to ring out above the hubbub.

They finally got settled. This is a process which always takes longer than it should — I calculated in their first year that, by wasting ten minutes of each lesson, over a year they wasted the equivalent of a whole half-term's worth of work.

Tired though I felt, I summoned the remaining joules of energy and set about explaining what we would be doing.

'Now, today is actually my birthday . . . and I know none of you have brought me a card or a present . . . '

There is mild outrage —

'You didn't tell us.'

'Wot?'

'Did you bring us cake?'

'How old are you?'

'Shh, shh — I'm afraid how old I am is top-secret information. I know none of you

76

have brought me a card or a present, because you didn't know it was my birthday, but the best present you could give me' — I'm really hamming it up — 'is a lesson where you all really concentrate on your work and make a good start on your pieces of writing.'

They roll their eyes. A few of the ones who are real supporters of my lessons smile benignly.

They know what they are to be getting on with. They have notes out, their exercise books lie open on the tables. They half settle down to the task. The best are well into their first paragraphs, the worst still looking for distractions.

'Adalia . . . ' I mime picking up a pen and looking intently at a piece of paper. She laughs.

'Sorry, Miss.' She switches her attention away from the conversation she was having and sets herself up to do some work.

I walk around the room trying to settle and start off the ones who are struggling, but every time I crouch beside a student the volume rises. I stand up, insist on silence, and the volume falls again. The pattern repeats itself several times, and each time I have to settle them again I become a little more irate.

'Girls, this is not on. I know some of you want my help, but every time I try to answer a question it becomes so loud I can't hear myself thinking. Settle down.'

Becky has her hand up. She sits at one of the tables at the back of the class. I signal I'll be with her in a second, but first I want to settle Abimbola, who is always the last to engage in any task. I ask her questions, draw out a first sentence from her, and tell her to write it down.

Becky meanwhile has started chatting to the person beside her.

'Becky, stop talking,' I say in a firm tone.

'Wot?' kissing her teeth. 'I was waiting for you, Miss,' she says, full of attitude and pure outrage.

I crouch down beside her and speak to her relatively calmly, though feeling a little angry that after teaching her and trying to help her for over a year she'd speak to me quite so viciously.

'Becky, I deserve to be spoken to with more respect than that . . . '

Telling her off is like a waving a red flag at a bull. She is indignant, and spitting out words so fast she can't know what she's saying. Meanwhile Abimbola, keen to use this scene as an opportunity to go off task, is mimicking my voice in a whiny tone: 'Becky . . . I deserve to be spoken to with a little bit more respect . . . '

All of a sudden it's just too much. My eyes sting and I stand up and walk out of the classroom. As I leave, Abimbola calls out after me, 'Happy birthday'.

I've never left a classroom before, or since, but I just couldn't take any more. I go down to the staff base and tell my head of department through sobs that 'They . . . (sob) . . . just push me too far. Every day is . . . (sob) . . . such a struggle with them . . . (sob).' Steph is cool and collected and says she'll go and sit with them.

I sit down with Kitty and, rather than being able to get myself together, I seem to just be crying more and more.

'They're so hard . . . They tell me I'm one of their best teachers . . . but they will not just work quietly . . .'

After about ten minutes I've calmed myself enough to be ready to return to the classroom. Steph is sitting at a table next to Abimbola, and is reading the few sentences she's written.

'Miss, thank you for letting me come in,' Steph says, getting up. 'You all seem to be doing some really *creative*, interesting work.'

'Thank you, Miss,' I say, smiling firmly to compensate for the red, puffy eyes. 'I'll take over. Thank you for sitting with them.'

The class work quietly for the remaining ten minutes, and then the bell goes.

'You may go,' I say in a harder tone of voice than I usually use. Most of the class leave, but Adalia, Aysha, Maria, Hebba and a few other supporters stay behind.

'Miss, we're so sorry . . . '

'Thank you, girls, that's really sweet of you, but none of you did anything you need to feel sorry about.'

Rather overwhelmed by their sweetness, I feel a little choked again and Adalia, full of life and emotion, tries to give me a big hug and starts sobbing herself, uncontrollably. Aysha joins in.

'Miss (*sob, sob*), we're really sorry.'

'Now, now, girls, you don't need to cry.'

'But Miss, (*sob, sob*), you're such a good teacher to us and . . . '

Seeing them cry sets me off again, but also makes me start laughing at the ridiculousness of it all.

'Oh, Miss,' Maria says sweetly, 'how old are you?'

'Twenty-five,' I say, caught off guard and feeling surrounded by goodies.

'Oh, Miss!' they all coo — 'but you look so young.'

After a meeting later in the afternoon, I return to my classroom to find an assortment of cards and flowers and mugs and teddy bears on my desk. With a big sigh, I collect my things together and head home.

I found Ella sitting on the floor of our tiny flat.

'I can't go back. Don't make me do it.'

She's so exhausted she can't summon up the energy to cry properly, and so is alternating between laughing hysterically and welling up. She is beyond sitting in a chair and crying like some kind of normal exhausted person. In the most sympathetic way possible, I'm convulsed with laughter.

Will met me in the restaurant with flowers, a book and a present of a first acupuncture session. He bought me a glass of champagne, and then looked at the time. He'd already prepared me for the fact that it was the crucial English match in the final of the World Cup, and so we walked down the road to wedge ourselves into the upstairs room of a pub. By the time we sat down to supper back at the restaurant, I was beginning to feel a little overwhelmed.

'Do you want to try the mackerel?'

'No.'

'It's delicious.'

'I'm kind of freaking out,' I admitted, looking at the fish I couldn't touch. 'I think I want to run away.'

'You can absolutely run away if you want to.'

'No. I don't want to run away.'

'Oh,' said Will. 'It's normally me who bolts. At around the three-month stage.'

'Great.'

He ate my fish, and I tried to concentrate on not feeling that I was trapped at a restaurant table. I sipped the wine, hoping to inebriate myself.

I tried unsuccessfully to explain myself on the long walk home.

'It's just the flowers . . . and the restaurant . . . and . . . '

'It's all too much?'

'No, it's lovely. It's just me freaking out . . . '

'I completely understand. Do you want me to go back to mine?'

'No,' I said, 'I want you not to freak out about the fact that I'm freaking out.' I felt it had been a rather overwhelming day. I was more than ready for a week off.

AUTUMN TERM
SECOND HALF

As the clocks changed the Sunday before we returned to school for the next segment of the year, the early morning on the first day back (after a week of half-term lie-ins) didn't seem so bad. Or rather I wouldn't have felt so bad had I not woken up feeling like I'd swallowed a cup full of drawing pins in the night. At 6.30 a.m. I called Julia.

'I'm just wondering . . . I think I've got tonsillitis. I feel a bit rubbish, but I think I'm OK to teach.'

'Come in,' said Julia. 'Teach your lessons, and then get a doctor's appointment — that's what I did.' Julia had had chickenpox and been wiped out for ten days of the previous half-term, but, despite feeling very strange, until the doctor had confirmed how properly unfit to work she was she kept coming in.

I could not bear the thought of trying to come up with cover work — i.e. work which will occupy the students, doesn't require teaching, and can be thrown in the bin on my return. And I imagined the students becoming distraught if they discovered I wasn't there — though, as far as I can remember, it was always a real treat to turn up to a lesson and discover a supply teacher. A treat for the class, not the supply teacher: the school has effectively provided them with a human sacrifice.

I'd spent the week's holiday toing and froing between London and my parents' homes in Norfolk and Suffolk — father in Norfolk, mother in Suffolk. My half-term coincided with Will's, and we daringly spent two evenings and a whole day in a row together. My flurry of fear at my birthday meal had passed, and I embarked on some boyfriend improvement at the most expensive shoe shop we could find. Rosanna, a friend from my schooldays, had seen him late one night cycling home in red trainers.

'You'll have to do something about those, Nones,' she said pulling an expression of horror.

'Yes, I know, they're hideous. I don't know why he wears them.' He was rather disappointed to learn his favourite pair of shoes had to be consigned to the bin.

The first day of the new half-term was bright and autumnal, and only a semi-real school day. Cecelia held an extralong meeting before we broke off to have tours of the newly refurbished Victorian block, which had had £8 million spent on renovations. My old dark classroom had had paint peeling off the ceiling. The wall of windows had been divided by a vast chimney which ran up from the boiler on the ground floor. I remember in one lesson in my first year my Year 11 class had started to complain about a smell rather like burning rubber. We had to evacuate into the hall when plumes of noxious smoke started blowing out of the ventilator. They coughed in disgust at the fumes, and squealed in delight at the opportunity to make even more noise than usual and waste yet another lesson.

Now the same room had been made much larger, and the chimney had been removed so that a whole wall of the classroom was made up of vast windows looking across London. Charcoal carpets had been laid, and all woodwork — doors, cupboards and cabinets — had been painted in a matching shade. New cream desks with charcoal legs, new baby-blue chairs, new whiteboards: everything new. All in all, if you couldn't have wood panelling or floor-to-ceiling bookcases, this was the next best thing.

Rather like the beginning of term in September, the return after the half-term break was to be staggered so that the students could find their way around the restored building. Everyone also received a short talk on how they were expected to behave there.

'We've spent eight million on doing up the Victorian building. We wanted to become an academy because we wanted to give you a better school. No chewing gum, no food, and no drinks except water. This school is not only for you, but for generations after you, and you need to look after it. No chewing gum.'

'Eight million? Eee.' The students were desperate to see the makeover.

The Year 11s careered around the hallways, poking their heads into the classrooms and excitedly greeting the teachers.

'Eeek! Hello, Miss!'

'Hello, Adalia, would you like to come into my classroom and put your gum in the bin?'

'Oh, sorry, Miss!' she laughed.

Waiting for my lesson with the 11s, I lugged the tables (which did not as yet have a layer of Wrigley's Spearmint and Juicy Fruit stuck to their undersides) into place and was irritated to discover that, because the chairs were so wide, and the legs of the tables so close together, you couldn't put a chair under the short side of the tables. What were the designers thinking?

Part of the GCSE course requires students to study a collection of poetry 'from different cultures'. To start the unit, it made sense to find out a little more about the cultural variety within the class. I set them the task of speed dating with each other to find out what their cultural heritage was and how this manifested itself — in their beliefs, in the clothes they wore, in the food they ate, and in their feelings about all these.

I took part in the activity, and made a beeline to interview one of only two white girls in the class. It was on my mind that my brother had recently commissioned a pro-gramme for the BBC exploring problems of cultural identity for White British students in multicultural schools. I asked her whether she felt at all uneasy about her White British status.

'Oh yeah, Miss, I know what you mean. But I'm proud to be British.'

Back in July I'd been to an evening of dub poetry and heard Linton Kwesi Johnson and his 'Revolutionary Friends' perform, or rather rail. They railed against the sus law, which allows police officers to stop and search on suspicion, and they railed against the fact that most of the people under suspicion were young and black. The law was abolished in the eighties but there seemed to be no boundaries between the past and the present. I came away with a feeling of unease.

I went to speak to Julia the following

morning. I told her I'd been to a dub-poetry night, and that I'd come away feeling white in a very bad way.

'Yeah, I used to go to those nights at uni. But not any more. Especially not because of my own situation — you know?' Julia is black, her partner white. 'I mean, I listened to their message and thought, 'That's not what I want'. There has to come a time when people think about moving on and the future.'

Back in the classroom, the thoughts of the white British student echoed Julia's. 'What happened in the past doesn't matter any more, yer. It's like time has moved on.'

The poets in the GCSE anthology rarely find anything but discord between the different strands of their heritage. The class didn't seem so bothered.

'I'm half white and half black, but I like being a mix, yeah. Because even though my friends make jokes about it, I represent unity.' Nia smiled broadly.

'I'm proud I speak Yoruba,' Abimbola added.

'Miss, I'm proud that I'm Argentinian,' Adalia confidently told the class. 'It makes me unique. And the culture . . . there is this ceremony you have, yeah, when you're fifteen. And speaking Spanish: it's so cool, because everyone speaks Spanish in a different way — so every time you speak to someone in Spanish, you learn something new.'

'And where is home?' I asked them.

All said home is where you come from, not where you live. They are Somalian or Nigerian or Afghan, not English — regardless of whether they were born here or not.

They said they were just themselves. No one confessed that they were caught between living in one place and belonging to another. At the end of my first year teaching this class I remember looking with them at Othello's 'travel's history', the story he told that seduced Desdemona. To draw them into the text, I told them my own 'travel's history'. I told them about growing up in Minnesota, where winters were so cold that a voice on the radio would warn 'young people, old people and slow-moving pets' not to go outside.

That unlocked the floodgates. There were stories of Nigeria, where rain was so infrequent that people rushed outside when it started; of mountain villages in Afghanistan and bombs dropping; of Peckham and the close communities on the estates; Adalia held court with memories from Argentina of abductions, gun crime and corruption.

Here again we were returning to the same territory: what they knew. Everyone was far more interested in hearing about each other than in listening to Jane Eyre's description of her past.

'But, Miss,' Aysha raised her hand and started her point at the same time, 'we're all part of more than one culture.'

'Fantastic point, and that brings me to our perfect Jerry Springer-style thought for the day . . . At school we are all part of a shared community — a community of shared experience and values. We have this community as well as having separate communities elsewhere. Please tuck your chairs under . . . Adalia, gum in the bin.'

The following lesson I wanted to introduce them to the idea of the global village and of hybridization. They were set off in their groups to debate an argument that I'd given each table. I made a dash for Becky's table. If I grabbed her attention from the beginning she was more likely to participate. Since the episode on my birthday when she'd pushed me to tears she'd been quieter in class. But, she hadn't apologized, and I hadn't spoken to her about why she might need to.

ME: Right, girls, what have you got? Ok, let me see, 'Are we living in a Mac Village?'
BECKY: *(sincerely)* I'd like a McDonald's.
ME: *(raising eyebrows)* Thank you.

BECKY: Oh, sorry, Miss.

ME: If I'd wanted an Indian takeaway a hundred years ago, where would I have had to go to get one?

BECKY: India?

ME: And now?

BECKY: I like Indian and Chinese.

ME: Who might object to a global village?

BECKY: Miss, can you help us with this?

ME: Yes, I'm trying to. Why might people in Delhi object to there being a McDonald's?

ABIMBOLA: But, Miss, in different countries McDonald's sells different things. For example, in Jamaica they sell spicy chicken. *(Miss beginning to run out of angles to approach this topic from.)*

BECKY: Miss . . . is London like a small world?

ME: *(seriously impressed)* How?

BECKY: Because there is everything here, people from everywhere. You can buy Nigerian clothes in the markets at Elephant.

ME: You've got it.

At lunch I sat with the head of Year 11.

'I think Becky's doing well,' I told him.

'Gosh, that one! You should have seen her in Year 7 . . . I can't remember the exact situation at home. I think Dad's gone and Mum's got maybe five kids. Her older sister was excluded when she was in Year 10. We've managed to hang on to Becky.'

'Well, I reckon she's going to get two Cs. She's working in class.'

'That's good to hear. I'll tell her you've been singing her praises.'

A few of the staff, counsellors who worked with individual students, and heads of years, were like vultures when it came to picking up snit-bits of praise for difficult students. They'd offer them up like presents to the students as a way of encouraging them to stay on the path of improvement.

★ ★ ★

In the evening, Sophie (who had worked in the classroom next to mine for all the previous year) and Bella (a maths teacher in my school) came round for supper. I was too exhausted to cook, so I collected three boxes of spaghetti bolognaise from the Italian restaurant down the road and poured them out on to plates. We sat round the small kitchen table in the flat — the large table was still a desk and covered in stacks of marking dutifully carried between home and school without ever being done. Just two years in, Sophie had decided to move to an equally, if not slightly more, challenging school nearby.

She regaled us with the pitfalls so far.

'So, I'm sharing a classroom, and when I say 'sharing' I actually mean there is another teacher in the class at the same time trying to teach. And all that divides us is a row of filing cabinets,' she said.

'What?' It is a laughably bad idea.

'Yes, so every time you've just about settled your class, the other class make it impossible to hear anything you're trying to say.'

'Oh, Sophie.'

'I know.'

'Does the other teacher have good control of his classes?'

'Yes, but that's not the point . . . '

'Yeah, I know — even if they are talking really quietly, it still makes it hard to concentrate. Oh, poor you.'

'Well,' I said excitedly. 'You know Teach First sometimes arrange for C-list celebrities to come into the classroom and teach a lesson?' Sophie and Bella are both also Teach First teachers, from cohorts previous to mine. 'Michael Gove, the Shadow Secretary for Children, Schools and Families, is coming into school to teach my Year 11s.' Teach First had rung me during the holidays to ask if I'd be happy for him to take one of my classes for a lesson.

'And there's a possibility that a film crew

will come in too,' the person on the other end of the phone had explained.

'Fantastic,' I had said, glowing with limelight.

'We're always getting Gordon Brown in,' Sophie told us. 'I remember telling a class that he would be dropping by, and they rolled their eyes and were like 'oh, Miss, he's *always* here.''

'God, it must be miserable teaching at a rough school out in the country with no celebrities and politicians dropping by,' I said.

'And how are things with Will going?' Bella asked.

'Yeah, good. I love him, but I'm not going to tell him for a while yet. I think it will freak him out.' I told practically everyone before I finally told Will.

★ ★ ★

On Tuesday the rest of the students returned. After their tours, normal lessons resumed. As my Year 7s came into the classroom, I stood at the board writing down the names of the ones who came in silently, took their seats, put their diaries on the tables, and wrote down the learning objective. It feels like a small miracle that they actually do all these things, without talking, because I have told them to.

In my first year, Sophie and I shared a Year 8 class. I taught them for two lessons each week, and so did Sophie. The last lesson on a Friday was one of Sophie's sessions. She could always tame them.

'Girls, I know you're tired. I'm tired, you're tired: we're all tired.'

No matter what I tried, I couldn't get the knack of calming them. They'd enter, and I simply wouldn't be able to get silence. I tried the various things that people suggested.

'Just stand at the front of the class, with your arms folded and a pissed-off look on your face and wait for them to be silent. Don't say anything till they're silent.' Two terms into the year I stood at the front with my arms folded and waited for eight minutes. I've heard of teachers who have waited for two weeks and then never had to ask for silence again.

I know that in classrooms elsewhere silence is the default setting of the students. And even in other classrooms in my school. But not yet in mine. Looking at my Year 7s, however, I felt so proud of them. I could hear mayhem in the hallways as they silently wrote down:

Learning Objectives:
1. To develop our understanding of symbolism.
2. To develop our speaking and listening

skills through class discussion.

3. To identify the persuasive language used to influence the reader in 'Suicide in the Trenches' by Siegfried Sassoon.

'No gum' is one rule; all lessons must have a learning objective is another. A learning objective is meant to tell the students exactly what skills they'll be developing during the lesson. 'They're a fad,' my head of department daringly told me, and I always feel that writing them is an approximate science.

The other rule about lessons is that they are divided into three parts: a starter, a main and a plenary. Teaching or hard graft is sandwiched between a fun activity to introduce what's going to be learned, and the plenary in which the students reflect on what they have learned.

'We're going to be reading a book called *Private Peaceful* this term. By Michael Morpurgo. Has anyone read any books by him?' A few hands go up.

'But before that we're going to read a poem . . . And before we do that I want you to all draw a poppy in the middle of your exercise books.' I hold up a book, and indicate where it should go.

'Right, you can start right away. You've got three minutes to draw a poppy. I'll draw one up on the board.'

I walk around the classroom peering at vast poppies which are flooding the page, and miserly ones drawn off-centre.

'Lovely, that's a beautiful one . . . No, you haven't finished, I want you to colour it in . . . No, I don't have a rubber . . . No, you draw it, it doesn't matter if it's not perfect . . . Chantelle, no, I don't want you to sharpen all the pencils in the box . . . Chantelle, why haven't you started?'

'Miss, can I borrow a pen?' she asks, looking up from her sharpening. She is sitting on her own at a desk, and seems quite absorbed in her task of sharpening the three hundred or so pencils in the box — she generally didn't seem to interact a lot with the other students in the class. As well as being almost six foot, she was slightly overweight. I guessed she might have some Irish blood in her, as her hair had a red tinge. She always wore it in the same way, pulled tightly back into a ponytail on the side of her head. As was the local fashion any wisps of hair that might escape were firmly stuck to her head with gel.

My box of biros, full at the beginning of term, had already evaporated. Half the Year 10 class needed a pen each lesson. I always forgot to collect them in, so would have to scrabble around on the floor to gather any that the students had been kind enough to leave with me. Scrambling around on the floor also gave me a chance to collect the wrappers and crisp packets they'd dropped once they'd finished surreptitiously eating the contents. I root around on my desk and find a pen for Chantelle.

'Ok, thirty seconds left to finish the poppies . . . and pencils down . . . Well done, Rose. Well done, Princess. Well done, Katie, Lilly, Flossy, Maude . . . We're just waiting for a two people now . . . Now one . . . Still waiting . . . '

'Chantelle, put the pencil down,' Princess hisses.

'Good, thank you, girls.'

'I want you to think, in pairs . . . Do we all have a person to work with?' I scan the room. 'Chantelle, please can you move next to Genesis. No, I said please can you move here . . . Good. I want you to think in pairs of all the things that a poppy symbolizes. What is a symbol? Can anyone remember?'

Nothing. But a few of the class know that the answer to this question is somewhere in the depths of their minds.

'Can anyone remember the statue in 'My Last Duchess'?'

Stella's hand shoots up, and a few others follow.

'It's, er, it's like something that makes you think of something else.'

'Great. Now you've got two minutes to come up with as many ideas as possible about what a poppy symbolizes. Go.' Chantelle raises her hand. I walk to the back of the classroom.

'Miss,' she giggles, 'have you seen what someone's written here?' She points at the desk. I look and see that someone has tried to etch into the desk 'Your mum is a cunt.'

'Oh,' I say, a bit shocked and seriously annoyed that someone has been writing on the desks at all. I lick my finger and try to smear away the words. It doesn't really work.

'Don't tell the others,' I instruct her, and she grins conspirtorially.

The volume rises, and I turn and wipe the poppy off the board to make room for notes. There was, at that point, no technology in the £8 million worth of new classrooms. No laptops, no printers, no internet, definitely no interactive whiteboards. We were all plunged into the dark ages of teaching. The overall effect was very calming. The bells had stopped working as well — or no one had been able to make them start working — and so I decided when, give or take a minute, the lessons were over.

'OK, everyone listening . . . ' I bang a tin of

chickpeas three times against my desk, and the room falls quiet. 'Everything that I write up on the board I want you to copy down on to your page around the poppy. What have people come up with? Genesis?'

'Um, it's like a symbol . . . ' — she's very careful to use the right words, and hesitates; I keep nodding all way through her sentence — 'of the war, yeah.' As she finishes her sentence, I draw a star next to her name on the board.

'Yes, it is. Thank you.' I write the word 'War' up on the board. 'What can we add to this? Stella?'

'It's what people wear to remember the war, to remember the soldiers who died.'

'Fantastic.' A star up on the board, and I write, 'To remember the soldiers who died.'

Rose is quiet and thinks carefully, blinking her eyes hard. She sits at the side of the room, always concentrating. Her hand is raised waiting when I turn round.

'Yes.' I nod to her.

'The red is like the blood.'

'Yes. That's, a good point. Can we take this any further? Does anyone know why it is that poppies are the flower we wear on Remembrance Day?'

'Yes, Stella again.'

'Um' — loud and confident she's going to

remember — 'um . . . I know I know, but I can't remember.'

'It's because poppies were the flower that grew in the fields out in Belgium after the battles, and after the soldiers had died.'

'Oh yer, that's it,' says Stella.

'It's like where the soldiers died their blood went into the ground and poppies grew,' intercepts Rose, refining her first point.

'And who knows when we wear poppies? I think I've already said the answer to this . . . '

'On Remembrance Day. Which is', Chantelle piped up, 'the eleventh of the eleventh of the eleventh of the eleventh of the . . . '

I'm going to have to watch Chantelle, I thought. In a class where everyone else was straining to be the model student, she stuck out.

'OK, I'm going to give you a poem now.' I hand out 'Suicide in the Trenches'. 'We're going to come up with an action for each one of the lines. Right. 'I knew a simple soldier boy' — what action could we do for that? Actually I think we need everyone standing up.' A few grumbles — oh, the effort of standing (most of the Year 10s would point-blank refuse). 'What are we going to do for this line? Good, everyone copy Rose.' Rose is standing bolt upright, head tilted back, hand raised in salute.

103

We come up with a sequence for each of the three stanzas, and it becomes our party piece for the next few lessons. Anyone who drops by is treated to a rendition, the students reciting the lines and adding the actions and sound effects.

When Harriet drops by to check on how this golden class are doing, she too is treated to the performance, which is beginning to fray slightly around the edges.

'What's this? Are these girls doing *A-level* work now?' she asks.

'Well yes, actually. You see, they are so bright I just have to keep finding them more and more challenging work.' And then, horror of all horrors, I suggest something. 'Perhaps they should do an assembly and perform for the whole school?'

'Well actually, Miss Crossley-Holland, I *do* have an assembly coming up, and it would work *very* well if your class could perform this . . . and maybe talk a little about what they have been *learning* in class.'

Up until this point I have avoided this kind of situation like the plague. 'Yes, that would be fantastic, we could definitely do that.'

'Great.' And then the classroom door swings closed behind her and, while some students grin in excitement, others look petrified. I myself feel a little sick as I say, 'Right, so we're going to do this in front of one thousand people.'

All called out their responses at once.

'No, Miss!'

'Yeah!'

'No,' says Chantelle crossly.

'Shut up, Chantelle,' a few retaliate.

'No, you shut up.'

'But there's 11s.'

'No, Miss, they'll think we're stupid.'

'Er, girls, shh, shh, shh, thank you, shhh, settle . . . Of course we can do it. And what I think is we need three students to be the readers. Are there any volunteers? You're going to need to memorize your bit of the poem.'

★   ★   ★

I proudly told Will about the lesson, and he said he'd try it with his students. He'd started regularly calling in the evenings for a quick chat. Ella, exhausted from her day's teaching, and further drained by the two and a half hour commute she was making, asked that we didn't talk about teaching for the few minutes she had after getting home and before going to bed to get up at 5.30. She occasionally broke her own rule and bemoaned the lack of support she was receiving at school.

The relationship with Will seemed to have all the elements of a relationship, but he was adamant we were still just seeing how things were going. We'd had an irksome conversation on his scooter at the end of half-term.

'So, Will, I was thinking . . . as you're kissing me, would it be all right with you if you didn't kiss anyone else?' I suggested tentatively.

After a long pause, 'Are you asking me to be your boyfriend?' — not said in the kind of voice that suggested that beneath his helmet he was smiling.

'No, I was saying, if you're kissing me, then would it be possible not to kiss anyone else?'

'But that conversation leads on to another one.'

'OK. Well, I guess I am wondering what this is?'

Will showed signs of being as panic-stricken as I had been in the restaurant on my birthday. 'I just don't want to rush into anything,' he tried to explain.

'Fine. But I wasn't asking if you were my boyfriend. It's just, if we're sleeping together, I want to know that you're not sleeping with other people.'

'No, of course I'm not.'

'Right, and can you continue not to?'

'Yes . . . I mean I didn't know what you were thinking . . . '

'I was thinking I'd see how things go.' Which was a lie. I was thinking I was happy to play along with this 'We're not boyfriend and girlfriend yet' because it seemed so blatantly obvious to me that we were a perfect match for each other, right down to the fact that neither of us was sure we wouldn't bolt.

Julia laughed as I relayed the conversation to her. 'What's the name of the game?' she sang. 'That's what you need to listen to.' She often prescribed listening to relevant songs as a remedy for turbulent times.

I shook my head.

'It's by ABBA.'

★ ★ ★

Towards the end of the first week back I was finding that, without the technology, the Year 10s seemed much harder to control. My energy was waning a little — there was a pile of unmarked homework in the tray on my desk, and I already felt ready for another week off. The Year 10 class didn't go in for waiting quietly with their arms folded for me to give them an instruction. I had to bamboozle them with Powerpoint presentations and clips of film and music, instructions and tasks and performances.

Poor Lakeisha looked at me mournfully

during Friday's lesson. She had finished her work and was ready to move on. A handful more were in the same boat. Others were still indignantly refusing to open their exercise books. They didn't know what to do until I went to each one of them personally and gave the instruction I had given to the whole class.

'Siobhan, I'd like you to think about the tone of voice you're using to speak to me.'

'No, you need to think about your tone.'

Several were sent out of the classroom, having had their two previous warnings. There would be more calls to make home.

I had to bite my tongue and not repeat the same refrains: 'This is too noisy, I'm trying to speak to a student and I can't hear myself think.' I calmly tried to tell them, 'This is not teaching, this is fighting. All I want to do is to help you succeed and achieve. And you can fight me all you want, but every day that is what I'm trying to do.'

'Skein, skein,' Coleen said. It means 'All right, I agree' in hoodie dialect. But my pleas had little impact. I didn't feel I had control of them even when they were silent and listening to me. I remembered Alex's stories about his lack of authority: in terms of the pecking order within my class, there were several positions above mine. By being so purely unpredictable and unbothered by the rules, they made me dread each lesson, not knowing what their mood would be.

At the end of a poorly planned and poorly executed lesson — a lesson where I just wanted them to get on with some work — I looked at the bin. It was overflowing with crisp packets. I considered giving up on having groups of tables and instead putting the desks into rows — and this made me feel cross, as it would have an impact on my three other classes. How was I meant to turn a drove of queen bees into worker bees? Drained of energy, I thought, I don't know if I can do this. I got on to the floor and started picking up the litter that hadn't made it to the bin. For every student like Becky who had turned a corner, there seemed to be a handful more on a downward slope.

The doctor had given me nothing for the sore throat, and I'd made the mistake of doing things during the evenings. I'd been to the theatre on Wednesday. Will and I had left halfway through — it had become a habit of ours. Before we'd gone to the theatre, I went across the road to the corner shop to buy some loo roll. I returned to my front door only to realize that I'd left my keys, my phone and the theatre tickets inside the flat. I sat on the pack of loo roll waiting for Ella to come home.

On Thursday I went to *Romeo and Juliet* at Covent Garden. It was exquisitely beautiful, and Kate, a friend from university, had arranged a backstage tour. We walked up into the rehearsal and costume rooms, and admired stacks of tutus. Kate was quite beside herself with the excitement of having men in tights wandering around. I was battling against heavy eyelids, wondering when I was next going to get enough sleep. I knew that, rather than having a lie-in on Saturday, I was going to attend a Teach First conference. Hours of workshops and talks.

By Friday of the first week back, Ella and I felt like one feels at the airport at five in the morning. We had that feeling you get when you've opted for a flight because it's £25 cheaper but it leaves from Luton at an ungodly hour so you've had to get up in the middle of the night and take a taxi — or, worse, you've decided to catch the last train and then just spend the night in the eternal light of the airport. And you've tried to bed down in a corner using a bag for a pillow, then given up and sat on your suitcases feeling as if you have given yourself jet lag before even leaving the country. That is what the end of the teaching week feels like.

After school, I dragged myself along to Portcullis House in Westminster for what felt like a rather exciting meeting. I found the place and sat in reception waiting for Michael Gove to appear. I had my smartest black winter coat on, and a reasonably scruffy school outfit. Surrounded by suits decorated with bright-red poppies, I felt a bit out of place.

I've got a vague feeling I'm meant to be quite smart for school. I got a message from the head in my first year that my dark-grey skinny jeans were strictly non-regulation. I bought a pair of black trousers from Gap, and wore them instead.

'You've changed,' Adalia said, eyeing me up and down. Her remark made it clear she did not approve of this new style direction I'd taken. It was obvious that Adalia was someone who would never put the need to look appropriate or be comfortable before efforts to look as attractive as possible. She'd worn heels for the previous non-school-uniform day, jeans that were sprayed on, and huge gold hoops in her ears. I'd given up tottering down the hallways in heels after the first few weeks. Nevertheless, following Adalia's appraisal, I reverted to tight black jeans, and have waited every day that I've worn them, for over a year, to be hauled into Cecelia's office.

Michael Gove took me through the security

area and into the canteen. We sat down with two cups of Earl Grey tea, and he set to asking me in his deep voice about my day. I launched into a diatribe about my Year 10s.

'They're exhausting . . . unbothered by the rules, for example . . . not motivated . . . ridiculous amount of time spent dealing with them . . . I mean, just today . . . But don't worry' — I realized I had been going on for quite a while about this specific class — 'you won't be teaching them. You'll be teaching my Year 11 class, who are much better behaved.'

He asked me about Teach First and about what it was like teaching in an inner-city school. I asked him what his plans for education were if the Conservatives came into power. He explained he wanted to make it financially beneficial for schools to take children from lower-income families. Effective schools should share the methods they'd used, and schools should be accountable to parents and the government if they chose not to follow the recommendations made to help them become more effective — or if they were failing. He asked me what I'd do.

'I think the British military should take over failing schools — or schools with discipline problems — or schools with disaffected students. Strict rules. Drill. Respect. Long runs. Consequences for not following the rules.'

Meeting over, I walked back from Westminster, along Waterloo Bridge, to the flat. I felt wearily aware that this pace of life was unsustainable. I dropped into bed for a small nap before rousing myself, eating a few slices of peanut butter on toast, and walking down to the South Bank to see *War Horse*, a play by Michael Morpurgo at the National Theatre. A small surprise was waiting for us there. Two of Will's students and a parent spied us as we were going in. His students' enjoyment of the play was enhanced as they strained out of their seats to try to see if their teacher was holding hands with the girl he was with.

Will and I sat in the front row holding hands and watching the life-size puppets of foals and horses prance and whinny across the stage. I'd quite like one of the puppets for my classroom. I imagine its imposing form dominating the space, its regal presence intimidating the younger students into silent awe. Perhaps my Year 10s would be unsettled by its dark glass eyes watching them. I told Will that my grandmother, in searching for a school for my father, had had a tour around the grounds of Gresham's, up on the north-Norfolk coast. (In the end he didn't attend the school, though I did.) The headmaster had nonchalantly pointed to a boggy area shaded by trees and explained, 'That's where the boys who keep crocodiles keep crocodiles.'

Wes, a Teach First friend who works at a school nearby, once entertained a table of teachers at the pub with a story about his most recent open evening. Leaving his science classroom moments before prospective parents were to drop by, he returned to discover his students trying to dislodge one of the two prize corn snakes from a suction pump. The second snake, during the commotion, had taken the opportunity to sidle off into the ventilation system. He'd intended to entertain the parents by showing them the snakes. Now he was left with only half a snake and a few cultures growing in Petri dishes.

I remember very vividly the pets we kept at the school I went to as a young child — a small Steiner-style school in the Minnesota prairies. One class had a small snake, and another a terrapin. There was a highly complex rotating timetable of chores and responsibilities. At some point in the term, each student would be called on to lower a thawed mouse into the tank and then we'd all gather around to watch the snake unhinge its jaw and tackle the impossible task of swallowing the mouse whole. The terrapin ate crickets. I recall peering into its watery tank

114

and seeing that there were two cricket legs poking out from its mouth at right angles. I'm not sure that a puppet, even a life-size one, would instil in my pupils the same feelings of horror and fascination. Though, having said that, in my first year a large buzzing bee sent my Year 11s, once again, screaming into the hall.

'Aaahhh, omigod what is that? Ahhhhh.'

'I'm going to get a classroom pet,' Will told me after I'd told him about the snake and terrapin. I rolled my eyes.

'Oh, Mummy, Mummy, I want a Siberian lynx, I must have it,' I said in the lispy voice of an imaginary student who spoke otherwise perfect Queen's English. I switched to the voice of a phantom parent: 'Mr Davis, we have a spare Siberian lynx and were wondering if you'd like it for your classroom.' The pupil again: 'Mr Davis, Mr Davis, the lynx has eaten Rupert. Mr Davis!'

After being transfixed for several hours by the *War Horse* puppets, Will and I walked along the river to Waterloo. I wanted to take him to a bar nearby. We cut through the station as a mist of rain came down outside.

'Siobhan,' I called out. One of the Year 10s was standing beneath a railway arch. She looked over, but didn't register me and wandered off. I stood unsure of what to do.

'What's a fourteen-year-old girl doing wandering around London on her own at eleven o'clock at night?' I felt uneasy. What was she up to? Did her parents know or care that she was out? There was little need to comment to Will on the contrast of seeing Siobhan and bumping into his own students. When I returned to school, I emailed to the head of child protection to tell her what I'd seen.

★ ★ ★

On Saturday morning I dragged myself out of bed with Will, and along to the Teach First conference with Ella. We shuffled along corridors to attend workshops led by superhuman educators. I became really excited listening to stories of tough inner-city schools in America where the students attend a three-day course at the beginning of the summer holidays before starting at the school. During the three days the students are drilled in the expected behaviour: silence in the classrooms; silence in single-file lines down the corridors; tracking of the teacher with your eyes at all times. The students are actually taught to watch the teacher moving around the room. This sounded like heaven to me.

'You are part of a cult,' Will insisted as I told him about this later. 'Children should not be educated like this.'

'Maybe the kids you teach don't need this kind of training, because they've already had it from their parents,' I argued, 'but in a school where the students can't listen politely to each other and you struggle to be heard when the corridors are full, I think it would be really helpful to have a bit of drilling.'

Will shook his head. 'No, it kills creativity.'

'On the contrary, history suggests that creativity has always flourished under oppressive rule.' It was a point I had prepared earlier.

At lunch I met up with James, a writer and, coincidentally, a friend of Will's. He had come to the conference as he was helping to set up a charity that places writers-in-residence into schools.

'I'm very keen to have a writer for school if you've got any spare ones going,' I told him between mouthfuls of sandwich. 'Ideally female and black' — to counterbalance the predominantly white writers we study, but also to provide a role model. I wondered how much the fact I am white and public-school-educated divides me from my students. Who could I be a role model for? Does class and race matter when it comes to being a role model?

Towards the end of the day we heard a selection of Teach First participants — past and present — tell us what they were up to. One former science teacher told us how she had finished her two years' teaching and then got a research job at a university. ' . . . And at 5.30 p.m. I didn't feel exhausted. I could go to the pub and have a few drinks with friends . . . But I didn't have any stories from the day to tell them . . . and so next September I'm going back to teaching . . . '

A warm fuzzy feeling settled over the audience.

As the conference drew to a close, at around 5.30, I sat in a hall with hundreds of other Teach First teachers listening to a group of friends who had formed a barbershop choir — the A to C-sharps. 'And when those dis-ad-vantaged pu-pils hear our final plena-ry . . . they will be exceptional, just like me . . . Let it be, let it be, let it be-ee . . . ' they sang to the tune of 'Let it Be,' and the audience cried with laughter at their tongue-in-cheek appraisal of the Teach First mission.

I had arranged to meet Will for the evening, and so as soon as we were let out I made a run for the station. At six on a Saturday the weekend was finally here. I was free, and buzzing with inspiration from the day and excitement about the evening ahead.

Will picked me up on his scooter and we drove to Battersea Park for the Bonfire Night celebrations. 'I've arranged a surprise for you tomorrow,' I told him. 'Guess.'

'Ooh, um, am I meeting your parents?' He looked worried.

On Sunday we drove down to Richmond Park to go riding, which was no longer a surprise by the time we arrived, because I hadn't been able to keep it as one. Will had suggested we spend a summer holiday horseback-trekking across England. I thought we'd better put in some practice beforehand.

'How much experience have you each had?' the woman at the stables asked us. Will claimed he was practically a professional polo player, and so was given an old mare and allowed to ride without being harnessed to an instructor — unlike me.

The three of us set off — Will galloping ahead down the bridle path, the instructor and myself occasionally being allowed to trot behind.

Will and I knew we had school work we needed to do on Sunday evening, so after returning from the ride we set off in the late afternoon for the pub. One drink turned into two, and the urgent marking and preparation became less and less urgent until it was decided it really didn't make any difference if

119

it was done the following evening.

I remember feeling incredibly content sitting in that pub. The weather had turned wintery cold. Despite Will's occasional murmurings about previous relationships having ended soon after starting, after two months we were getting closer and closer. School seemed a million miles away that Sunday. If I'd spent the day marking, it would have made the week ahead less stressful — and this knowledge made the hours not spent marking all the more delicious. The benefit of having an all-consuming job was the pleasure of the hours spent letting essential things on your to-do list fall by the wayside.

We broke the rule of not staying together on Sunday nights. Sunday nights are for getting ready for the school week ahead. If you don't get enough sleep on Sunday — which you never do — the whole week is made up of early-morning promises to yourself that you will give yourself an early night.

★   ★   ★

Back in school on Monday, feeling a little sleepy and rather dreamy, and with incredibly sore muscles, which made me walk down the hallways like John Wayne, I watched the presentations the Year 11s had prepared on issues surrounding globalization. Adalia's group — the last one to take the stage — centred their discussion around the fact that the Iranian government had banned TV satellite dishes, why this was, and what the impact of their ruling might be.

They developed a small sketch: a domestic scene in Iran before satellite dishes, and the same scene played out after the wife had been watching uncensored Western television.

Predictably, and stereotypically, in the first scene the Iranian father was served by his unquestioning wife (Adalia). In the second, his wife, having been corrupted by the influences of Western television, was unwilling to play the domestic servant.

It would never have occurred to Adalia in a thousand years that her small sketch might offend. She cared deeply if she saw someone was upset, but she took life lightly and I don't imagine she spent time worrying about the repercussions of her actions. Becky, by contrast, was quicker to see the injustice of a situation — but a sketch highlighting Islamic gender stereotypes would not ruffle her feathers. Her only dissatisfaction in this lesson had been when I had reclaimed my board markers, which she had taken to graffiti her exercise book with. I looked to two feisty, articulate Muslim students, expecting them to respond. Neither said anything.

The end of the lesson had come too soon, and there was more that remained to be said. 'I enjoyed your presentation, girls . . . I think the issue in Iran is perhaps more complex . . . I'm sure the Iranian women are aware of Western culture, but the issue is perhaps that the government doesn't want to promote Western values.' (I'm aware that this doesn't really tackle the issue of reducing a culture to its stereotypes.)

As the rest of the students left, I approached the two girls I had been watching.

'Miss, Islamic culture is all about protecting the woman. That is why I wear a headscarf.'

'Yes, Miss, at home it is my aunt who makes all the decisions,' said Hebba.

'I'm sorry girls, I know I didn't handle that very well. You both need to share what you know with the class.'

Having spent my last ten years of education in whiter-than-white institutions, I had mistakenly presumed that in a multicultural environment there would be greater understanding of different cultures. But, even though we'd devoted several lessons to exploring each other's pasts and cultures, common stereotypes held strong. Hebba wrote me a note the following lesson.

By the way, I was thinking that me and you are in totally different worlds yet cross each other but shall never be in the same position and feel the same way. Don't you agree? It is quite amazing. You know, I would want to bring you once to Afghanistan you would see such a different world. I know that even though I'm from Afghanistan I am still different to them. I think I have just accepted both worlds and sort of made my religion my culture.

I was thinking let me write something on culture, yes I know you must be thinking, hasn't Hebba got a life but I was in the mood.

I remember first properly noticing Hebba when she stayed behind after one of our first lessons the previous year. She was newly arrived from Afghanistan; I was newly arrived from my six weeks' intensive teacher-training course. Hebba had stayed behind to ask for more help with English — she spoke little English, but was determined to fix that. I barely knew what I was doing inside the classroom, but said I'd do what I could to help.

A few weeks later Maria arrived from

Romania speaking next to no English. They were two of my brightest students, and in the time it took me to drag the rest of the class through pieces of coursework they learned English by themselves. They both had something over most of the class: an understanding greater than their years of how valuable an education would be to them, and knowledge of more of the world than one London borough.

It must have driven them both mad at times to have to spend so much time waiting for me to finish dealing with the small but constant distractions provided by their colleagues. But, rather than giving up and deciding to fill in the wasted time with a small conversation, they waited quietly. In the first year when I marked their essays written in broken English I felt guilty that I wasn't giving them more time. In my second year with them I still felt they didn't get their fair share.

★   ★   ★

Michael Gove had decided he wanted to set the Year 11s the task of deciding whether mixed faith schools were better than single-faith schools.

On the day he was to visit, I went into

school a little on the early side to make sure my classroom looked presentable. At 7.50 I had a near heart attack as I realized that the whole-school assembly that my Year 7s were starring in was also going to be this morning. I ran down the endless flights of stairs to the hall, and was semi-relieved to see that no chairs were set out. The gods had been merciful — for some unknown reason assembly was cancelled — and we were going to have another week to practise. The performance of 'Suicide in the Trenches' was looking fairly shambolic, though Genesis, Rose and Princess had learned their stanzas perfectly. The rest were to stand in rows behind the speakers, school uniforms perfect, poppies in their lapels, and swiftly move through the actions that accompanied and exemplified each line of the poem. I was convinced it was going to be very embarrassing for everyone involved.

Michael Gove arrived with his entourage of a cameraman, a sound engineer, a photographer and two representatives from Teach First — former super-teachers. The Conservative Party wanted a short film about Gove's experience as a teacher, so we set to staging various scenes: a shot of Gove walking into the school, a shot of him in the staffroom with other teachers looking on completely bemused as he sat down and pretended to finish his last minute preparations for the lesson, a shot of students going absolutely mental in the corridor because there was a camera pointing at them, a shot of the ceiling as the cameraman was mobbed by the students in the corridor.

Upbeat music and shots of the students milling, taken though the wire fence. Shots of the corridors taken before the students realized they were being filmed.

MICHAEL: I'm preparing actually to teach a class of sixteen-year-old girls. Now, teaching requires bravery and commitment and dedication, and I suspect I'm going to find out in the next hour or so just how much bravery and commitment when, like me, you have no professional qualifications and no expertise.

(Loud music again and shots of some of the individuals in the class looking studious. Shot of the whiteboard which has 'November 19th 2007' written in the top right-hand corner.)

MICHAEL: Good morning everyone, my name is Mr Gove. It's lovely to see you, even though it's horrible weather out there. Thank you all for coming along on time. First of all I just want to say a little bit more about who I am, because, um, I'm a politician, I'm a Member of Parliament, I'm a Conservative . . .

The film of the lesson continues, and we come to a scene where Michael wants to set the students the task of writing their own sound bite. First he has to explain what one is.

MICHAEL: A sound bite is like a slogan that's used by politicians. So have any of you heard of the phrase 'tough on crime, tough on the causes of crime'?

CLASS: . . . (Complete silence — students stare blankly at Michael.)

MICHAEL: No. Have any of you . . . have any of you heard of the phrase 'ask not what you can do for your country but what your country can do for you'?

CLASS: . . . (Deafening silence — shot of Adalia looking bored.)

MICHAEL: Have any of you heard of the phrase 'Why take two bottles into the shower, when you can take just one with Wash&Go?'?

CLASS: (Relieved laughter.)

MICHAEL: That's a sound bite. It's a slogan. It's a way of remembering something by putting it in a little pithy phrase.

(Music plays and there are more shots of the students. Adalia again gets a close-up — she's a very pretty student, and this time she is fully rolling her eyes from one side to the other as Michael sits by her table explaining something.)

MICHAEL: When I worked in newspapers, my job was to do the boring bit here *(pointing to the front page of a news-paper)*, the boring bit with all the facts. But there was someone else, the editor, whose job it was to find the slogan to persuade people to read. 'Too Fat to Work' *(he looks at the newspaper, reading the headline, then at the rest of the class, showing the doubt on his face)*. Too fat to work? Too fat? I'm going to read on — that is amazing.

When the DVD arrived by post a few days later, I played it through to the Year 11s. Becky's face looked angry each time she appeared on the film.

'Omigod! It's you, Aysha . . . Aw, you look so cute!' They screamed each time they saw each other or themselves in a shot. It wasn't possible to hear a single word said.

Harriet, the deputy head, was particularly unimpressed that I was using the students to win votes for the Conservatives. I'd never voted for the party, but every day spent with students who lacked a sense of the need to work for their futures made the harder rules of the Conservatives seem appealing.

What the film didn't show was my Year 10s, fronted by Coleen, banging on the door, beside themselves with excitement, while the cameraman tried to film me giving my verdict on the lesson. It also didn't record that when I finally opened the door Siobhan flew in, limbs and fake nails all over the place, asking me which of the men in the room was my boyfriend. In an all-girls school, male visitors tend to cause extreme behaviour. In fact men tend to cause quite a stir even if they are spotted on the road from the window of my fourth-storey classroom. Male teachers are sometimes the objects of a few quiet crushes, but it's always new blood that inspires more violent reactions.

I was secretly quite glad that my Year 10s had displayed such outlandish behaviour entering the classroom. It meant that Michael Gove and the rest of the visitors had a taste of what it's like when you haven't read the students the riot act in the days preceding the visit. I didn't want the guests to leave wondering what all the fuss was about inner-city schools.

* * *

Autumn term is the cruellest term. In the last few weeks before the Christmas holidays, each day I felt a little bit more drained. I asked the Year 11s to write brief thank-you letters to Michael Gove, and, collecting them in, I saw that every single short note had at least a couple of small mistakes. I corrected them and handed them back to be rewritten.

'Why are we writing these out again?' Becky asked, irritated.

'Because there were mistakes in all of them,' I explained.

'But that's just how we write,' she retorted, seeming annoyed, but also as if she genuinely did not see what the issue was.

Aysha had asked Michael why he was a Conservative. He said he thought the idea of greater personal freedom was appealing. School feels like the nanny state at its fiercest — all responsibility lies with the teacher. Feeling depressed about the students' dependency, I dropped in to see my colleague John.

'Look, Nony, the girls know that making

sure there are no mistakes in their work is *our* responsibility, because we correct their mistakes for them.'

'Um,' I agreed.

'Getting coursework in is our responsibility. Their grades are our responsibility.'

'But what favours are we actually doing them?'

John shrugged his shoulders.

My energy was flagging, but knowing Julia was going to come in and observe me teaching the Year 10s gave me the kick I needed to try to reassert some authority. I asked her to come along to the beginning of a lesson a few days before she was due to formally assess me. I'd decided to introduce a new seating plan — a move that was guaranteed to generate anarchy.

Sure enough, Coleen refused, loudly, to sit in her new seat.

'No, I don't care, I'm not sitting there,' she said as I indicated that I wanted her at the front of the classroom. Coleen moved to a desk of her own choice, incoherently grumbling.

'Coleen,' Julia's tone of voice meant business. 'Could you come out into the hall please?' Coleen trudged out and didn't return. Why would she follow other people's instructions but not mine?

Mini-crisis dealt with, the rest of the class were subdued by the fact that, by inviting Julia along to the start of the lesson, I had temporarily outmanoeuvred them.

A few lessons later Julia was *in situ* at the back of the class. I'd run through the lesson I was going to teach with Ella the previous evening. It was a lesson on the Victorian education system, to help the class understand more about Jane Eyre's school days.

'I know, why don't you dress up as a Victorian teacher?' Ella had suggested.

'That's brilliant. We'll act out a little Victorian classroom scene.'

The girls entered in dribs and drabs, automatically moving to the new seats they'd been allocated. Coleen came in, and I quietly asked her to come to a desk at the front. She slumped down looking pissed off.

I was wearing my university mortar board and gown, and a pair of dark rimmed glasses. I held my longest ruler in my hand, and started slapping it down on the desks.

'Sit up, you miserable child.' Slap.

'What are you laughing at, you disgusting student?' Crack, the ruler hit the table in front of Coleen and splintered into pieces. She laughed and sat up.

'All right. *Calm* down,' she said, playing along. The Year 10s were heckling far too much to be convincing Victorian students. No one seemed to have any idea whether I was acting or not — and I had no idea myself.

'You,' I pointed at Ummi, 'come up here.' It was cruel to pick a compliant student. Coleen was the more obvious choice, but I feared that, even though she'd been amused at the ruler breaking, she wouldn't play ball in the next activity. Ummi came up to the front of the classroom and I Sellotaped a piece of paper saying 'Bad Child' to her jumper. I told her to stand on a chair, and instructed the rest of the class not to look at or talk to her.

The lesson went downhill after the dramatic start. We grappled with a piece of text from *Jane Eyre* about Jane's schooldays. I made the same mistake I'd made when I'd given the first chapter of *Great Expectations* to my first Year 11 set: there were too many words they didn't understand. I was trying to move too quickly. Nothing made sense, and they lost interest. Every time I tried to help individuals and pairs, as soon as I turned my back Coleen had swung herself round and was chatting to the girls behind her.

Studying *Jane Eyre* had, on the whole, been quite a challenge. The class were most gripped watching the DVD — especially when they discovered Bertha was living in the attic. 'I'd kill 'er,' Folashade commented. (There was always an ongoing commentary on the action while DVDs played.) 'No, I'd kill 'im,' Coleen shouted passionately.

At the end of the lesson Julia was observing, I asked them to take out the self-assessment sheets I had given them previously but hadn't really explained.

'Who can't find the sheet, raise your hand.' I quickly handed out new photocopies.

'Right, Chamel, tell me which box you have ticked off. What do you think you've learned this lesson?'

Chamel read out the sentence next to the box she had ticked. It was not what I was expecting — which was something about understanding what Victorian education was like. I was thrown for a second, and then realized she was reading from the self-assessment sheet from the previous piece of coursework — the creative writing. Bollocks!

Julia's feedback was like observing yourself in a magnifying mirror under strip lighting. 'Great effort with the dressing-up, but . . . what was the focus? And you said, 'Hands up' but then listened to answers shouted out . . . And the girl with the self-assessment at the end . . . '

'Yeah, I know.' I had already formulated a list in my head of things that had not worked.

'And Coleen . . . ' I said, trailing off and pulling a comedy grimace.

'Well, at least she was engaged — '

'For some of the time,' I broke in.

The whole lesson had the hallmark of someone who knew what they were meant to be doing but hadn't taken the time to really think things through.

★ ★ ★

With only a few weeks till Christmas, a large tree was erected in reception, decorated with gaudy baubles. The dining hall too had been given the tinsel treatment.

Both sets of Year 7s were gripped by the book we had devoted many a lesson to reading. I'd read *Private Peaceful* during the summer holidays, and sobbed uncontrollably at the death of the soldier, something that had already taken on a new meaning for me. In April of my first year teaching, during the Easter holidays, one of my closest friends from university, Joanna Dyer an army officer, was killed out in Iraq by a roadside bomb. I'd told my classes when I returned to school, taking in a few photographs of her and a front page of one of the newspapers which had her picture blazoned across it. The younger students made cards with RIPs scattered across the pages. The older students — my terrible Year 11s — had been stunned into quiet for a whole sixty-minute lesson. In the weeks after her death I'd been rather stunned too.

And ever since then everything has been altered. There have been moments, walking across the playground on a crisp, sunny day, satisfied with a lesson just taught, that I've suddenly been struck with the sadness of Jo not being able to have an ordinary day.

Reaching the last pages of *Private Peaceful* again, and knowing what was coming, I started choking up. At the end of our third year of university Jo watched me fall to pieces after breaking up with a boyfriend of two years, just a month before our finals. She told me to have 'strength', and it became a motto between us. Digging my nails into my hands, I tried to conjure up some of her strength to keep reading without sabotaging the end of the book — but I kept faltering.

'Camilla, would you continue reading?' I asked, voice cracking, face scrunching up trying to hold back tears.

'No, Miss, you read.' The class were annoyed I'd pass over reading at such a point. And so, with tears streaming down my face, I read the ending through twice — once to the top-set Year 7s and once to the lower set.

Both times I finished and looked up to see several others with red puffy eyes and snotty noses. Stella was sobbing openly.

'It's so sad, Miss,' she said, coming up to me as the others returned their chairs from the front of the classroom to behind their desks.

'Yes, isn't it.'

'Are you OK, Miss?' Princess and Stella lingered by me. I think they were worried to see their teacher so dissolved.

'Yes, it's just very, very sad' — the rest of the class were listening — 'and it makes me think of a friend I had who was killed out in Iraq earlier this year.'

'A girl, Miss?'

'Yes.'

'Oh,' they cooed, understanding.

'Was she in the army?'

'Yes.'

'Oh.'

'That's so sad.'

'Yes.'

The end of the lesson had come, and they left quietly, some still wiping their eyes. I took a deep breath and went down to lunch to confess to Emily how emotional I'd been.

★ ★ ★

The following Monday morning I frantically pinned poppies to the lapels of the Year 7s' blazers. They were standing on the great stage in the dining hall, behind a heavy curtain. At 8.15, with fifteen minutes till the assembly began, we had about a quarter of the class. I was convinced the whole thing was going to be a complete disaster, but tried to keep these pessimistic thoughts hidden behind a smile and lots of words of encouragement. At 8.29 the last few girls made it on to the stage and I hushed them as Harriet spoke through a microphone to the thousand students on the other side of the curtain.

After Harriet had introduced the class, the curtains opened and I slipped away down the stairs stage left. I stood to the side of the hall, halfway back. Please, God, let this not be a disaster. One student said the title of the poem into the microphone: 'Suicide in the Trenches'. Please don't let it be public suicide on stage. Another student, knee high to a grasshopper, announced the poem was by Siegfried Sassoon. Chantelle took the mike and my heart jumped. She explained that we'd been studying this poem in class. This was unplanned and unpractised, but clearly Chantelle had decided at the last moment that she wanted to get involved in the fun with a bit of free-styling. Then Rose began the first stanza.

The hall was completely silent, and there was something very impressive about such tiny students, before such a huge audience, reciting a poem by heart:

I knew a simple soldier boy
Who grinned at life in empty joy

The rest of the girls, in their navy blazers and red poppies, acted out each line, and when the last stanza was finished the audience breathed out a sigh of 'Aw' before rupturing into applause.

'Miss Crossley-Holland,' said John, coming up to me. 'Are they your girls?'

'Yes,' I said.

'I thought that was really impressive.'

'Really?'

'Yeah . . . I mean, we see a lot of dance and drama sketches, and it always tends to be the same thing — but that was actually entertaining, and I rarely think that about assembly.'

'Thanks.' What little legends, I thought, filled with relief that the event was over.

When we all saw each other for a lesson the following day, there was still much excitement about the success of the assembly.

'I have a very important secret I want to tell you all,' I said. 'It's really important that you don't tell anyone this.' I eyed them all very seriously. 'If you do tell anyone and I find out, I will have to throw you out of the window.'

'Miss, you wouldn't actually do that,' Chantelle called out.

'Yes I would,' I said, 'and to prove it . . . ' I picked up a newspaper article I'd cut out thinking I might put it up on my noticeboard. 'Look,' I read out the headline — 'Teacher Kills Student for Doodling.' I'd thought there was something darkly amusing about an Indian teacher losing his rag with a student. I'd shown it to a few people in the staffroom, who'd thought it was inappropriate and not funny at all.

The Year 7s didn't seem particularly perturbed by being shown the article, and I swiftly moved on.

'The secret I want to tell you all is that you are my absolute favourite class.' They were. There wasn't a lot of competition, but theirs were the lessons I most looked forward to — they were the class it seemed most magic to teach, and in the minutes preceding their lessons I didn't get a sinking feeling in the pit of my stomach.

This didn't take away from the fact that they still needed frequent reminding of the rules.

'Princess, don't do that.'

She was playing up, but only slightly: she quickly forgot that she had been told several times not to play with her pencil case while someone else was talking. Like Stella, she is small and eager and has the look of a cherub. I've noticed that frequently when I ask a question — 'And who can tell me what they thought about doing the assembly?' — her hand shoots up and she starts telling me before she has been called on. It's very difficult to be stern when she did such a sterling job reciting a stanza before the audience, helping me organize the rest of the class into rows, helping me pin on poppies. And it becomes almost impossible to be strict when she has just given me a Christmas card at the beginning of the lesson. Scrawled and misspelled, it was to 'my favourite teacher Miss Crossly Holand'.

I notice a few more cautious students hold their Christmas cards back till the end of the lesson — no doubt waiting to see how the hour went.

Another of my prize cards this year was from Amaal, who, with her pouted lips and open eyes, reminds me of an owl. She is also of the variety of student easily distracted by objects on her desk. A few lessons ago I kept her back with Poppy.

'Repeat after me,' I said: 'I Amaal, and I Poppy . . . ' But the two of them couldn't figure out who was meant to say what, and so giggled their way through the whole of their vows. 'I Amaal, and I Poppy, promise to behave perfectly in Miss Crossley-Holland's lessons. We will not undertake silly things like painting our nails with highlighter pens. If we misbehave again we understand Miss Crossley-Holland will think up a very serious punishment.' They left the room quite happy.

When I watch Amaal, I can see her thinking carefully. She likes to check specific details. 'What is the plural of 'duchess'?' 'I want to talk about the structure of the book, but I don't know how to start.' In her Christmas card she asked me, 'Please will you mention me in your column? Lol.' To liven things up in class, I'd occasionally photocopied a copy of a recent column I'd written for the *Guardian* which mentioned an incident that had happened with that particular group. Generally the students were less excited to see the pieces than I imagined they might be.

Both Amaal and Princess are Muslim. I remember that out in India, at the school where Ella and I taught in our gap year, students would happily assimilate the various religions. One girl said that she was a Buddhist Christian. I don't think the same amalgamation is going on in London, but Christmas is just for everyone in a multi-faith school.

I wrote about the Christmas cards and Amaal's inscription in a column that fortnight, adding a note about how much I appreciated the amount of freedom we had within the English department to follow a course of study we each devised to suit our students. Ella returned home from school every day having taught the lessons her whole department was teaching, learning objectives and outcomes having been agreed. Having finished *Private Peaceful* with a few lessons still to go before the end of term, I decided to try to devise a lesson or two about the Christmas truce of 1914. I wrote a column celebrating the fact that I was able to introduce new material at will.

Steph read the *Guardian* and picked me up on the piece.

'A friend of mine read it, Nony, another head of department, and said you're delusional. It's anarchic to have teachers just teaching their own thing.'

I grinned guiltily. Steph's big drive this year has been to try to get us all working together — teaching the same material — 'consistency across the department. We can't have a department full of mavericks.'

'Ye-es, in principle I agree.' But I thought the idea of being prescribed what to teach seemed to take all the fun out of it.

Will had been fighting a similar battle at school. The senior management had wanted to see evidence of everyone's planning for the term. Will's planning takes place in the seconds before he enters to the classroom — or the seconds before the instructions come out of his mouth. I think I'd give myself a heart attack if I waited till the students were in the room to decide on what we were going to do.

★ ★ ★

Will's term ended with a Christmas carol concert in a local church. I went along. For two hours I sat next to the art teacher listening to small children belting out carols, stretching their mouths as open as possible, wobbling on the top notes. The girls wore small navy-cord pinafore dresses with woolly tights, the boys navy cords and polo shirts. They looked like something out of a Ralph Lauren advert. The church was lit with candles, and the parents — mothers dressed in velvet and sequins — sat listening. My own students were still wearing socks with their skirts. To keep warm, many had rolled-up pyjama bottoms on under the skirts, which occasionally became visible when the girls walked or when a pyjama leg slipped down.

What Will had been most keen that I hear was the parent-teacher choir, of which he was the only male member. 'Sing strong and wrong,' the music teacher had reassured him.

In the final rendition of 'The Twelve Days of Christmas', we all rose to our feet to sing and perform the song, with the head teacher leading the way. I met her after the performance. 'She'll probably offer you a job,' said Will. And indeed, within three seconds of meeting her she asked if I could be persuaded to move schools.

'No, I can't come and work for you,' I said, 'because if I did, I would take Will's position.' Will looked on nervously.

Out in the cold night, I wrapped my coat more tightly around me and put a helmet on. On the back of Will's scooter, the wind cut through my tights. It had some how got to be 9.30 and we hadn't yet had supper. We drove to a sushi restaurant before returning to his. I sat and looked at the raw fish, and again felt a sick panic rising. I told Will, and he gobbled down my portion while I sipped miserably at the miso soup.

On the freezing-cold drive back, he suggested we spend the New Year out in

Ireland with his closest friends — a couple with two small children. 'What do you think?' he said.

I thought it sounded completely terrifying. Staying in a house with grown-ups and their *children* for a week — with Will for a whole *week*. Nowhere to run away to.

'Yeah, that'd be cool.'

My term ended with a staff party at a hotel. No one sat on a photocopier or snogged in a store cupboard, there was just scandalously bad dancing — 'Wouldn't the students laugh if they could see us now?' Only if they were feeling particularly kind. The party started at midday, and by six o'clock we'd spent six hours chewing through a rather miserable Christmas dinner and listening to the world's most depressing DJ. By then many of the staff had slunk off, others perhaps should have, and some were clearly going to need to be carried off.

I ended up sitting, during the afternoon, next to Cecelia, the principal.

'If you'd like to give me an early Christmas present,' I said, trying my luck, 'permanently excluding a few of my Year 10s would be ideal.' She laughed, obviously thinking I was trying to be amusing.

'Adalia Casas was telling me how much the school has changed since she was in Year 7,' I told Cecelia, moving on to a different topic. Adalia had dropped by my classroom after school one day to say hello. I'd asked her if she'd be willing to write something about Michael Gove's visit for the school newsletter, and, unprompted, she started telling me about how different the school was now from the school she'd arrived at four and a half years earlier.

'It was well bad, yeah. I was properly scared.'

'What, in the hallways?' I asked.

'Yeah. You used to have to fight to get through, and people would just hang around and not go to lessons. And . . . ' she started laughing, 'the girls from this school didn't — you know — have a very good reputation. There used to be all these boys outside the gates.'

'What? Just coming to pick girls up after school.'

'Yeah!'

We both raised our eyebrows.

I caught the Tube home from the hotel, relieved to get away. I had three nights of Christmas parties with friends planned, and I wanted to go and hibernate.

In *Overboard*, Goldie Hawn plays a wealthy heiress who, suffering from amnesia, is tricked by a carpenter she once refused to pay. As retribution, he has her believe she is his wife and the mother of his four unruly children. After her first few days of real graft as a housewife, the carpenter returns home in the evening to find her traumatized by the day's work, mumbling, 'Ba . . . ba . . . ba . . . ba.' When Ella returned home, she crashed on to my bed.

'Ba . . . ba . . . ba . . . ba,' she said.

'Ba . . . ba . . . ba . . . ba,' I replied.

SPRING TERM
FIRST HALF

The new term began on Monday 7 January. I was exhausted. As the holidays had progressed, I didn't feel that I was getting any rest: I was just getting more tired. Christmas with all four of my parents — mother and stepfather, father and stepmother — had been strenuous. The prospect of Ireland seemed terrifying — and the most terrifying thought was that I'd just feel sick with anxiety the whole time I was out there. I worked myself into a downward spiral about panicking about things, and very quickly I was panicking about panicking. I pleaded with my doctor to give me some Valium to try to induce a relaxed state while I was in Ireland with Will's friends Kate and Jerome and their children.

In the end, the trip to Ireland was lovely. Keen to keep the Valium for himself, Will had tried to talk me through spells where I thought my head was spinning out of control.

'Will, I think I'm going crazy.'

'Who's your favourite playwright, Nony?'

'Um, I don't know. Tom Stoppard?'

'No, the other one.'

151

'Oh, Beckett.'

'What did Beckett say?'

'I don't know.'

'Anything but thinking.'

I weakly attempted laughing.

I have a track record of hideous New Year's Eves. Two remain very vividly in my mind. An ex-boyfriend and I were fighting and so involved in our argument that for two years running we didn't realize that midnight and the start of the new year had come and gone. This New Year I managed to inebriate myself with champagne and wine into a relative state of calm. Will, Kate and Jerome and I sat in their upstairs sitting room drinking vodka and playing games. Midnight came, we kissed our respective partners, and the four of us remained warm and snug inside while the rain lashed against the windows. At one o'clock Kate decided it was time for bed, and I shortly followed. I took my glass with me, and stood at the top of their wooden stairs in my socks. I took a first step and then bounced down the rest of the staircase on the base of my spine. The glass smashed out of my hand, and I landed at the bottom and sat in a pool of wine, broken glass and tears. Will spent the first night of the new year holding a bag of frozen peas against my back and waking me up to administer painkillers.

I tried unsuccessfully to explain to Will what I was so worked up about. I knew that breaking up with him would get rid of the near-constant feeling of panic, but I also knew it wouldn't solve the problem. And at least Will seemed rather indifferent as to whether I was feeling fine or fighting off waves of nausea for which he was the cause. I suspected any future guy might be a little more put-off. And, despite his presence making me feel queasy, I didn't want not to be with him.

Returning to England, I booked myself in for some therapy. The doctor with whom I'd pleaded for drugs had advised counselling as a better long-term solution. I texted Julia to tell her I'd lost the plot. 'Stop being so hard on yourself . . . Don't let your demons get you down . . . Play 'Shine' by Take That,' she replied. 'And don't worry: everyone's fucking mental.'

Approaching the end of the holiday, I made a list of all the things I needed to do, over the weekend, to ensure my return to school was not like diving into a pool of piranhas. What had I been thinking, spending the days freaking out? There was piles of marking to be done.

Back in the flat with Ella, I immediately felt less sick. Ella and I reasoned with each other on the Friday before school.

'There's no point trying to do school work while the flat is such a mess,' I informed her.

'Yes, Nony, let's tidy this morning and then mark this afternoon.'

We put on Paul Simon's *Graceland* — an album we always played if we wanted to sort things out in the flat — and set to cleaning and trying to rearrange the few bits of furniture so as to create the illusion of more space. It was a puzzle we constantly worked at. Periodically we switched the rooms round — two rooms could be made into bedrooms, and the third would become a kind of very squashed dining room-cum-sitting room-cum-study.

By the evening we had a sparkling flat and we'd done lots of marking. No, I'm lying: we hadn't. Distracted by *Vogue*, we sat leafing through its pages, made home-made green-pea soup for lunch, and wrote lists of the pieces of clothing we desperately needed to buy.

Evening arrived in no time at all, and we retired to the bar across the road and were joined by Will and Leo, a teacher whom Ella had just started dating. I watched the three of them become paralytic — smugly keeping myself sober in the knowledge that Saturday was going to be a big marking day.

The weekend passed without my so much as opening a student's exercise book. On Sunday I spent an hour planning a few lessons, then realized that I'd left the really important, the really urgent marking that I'd been saving up to do over the holidays at school. I gave up and went to Will's to watch Harry Potter.

★ ★ ★

Arriving at school on Monday, I remembered that I'd intended to come in during the holidays to rearrange the desks and spring-clean. No marking had been done, and I couldn't have been further from feeling rested and rejuvenated.

I pushed the tables into squares, so two students would sit facing another pair, and welcomed the Year 10s back to school.

'Hello, Folashade, nice to see you . . . ' Folashade didn't notice I was speaking to her.

'Hello, Coleen . . . '

'Uh.' Coleen briefly looked at me, bored already.

'Hello, Ummi.'

'Hello, Miss, did you have a nice holiday?'

'Yes, thank you, Ummi. That's really sweet of you to ask.'

After the lesson, I reflected that I might as

well not have been there. With the desks in squares, the girls started talking to each other immediately and basically did not stop for the duration of the lesson. Coleen's behaviour had been massively disruptive, but it hadn't stood out from anyone else's.

'Coleen, stop talking, please.'

'Why you looking at me? I'm not the only one talking. Man!' She turned to another student: 'If you ever do one thing wrong in this school they don't let you forget it.'

I pushed the tables back into rows.

With the Year 11s I started reading *Catcher in the Rye*.

'OK, I'm going to try an American accent,' I told them, feeling confident that having lived for seven years in Minnesota I would do a convincing job of bringing the text to life. 'If you really want to hear about it, the first thing you'll probably want to know is where I was born, and what my lousy childhood was like . . . ' I began.

'No, Miss,' Abimbola called out.

'No, don't, that's annoying,' several more joined in.

I dropped the accent and continued in English for a page or two before deciding to ask Adalia to read. She wasn't following along like the rest of the class. She roused her head from the desk and started reading. After the lesson I went to speak to her.

'Do you know why Becky's not in?' I asked.
'No,' she shook her head. Damn, I thought.
Becky's missed the beginning of the book
— she's going to be confused.

On Monday evening I started on the pile of
marking left over from the previous term. I
read Ummi's essay on *Jane Eyre* and was
filled with a glowing pride. The work was all
her own. I'd asked the Year 10s to write an
essay exploring the ways in which Jane Eyre
was a woman before her time. We'd written it
once, cobbling together paragraphs written in
each lesson, but it didn't really work. I told
them we'd have to write it again. That went
down really badly until Chamel came to my
aid and explained to the class that I wanted
them to get higher grades. I'd tried telling
them the same thing, but they paid more
heed to Chamel. I taught them how to write a
paragraph — how to write a point to start it;
how to make sure that you find a quotation
that backs the point up. Then I showed them
how to structure an essay. They wrote the
essay again. Ummi had used the structure but
had also thought carefully herself, and the
result was satisfying.

Coleen had put the same amount of effort
into her essay on *Jane Eyre* as she had put
into her piece of creative writing. The result

was barely more than a paragraph. She hadn't used the time I'd given her in class to restructure her work, but had simply copied out the first weak attempt, ignoring once again the questions, comments and corrections I'd written in.

★   ★   ★

On Tuesday, during lesson four, I realized I'd been bitten (not by a student). Late Tuesday afternoon we had a rare staff meeting, to prepare for an imminent visit from Her Majesty's Inspectors. We'd had no tip-offs, but management feel the arrival of inspectors in their bones. The briefing went something like 'Don't panic, we've got a great team. Don't panic, remember that the inspectors might be looming outside your door at any time — you might not even be aware they are watching you — but don't panic. Here is a checklist of things to make sure you're on top of. You'll notice that the list is printed on cream paper: all correspondence to do with HMI will be printed on cream paper, not red, because red is the colour of panic.'

I found it quite difficult to concentrate during the meeting. I was sitting in the back row, and I needed to show the rest of the English department (also in the back row) my elbow, which was very swollen and red.

At home, Ella and I swapped teaching stories of the day over chicken Kievs before settling down for some marking (more of the marking that should have been done during the holidays). Everything seemed to be going well — I noted it was taking me five minutes to mark each student's work and therefore I would be finishing at ten. But then at 8.30 something strange happened: every muscle in my body hurt, and I suddenly had to crawl to bed, unable to do anything more.

At six o'clock on Wednesday morning I called in sick. Most mornings at six o'clock I think it would be nice to call in sick, but when it comes to doing it it's horrible. I sat down morosely at my laptop to email in cover work, thinking how the poor cover teacher would be so abused by my classes. The students would trash the room. The Year 10s probably won't even notice I'm not there, I thought.

I hobbled down the road to the doctor's. I had to carry my swollen arm. Every step I took made it hurt more. The doctor looked at my arm and I described my symptoms. He was bemused. He told me I was not well enough to go to school for a couple of days, and so I lay in bed thinking how much I wished I was well, rather than afflicted with an unknown disease — probably tropical — and unable to enjoy the precious time off.

Two friends from separate circles were having birthday drinks on Friday night. I felt better. Or rather I felt well enough to chat quietly to some friends in a bar, but hadn't quite felt up to controlling the chat of the one hundred and twenty students I see on a Friday. I knew people from school would be at one of the parties, and it seemed very bad form to have the day off and then go for a drink — so I went to the other one, praying I wouldn't be found out.

On Saturday night Will went to stay at his parents' in Oxfordshire, Ella went to stay with Leo, and I thought it would be sensible to get a reasonably early night. I saw Lucy, a friend I'd met through Teach First, for lunch on Sunday.

'I was awake till five this morning — I'm feeling a bit sleepy,' I told her.

'God, Nones, why?' Lucy looked more bemused than concerned.

'I was worried about burglars.'

'Oh, Nones.'

'At about four I actually started thinking about monsters in hoods climbing up the front of the flat and coming through the windows.'

I reflected that the feeling I'd enjoyed in

160

September of being on top of the new school year, on top of marking, really enjoying lessons, had been short lived. I needed to get more sleep and more exercise, and take the reins again for each of my classes so that each lesson didn't feel like donating a quart of blood.

★   ★   ★

I braced myself on Monday entering my classroom. But the damage was limited. Lots of sheets of A4 lined paper were strewn about the place. Some students had obviously managed to write their names at the tops of their piece of paper, but not got any further. I removed the crisp packets stuffed into the cupboard at the back of the room.

Over the weekend I had marked the Year 11 mock exams. The class were predicted mostly Bs with the odd A, and had achieved Ds and Es. Becky had completed only one side of A4. She'd answered one question and then clearly given up. I knew that she, more than the other students, had a long way to go. I hoped their individual results would give them a much needed kick up the backside. I entered their marks into the computer system.

'Reading your exams papers was heartening,' I told the class before giving them their results. They stared blankly, and then looked distressed. I couldn't understand what the problem was until Adalia confidently put into words what everyone else was thinking.

'What does 'heartening' mean?' she said, scrunching up her nose. All breathed a sigh of relief as I elaborated.

'Your grades aren't actually very good, because you're all still not writing enough. But what you are writing is of really good quality. So all we need to work on is just working much, much faster and writing much more.'

When I put Becky's exam paper on the desk in front of her, she took her eyes off the doodle she was drawing for a second, looked at the grade, flushed red, and then intently continued with her drawing, deaf to anything else happening in the room.

'Don't worry, Becky, you'll get there,' I told her quietly. 'We've still got a couple of months.' She didn't look at me.

The Year 10s entered the room on Monday morning in their usual ungainly way. I spent a few minutes politely asking Erez to take off her coat.

'Please take off your coat, Erez.'

Erez looked at me blankly. She did not move.

I know the routine. I asked a few others to

remove a scarf, a bag from the table, a hat and, working my way around the room, found myself back asking Erez to take her coat off. This time, at a snail's pace, she began shuffling out of the black sleeves and shifting herself forward to shrug the coat off. Operation completed, she stared blankly at me.

Coleen was sitting at the front. She was my next target.

'Please could you take out a pen.'

'Don't start on me — I'm not in the mood.'

I paused. I looked at her blankly. My face gave no clues, but in my mind I was running over my options, the stock phrases I could trip out to manage the situation. The trouble was, I was tiring of this discussion.

'No. *I'm* not in the mood,' I said. 'Take out a pen and write down the learning objective.'

'All right . . . no need to get angry.'

'I am not getting angry,' and then, feeling the blood boiling in my head, added, 'but I can clearly see that you are finding it difficult to control yourself.'

This is bad teaching. Really bad. I'd retaliated, and it made me smart inside. I'd sunk to the level of answering back.

I don't run out of patience with the Year 7s.

'Chantelle, what do we put around a quotation?'

'Quotation marks?'

'Yes, exactly. And, Genesis, why do we put quotation marks around a quotation?'

'Because they show the words are from the text.'

'Fantastic.'

I'm willing to defuse the Year 11s who are having an off day with distractions or humour. Willing to crouch down beside Becky and ask her questions which I know she can answer, so that we get the ball rolling. But with Coleen, who presents me with the same confrontation day in, day out, I had run out of calm responses.

After school on Monday I went along to a workshop Julia was running on combating bad behaviour. She divided us into pairs and gave us a situation to role-play — an example of challenging behaviour that she had encountered in one of her lessons. I sat with Sam, an NQT and a member of the maths department. Julia handed us a folded-up slip.

A student arrives to lesson ten minutes late. She kicks open the door and then loudly announces to the rest of the class, who are working quietly, 'Look, I'm early.'

I got to play the role of the student. It was brilliant. The room of teachers giggled as I kicked down the door. It was fantastically entertaining trying to watch Sam rein me in.

I sat down, still in role, and shifted my chair so that I had a view of the rest of the class (this was something I had learned from Coleen). I slumped back in the chair. I had all the control. Sam, playing the teacher, nervously tried to continue addressing the rest of the class — 'Just continue with the work you are doing' — and then gave me the worksheet that the others were working on and told me quietly what I needed to do. The quieter she was, the louder I was.

'What? I don't get it, Miss.' I folded my arms and refused to look at the worksheet, then decided to sweep it off the desk and on to the floor. More laughs from the rest of the class.

The kids get to have all the fun.

As a general rule, the things that the students are raucously squawking about I don't find funny.

'Look,' I've overheard Abimbola say, 'she never laughs.'

Taking the bus home after Julia's workshop, I spied two students out of the window. Our green and blue uniform is very recognizable, and the roads along my route home are littered with students loitering on their way from school. As the bus drew closer, I saw that Adalia and a girl from another class

165

were in a supermarket trolley being pushed along by some boys obviously from a nearby school. They were laughing their heads off. I smiled and thought that if I had to guess which one of my Year 11s would be most likely to be larking around in a supermarket trolley, I would have plumped for Adalia. She misbehaves in the most amiable of ways. I don't believe she has ever arrived at my class on time, but she always apologizes smiling sweetly.

I paused and wondered whether a responsible teacher thing to do would be to report Adalia's freewheeling at school. Surely not.

★ ★ ★

'It's like the story of Sisyphus,' Will told me as I admitted I'd lost my cool with Coleen earlier on. He'd called to fill me in on his day.

'I don't know that one,' I admitted.

'God, your general knowledge is bad,' he reflected.

'Ha, ha. Whatever.' It's a long-running theme. I reminded him he'd had twelve years more reading than I had. 'Tell me who Sisyphus was.'

'He's the one condemned for all eternity to roll a boulder up a hill, only to watch it roll down again.'

'No. That doesn't work — it's not the same. If I thought that about Coleen then I'm admitting defeat.'

'Give up on the ones who don't want to learn and concentrate your energies on the ones who do.'

'No. That's not being a good teacher.'

'You can't save every child.'

'I'm not trying to save them. It's my job to teach them all.'

'What is it that bothers you so much about Coleen?' my therapist asked me as I described the incident to her.

'Um, that she just doesn't care,' I offered. 'That she doesn't care whether I help her — or doesn't seem to. She doesn't want to do better . . . or acts like she doesn't want to do better. And she's rude and aggressive, and she doesn't see what the point of doing English is.'

'So, she undermines everything you stand for and believe in?'

'Yes, I guess she does.'

The first handful of sessions with the therapist had had a noticeable impact. I told her I couldn't sit opposite Will in a restaurant without freaking out: she suggested I sat beside him for now, or that we avoided restaurants. She seemed to think I'd come to her at a good time — before I'd properly lost the plot. We didn't dive into what my issues were: she tried to build up a picture of my life, and I suppose at the same time tried to get me to see a picture of it.

★ ★ ★

The glory days with my Year 7s seemed to be drawing to a close. They were in their second term at the school and, after carefully observing the years above them, had started adopting some of their bad habits. They had grown loud. And the louder they grew, the less I enjoyed being in the classroom with them.

The half-term's work revolved around reading, writing and telling urban myths.

'What do you notice about the beginning of an urban myth?' I ask them. Stella's hand shoots up.

'You always have to say that it happened to someone you know.'

'Exactly.' I write the point up on the board, and they copy it down into their exercise books.

We establish that you need to tell an urban myth in the first person, and you always try to pass it off as a true story. The class have a go at writing the first sentence of one, and then read out the results.

'Chantelle, are you going to read yours out for us?'

'Yes, Miss'

'Everyone listening.'

'You lot are never going to believe this, but I swear it is 1,000 per cent true. It happened to my best friend's sister's aunt's hairdresser's mother's cousin's friend.'

With a few minutes left in the lesson, I announce I am going to tell them a story. 'But I'm going to tell you a true story.'

'What, really true?' Everyone looks distrustful and confused as to whether I am using the conventions of an urban myth or am about to tell them something that actually happened.

'No, this is a 100 per cent true story. And I know this story is true because it happened to my sister when we were living in America — I've told you that I lived in America when I was younger, haven't I? Well, in America you can pass your driving test when you're sixteen, and my sister had *just* passed her test and wanted to go to a party.'

Everyone is listening.

'And so she asked my dad if she could take the car and come back on her own. He said all right, 'but you have to be home by 11.30' — because she was only sixteen, and that's pretty late for a sixteen-year-old to be out.

'Well . . . she drove to the party at her friend's house and had a lovely evening and almost forgot about the time, and at 11.30 she realized she was meant to be home already, so she ran out to her car, which was parked on the road. She opened the door, and realized in her excitement earlier she'd forgotten to lock the doors.

'So she started driving, and when she stopped at the first set of traffic lights she saw a car drive up behind her. As the lights changed and she drove away, the car behind her started flashing its lights. She didn't know what to do, but she felt a bit scared so she speeded up, but the car behind her speeded up too and started beeping its horn: 'HONK! HONK!' I make the noise as loud as possible, and there are a few nervous giggles. 'And then Ellie, my sister, took a left off the main road and then a right on to a smaller road — the road which leads to our house — and the driver behind her took a left and then a right. Ellie was getting really scared, but she knew she was almost home.

'She pulled into our driveway, and the man in the car behind pulled into our driveway. Ellie put her hand on the horn and did not take it off — HONNKK! And my dad ran out of our house in his pyjamas, and he was really cross because Ellie was late home. But

Ellie just rolled down her window and said 'Daddy, Daddy, there's a man following me in the car behind.'

'And at that point the man in the car behind got out of his car and ran towards my dad with his arms stretched out. 'Sir,' he said, 'there's a man in the back of your daughter's car and he's got an axe — I saw him raise it at the traffic lights'. Well, my dad just ran to Ellie, opened her door, and dragged her out by the arm, and the man from the car behind opened her back door and jumped on to the man in the back seat.'

Twenty-six sets of eyes are bulging out of their heads, twenty-six hearts racing. I keep a serious face as they come to, laughing and asking, 'Is that story really true?' Others explain that of course it wasn't. I simply said, 'What do you think? . . . It's lunchtime. Please pack away your folders and tuck your chairs under.'

I'd first heard the story at school in America — I'd been terrified, and relayed it to my father in the evening. I believed it had happened to a friend's friend.

'Ah,' he had said, putting the tips of his fingers together, his eyes lighting up. 'I've heard that very same story.'

'What? It happened to someone you know too?' I'd asked, amazed.

★ ★ ★

Midweek, as I was dropping into Steph's classroom at the end of the day to say goodbye, she paused and looked at me grinning.

'Nony, I've put together a job description for that 2ic job I mentioned' — a job as second in command. Though the title sounds like a position on a space hub, in fact it is a role supporting the head of department. John was already 2ic for Key Stage 4 (the GCSE years), and what Steph wanted was support with Key Stage 3 (Years 7, 8 and 9).

'Oh,' I said, excited. But then I remembered I had too much on my plate already: a very challenging job, a newspaper column, a boyfriend.

'You should go for it,' said Steph.

'Yes,' I said, 'but I don't know . . . I'm not sure I'm good enough at just looking after my own classes as it is.'

'Well, have a think about applying, even if it's just for the experience.'

Walking to the bus stop, swathed in layers of winter clothing, I grimaced at the thought of willingly taking on more work. A year ago, when I started, I thought I wanted to aim for the top and be a super young super-head in a tough inner-city school. But something had happened since September, and I was now more interested in arranging surprises for Will for the coming weekend than in planning my ascent into power. Maybe I can do it, I thought. Maybe it wouldn't be too bad . . . I could do it . . . I'll just shuffle things round . . . It's not like I write that much during term time . . . And . . . and . . . and . . .

Will came round for supper, and I asked him what he thought.

'I absolutely think you should not take it,' he said. 'You've got too much to do already.'

'Yes, but I could probably just — '

'You'll always be able to move into management positions if you want to, but you've got a book to write now and school is stressful enough without trying to organize other teachers.'

'Yes, yes, I know you're right — but maybe I could just . . . I don't know . . . just do it.' Bollocks to being told I can't do it, I thought. I could do it all.

As I pay for my therapist's advice, I take it much more seriously.

'We're trying to come up with ways to decrease your stress levels. Do you think it would be wise to take on more?'

'Um. No, But, maybe I could just . . . I don't know . . . just be a bit more efficient. I rather fancy the money.'

She laughed. 'Well, yes, there's always that temptation.' She paused. 'What does Will think?'

'Will?'

'Yes. What does he think about you taking on a larger role?'

'He thinks that I absolutely shouldn't do it. That I've got enough on my plate already . . . But I really want to support my head of department . . . and I like the idea of having more say in the direction our curriculum takes . . . and . . . and part of me really wants to do this. Oh! I know it's a bad idea.'

'Have a careful think about it, that's all.'

Day to day I could feel I was falling down a never-ending spiral of tiredness. I couldn't understand why my friends from university — who were all putting in obscene hours as lawyers and bankers — didn't seem to be suffering from lack of sleep. The therapist tried very hard to get me to see that it really wasn't surprising I was feeling tired and run-down: that's what happens if you pack your days and evenings and then spend the night sharing a mattress which is too small with a boyfriend. I had this misguided notion from somewhere that I was invincible, but began to see that actually I was very un-invincible. I brightened at the thought that Friday was going to be a day off school.

I'd booked myself in for a Teach First career day.

'I'm sorry,' I told the Year 11s, 'but I'm not going to be in on Friday. I'm going to a day which is all about continuing a career in teaching.'

'Miss, why would you do that to yourself?' Abimbola asked, her voice full of disdain at the thought of teaching. It had always been clear that, although the class quite liked me, they thought I was capable of a better job — a better job, in their opinion, being almost everything bar emptying dustbins. Once rubbish has touched the floor, the students treat it as if it is radioactive. A sealed pack of crisps put in a clean bin is ruined. On Thursdays at break time I stand outside with Richard, an art teacher. We chat away hoping not to be distracted from conversations about books and exhibitions by playground fights. When the bell goes, the students have to be swept to their lessons. We walk behind them picking up a few crisp packets that fly our way. The students who see this practically gag.

'Well . . . ' I started trying to answer Abimbola's question.

'I mean, Miss, you've got a good degree, why would you teach here?' Abimbola continued.

Nia turned on her. 'What do you mean teach *here?*' Others echoed her disapproval.

'Well, this is a school in south London, innit?'

'Um, I can answer your question Abimbola,' I interjected. 'I like teaching here because it's challenging and difficult sometimes . . . and,' I continued, 'I really believe that everyone deserves a really good education regardless of where they live — so that's why I chose to teach here.'

'Skein, skein.'

I didn't tell them I too was thinking more and more frequently that there must be easier ways of making a living.

Like race, class and circumstance, opportunity and wealth are sticky subjects. Abimbola had asked me a much easier question in my first year.

'Miss, are you posh?' she said.

'Has it taken you this long to notice?' I asked.

So much of the time teaching the Year 11s I wanted to shake them and say, 'Stop wasting time. You don't know what you're missing out on. Why won't you do something about it?' When your students fail to see something, it naturally feels like a failing on your part. Why wasn't I a good enough teacher to make them work harder? How did Julia do it?

Her students were orderly: she narrowed her eyes at them and they fell into silence. When students handed her a piece of work saying it was finished, she would raise an eyebrow. 'Read that line,' she'd say pointing to their first sentence. 'Does it make sense?' Of course it didn't. 'Do it again. And *don't* tell me you're finished.' And the result was that not only did her students get exceptional results, they ended up caring, and taking a real sense of pride in their work. I spoke to my students reasonably and waited for them to become motivated themselves because I thought perhaps that was a better way. But it wasn't if they never did find that motivation.

★ ★ ★

At the other end of the spectrum, Will had decided that his class should get a tortoise, as no offers of unwanted lynxes had been forthcoming. His students had raised half the money; the bursar contributed the rest. Will had had several sleepless nights worrying about the responsibility of having a pet on top of the responsibility of having a girlfriend (he'd now conceded that we were in a relationship). On the last Sunday of January, he and I drove to a pet shop and picked up a tortoise he'd already been to see a few times.

We spent several hours in the pet shop playing with the rabbits and watching the fish. We booked a taxi to carry the coffin-sized tank it was to live in, and I carried the tort — the size of a halved orange — on the back of his scooter, praying that it wouldn't be dead by the time we arrived at Will's school.

★ ★ ★

Waking up miserably bleary-eyed on another cold, dark Monday, I decided it would be insane to willingly make my life more difficult. The sensible thing to do was not apply for the 2ic job. I went to see Steph with my decision.

'Steph, I've decided I'm not going to apply for the position,' I told her. 'I would really like to do it, and I really want to be supportive towards you, but I just feel like I have so much on and there aren't enough hours in the week as it is to plan and mark, and I'm not on top of my own teaching . . . Sorry.'

Steph looked at me and I looked at her.

'What does Will think?'

I don't know when it was that everyone began to think Will's opinion on my job was of the greatest importance.

'He thinks I shouldn't do it. That I should concentrate on writing.'

178

'Oh . . . go on,' she said. 'You can do it. I know you can't put in lots of extra hours in the week, but that's not what it's about. It's just about taking on a few of the responsibilities, helping with a few things . . . '

'Oh . . . ' I replied, visibly weakening. 'I'll get my letter of application in.'

Will texted during the day to say they'd decided on a name for the tortoise. 'Ferrari Cappuccino Tort.' Ridiculous.

* * *

Year 11's parents evening fell at the end of January. Small desks were laid out in rows in the hall. One chair was placed behind the desk for the teacher, two in front for the parent and the student — but many parents came with several smaller children, or with a friend who was going to translate, and so there'd be much scrabbling over extra chairs. There were no appointments: parents simply queued up if they wanted to see you. Inevitably this led to small disagreements about who'd been waiting for the longest time.

I gave the Year 11s fairly glowing reports — probably more glowing than they deserved. I was especially pleased to see Becky's mum. Becky seemed, slowly but surely, to be sorting

179

herself out. I thought it was heartening. Although she still occasionally seemed to flare up like she used to, it had become much easier to coax her round — 'You're doing really well . . . I've been so impressed to see how much you've sorted yourself out . . . I was telling a teacher only yesterday how well you're doing . . .' It was also easier to handle her because the rest of the Year 11 class no longer constantly exploded in different directions, so one or two confused and frustrated students seemed easily manageable.

I heard that things hadn't gone so well for another student who at one point had seemed no more challenging than Becky. She had been permanently excluded the year before from the same class, when they were Year 10s. She'd threatened to mug and beat up a young teenage girl if the girl didn't hand over her phone. The girl happened to be pregnant, and had ended up miscarrying in hospital after the threat was carried out. I wondered where things had gone so wrong for an ex-student. She'd been mischievous but bright. I remembered that Ella had come and spent the day watching me teach to see if she wanted to apply for Teach First. She'd sat with the student, who with all Ella's attention and enthusiasm had been transformed and offered perceptive and sensitive thoughts about the poem we had been studying. It didn't make sense that she could be so brutal.

'Becky's been doing so well . . . just in time for her exams . . . Just fantastic to see how hard she's trying . . . '

I told Becky's mum how pleased I was that things were going better for Becky. After years of hearing the opposite, she seemed jovially surprised to hear such praise.

* * *

By the beginning of February the Year 7s had finished writing their own urban myths. I'd noticed that Chantelle, who had hitherto never required more than a stern eye to show her I was watching her, was beginning to play up. Previously she'd always been the first to finish a piece of work. She tried reasonably hard, but once she'd finished a piece, in her neat, controlled handwriting, she had no interest in developing or extending it. She liked drawing, and spent much time working on illustrations. I noticed that she had started writing and rewriting the date and lesson objective, tearing pages from her exercise book which she didn't think were neat enough. She seemed frustrated, and had started to ignore my instructions. I'd given her three warnings in one lesson, and then sent her to sit in another teacher's class. The following lesson I wanted to get her back on track.

While the others were working and Chantelle was staring into space with an annoyed expression on her face, I went and crouched beside her.

'Chantelle, is there something that is making you angry?' She nodded. 'What is making you feel angry?'

'Things at break,' she said.

'Well, I think that while you are in class it's really important you do your best to really concentrate on what we are doing and not think about what's going on outside the classroom . . . What could we do with the things that are making you angry?' I looked in an exaggerated way over to the window. Chantelle smiled.

'Throw them out the window!'

'Exactly.'

I phoned home to speak to Chantelle's mother. She was concerned that Chantelle was bothered by things at school, though she didn't know what the 'things' were exactly. I was concerned that the hold I had on Chantelle was weakening, but I also knew we had a track record of lots of successful lessons to counterbalance the most recent difficult ones.

Back in class, once the Year 7s had written their urban myths, I set them the task of sharing their stories on their tables before choosing one to develop into a performance piece for the rest of the class.

The students who had come up from primary school so well trained and able to listen to each other politely, had all turned into mini-volcanoes spewing out noise. They'd completely lost interest in hearing anything the rest of the class might have to say. I watched Chantelle on her table as Rose read, and made a note that I needed to speak to her after class.

Though unwilling to listen to each other, they'd still listen to me once I'd spent a few moments trying to get quiet. They wouldn't start talking again as long as what I was saying was something they wanted to hear.

I ended another lesson with a new tale, this time about my flatmate, Ella — 'I've told you about her before, haven't I?' — and this boyfriend, Timbo, who she was with at university.

'Timbo? That's a funny name,' a few said, wholly suspicious as to where the line was, in my stories, between fiction and fact.

I told them how he drove her down to the river in Oxford for an evening picnic to celebrate their one-year anniversary. As they

183

were driving to the spot, they listened to the radio and heard that a man had just escaped from the local prison.

Rose smiled at me. She was not going to fall for this.

' . . . Fuzz, crack,' I made the sounds of a radio, and then mimicked the voice of a newsreader: ''The man is highly dangerous and people are advised to stay at home and lock their doors. He is easily identifiable as he has a hook instead of a right hand' . . . fuzz, crack.' Ella was scared but Timbo told her not to be silly.

'It started raining just as they reached the picnic spot so they parked under a tree and laid the picnic rug out on the back seat of the car.'

''What's that noise?' Ella asked, jumping. Timbo laughed at how easily freaked she was. 'You're imagining things,' he told her.

'It was beginning to get quite dark outside, so he turned on the light inside the car. This made it even harder to see out into the rainy evening.

Scratch . . . scratch . . . This time they both heard it. 'Stop worrying, it's probably just the branches of the tree above.''

''I don't like this,' Ella whimpered. 'Sorry, can we just go back into town and finish the picnic in my room?' Timbo rolled his eyes.

The evening hadn't quite turned out as he'd planned. They climbed into the front seats, and Timbo started the ignition and drove off back into town.

'They pulled up outside Ella's college and Timbo jumped out of the car and ran round to open Ella's door. And do you know what he saw?'

'Miss, you're giving me nightmares,' Stella said.

'Yes, Ella still has nightmares about it.'

'Miss!'

'He saw a hook hanging from the door handle of the car.'

'Oh, Miss!' the ones who got it exclaimed. A few waited for a bit more explanation from their friends.

'Everyone may go. Please tidy your desks and tuck your chairs under. Chantelle, please stay behind.'

'Chantelle, do you think Rose feels confident when she speaks in class?'

Chantelle looked at the ceiling, thinking.

'Um, yes.' She seemed to have really taken some time over coming to this conclusion, but it was, alas, not the answer I was looking for.

'Really? When Rose speaks, does she speak loudly?' I played at being a barrister and questioned her into a corner.

185

Chantelle thought again.

'Yes, quite loudly.'

'Really? I'd say she was quite quiet when she speaks.'

I raised one eyebrow into a question mark, and Chantelle read the sign that she needed to rethink her answer.

'Yes, she is sort of quiet.'

Right. Now we're getting somewhere.

'Now, do you think if someone doesn't feel very confident they'd speak loudly or quietly?'

'Um, quietly?'

'Yes, I think so. I think if someone doesn't feel very confident, they'd speak quietly.'

Chantelle nodded.

'Now, if you felt unconfident about speaking out in class and you saw that people weren't listening to you, that they were playing with their pencil cases or talking to someone else, would you think they were interested in what you had to say?'

Chantelle shook her head.

'Right, so why is it important that you listen carefully to Rose and all the other students in the class?'

Chantelle paused. She is thoughtful and perceptive. In lessons, she spends a lot of time fidgeting, looking like she's not listening, and then she always comes out with the right answer when I ask her a question directly. Perhaps she is too bright; perhaps a lot of the time she is bored. Nevertheless, she must show respect to others.

'Because other people won't feel confident about sharing in class.'

'Yes,' I nodded very solemnly. It was time to go down to lunch.

'And so, Chantelle, in tomorrow's lesson I want to see that you are encouraging other students to speak by listening carefully to them. Can you do that?'

'Yes, Miss. Sorry.'

The Year 7s were always at their worst on a Wednesday afternoon. They had history in the previous lesson, which was taught across the hallway by a long-term supply teacher. His door was closed, and so was mine, and the hallway lay between, and yet I could still hear them rioting in his room. As they surged from his class to mine, I braced myself, for the fact that they still had the taste of blood in their mouths. In our next lesson Chantelle was marginally better, but the rest of the class spent the hour not listening to me. They were certainly not listening to each other. My voice was hoarse. I had no energy. I cannot keep them quiet, I thought: I have lost the will.

★ ★ ★

On the first Wednesday of February I went along to the deputy head's office, where the interview was taking place for the 2ic job. It turned out that I had been the only person to apply. I took along the carefully typed-out notes I had prepared. An educational consultant from the borough had been in to assist the English department over the last few days, and she had filled me in on the changes in the curriculum taking place on the national scale — all of which had been news to me, though it probably shouldn't have been.

A new national strategy was just being launched which was intended to simplify and combine previous initiatives. It still looked pretty complex to me. I'm sure there must be a simpler way to show teachers what needs to be taught. Julia had rolled her eyes at the new document.

Ignoring all advice given explicitly by Will and implicitly by the therapist, I prepared myself for the interview.

I sat in the small office with Cecelia, the principal, and Steph. They ran through ten questions. What had I done to prepare for the interview? What did I plan to do if I were given the position? Did I feel I set an example in my own teaching? How would I define the difference between a good lesson and an outstanding lesson? How would I manage the workload? . . . In a voice slightly quieter and less sure than normal, I gave the answers that I thought were the right ones.

The two of them took turns asking the questions, smiling as I finished each answer. Only on one question did I become unstuck. What would I do if a member of the department failed to do what I'd asked? What would I do when the good working relationships I had with the rest of the department were put under pressure and I had to ask them to do something they didn't want to do? The thought, for example, of telling Julia that she had to teach a unit she didn't want to made me squirm in my seat.

I returned to my classroom after the interview, and Cecelia found me there twenty minutes later to tell me I'd got the job.

'Congratulations on your promotion!'

'Er, thanks,' I said to John as the two of us walked out of the school at the end of the day.

'That's the strangest reaction I have ever seen,' he replied.

'Yeah . . . I know.'

'Now, don't make me look bad eh?' John and I now held very similar posts within the department.

I didn't tell my parents for a few days.

Denial seemed like a good option. Will arrived that evening with a bottle of champagne.

'This was on special offer — I didn't get it to celebrate your promotion.'

'Oh, I don't want to talk about it,' I said, beginning to wonder if I'd made a big mistake and if part of me was conspiring against myself to bring on a full blown breakdown. We didn't talk about it, and drank the champagne.

Instead, we talked about my Year 7s.

'I can't do it,' I told him. 'I can't make them listen.'

'You need a positive reward — put a sticker on the shoulders of all the students displaying good listening skills.'

Of course — so simple. The next day, aware that a system where I didn't touch the students would be preferable, I prepared 'Active Listening' cards, with boxes to collect stars for each lesson. I spent several minutes with the Year 7s thinking through what listening is and how you show someone you're listening. I told them the rules of engagement — nobody is allowed to ask for a sticker, or to point out that I haven't given them one.

'I will walk around the classroom during the lesson and give stars to those students who are really listening well to each other and to me. At the end of two weeks we'll count up the stars and give rewards to those who have the most.'

Silence fell, and lasted throughout the lesson. People strained to take in contributions made by others in the class. They were desperate for sticky gold stars.

It's so easy when it goes well. At the end of the lesson you feel like a balanced individual. Why can't it always be like this?

★   ★   ★

Coleen had of late become more and more inert in lessons. I weakly asked her to take her head off the table, but didn't insist. Let her lie there, I thought: I'll teach the rest of the class. Erez also chose to keep her head under her folder for much of the lesson.

Months on from when they were supposed to have handed in their creative-writing pieces, I was still chasing up some of them. The last few pieces were extracted from the bottom of bags, dog-eared, stained and looking rather on the light side. I thanked the students in question, and stuffed the pieces into a folder to mark in the evening.

Charlotte, a university friend who lives down the road, suggested I came over and marked at her place in the evening. We sat at her table. Charlotte was working on something for her law conversion course; I took out the scraps of paper to be marked.

'It's so weird, Nony — you're actually a *teacher*.'

'I know.'

I scanned through Folashade's piece. It sounded familiar. 'Can I use your laptop, Charlotte?' I typed in the first few lines.

Folashade had pleaded with me, 'Miss, I really love writing poems. Miss, can I write a poem instead?' I'd dithered. I thought she was more likely to get the marks by writing a descriptive passage about a prison cell, as I'd suggested, but I didn't want to be prescriptive and limit an imaginative response — and so I gave in, certain that Julia wouldn't have.

What she'd ended up giving me was a page of scrawled writing. The short poem — about how she would always be near to her 'dear' — which had a certain catchiness, but would not get her any marks for creating a sense of time or place, sounded somehow familiar to me. I googled it.

At the bottom of the piece I wrote the following:

'Folashade — or should I say Shakira? Please see me.'

'That's so funny, Nones. I can't believe she

just wrote out the lyrics. That's so blates obvious.' (Charlotte shortens any word she can to a single syllable.) 'And to choose Shakira . . . '

Coleen had also handed me a redraft of her piece of creative writing. She'd completed the first draft in a few minutes. Rather than tearing it up, giving it back to her, and telling her to hand something decent in, I had painstakingly tried to edit her work, listing questions in the margins to help her expand the piece. She had since had hours of class time to develop it, but had somehow produced nothing more than the sentences she had first handed in. Her coursework folder was looking painfully unheathly.

Another problem I'd started to despair at was the fact that several of the most difficult students were often absent. It was a mixed blessing.

'Has anyone seen Erez or Mahima today?'

'Yeah . . . I think they are in,' another student would tell me. I'd check on the register: yes indeed, they were in — but not in my lesson. After emailing round trying to discover if there was any good reason why they weren't there, I had to fill in forms and contact their parents to say they'd being playing truant — and then try and get them to turn up for detention (and, considering I couldn't get them to turn up to class, this wasn't an easy punishment).

I had actually succeeded in getting Erez to return for one detention after a lesson where she had refused to write anything. All attempts to speak to her had been met with blank stares.

'Erez, Erez — look at me please when I'm speaking to you. Erez, can you tell me which your favourite subject is?'

More blank stares.

'Right,' I told her, sitting opposite her, 'here are your options. I've written the choices down for you. All you have to do is tell me which option you choose.

(a) Miss Crossley-Holland completely gives up on you and lets you write nothing every lesson.
(b) You let Miss Crossley-Holland try to help you get a C grade in your GCSE English.'

We sat silently for a few minutes. Then she picked up a pen and put a tick next to option (b).

'OK, that's good to know Erez. You can go, and I look forward to seeing you in tomorrow's lesson.'

Erez looked up towards the window in my door: her friends were waiting outside. I felt pleased with the millimetre of progress made.

'Hurry up.' I looked at the glass on my door after Erez had left the room. In Vaseline, the girls waiting for her had smeared the words 'Hurry up' on the glass. Shit. I furiously emailed the head of year.

When the students who were properly absent from school for one reason or another would return after missing a few lessons, they would be further behind than ever, and within seconds of realizing they didn't know what was going on, they clamped down or flared up.

One student whom I'd noticed had been more and more frequently absent was Siobhan. She seemed to have racked up a number of short term exclusions. I wasn't sure what they were for, but reflected for a moment on the times I'd found her hiding under a desk to listen to me speaking to a student after class. She could be excluded for any number of her misdemeanours, I thought.

★ ★ ★

With the prospect of another Saturday being taken by a compulsory Teach First day, I felt miserable and come Friday evening dissolved into tears on the phone with Will.

195

'Leave. Your work should not be making you cry,' Will said on the other end of the phone.

'No,' I whimpered. 'I'm just tired . . . and I had a crap day. And I'm cross that I have to go to a stupid conference on a Saturday.'

I'd reached a low ebb, and felt rather out of love with teaching. Controlling errant behaviour — or not controlling it — was sapping my energy, and I felt, once again, I was having to fight my older students in order to teach them.

But I knew part of my dissatisfaction was also because I was giving less time and energy to sorting stuff out at school and instead devoting hours to whiling away the time with Will. And on nights spent together we invariably lost more sleep. I thought about my first year, when I'd thought about nothing but teaching — how I'd regularly stayed up till ten in a marking frenzy, arrived into school an hour early to polish off preparation for the day, spent whole Sundays marking.

This is too hard, I thought over and over as I went through the routine of waking up tired, having an unsatisfactory day, and then spending the evening doing something other than marking. I had signed up for something which required as much as you could give. My stepmother — also a teacher — had told

196

me early on that, as a teacher, you always feel there's more you can do. But I felt there was loads more I could be doing, and that by not 'getting on top of things' I was allowing myself to become more and more dissatisfied. In my first year I'd regularly torn my hair out, but had never spent much time thinking I might not want to teach long-term.

I felt the Teach First mission looming large above me and heard the voices of the organizers — 'What are the factors you've identified that stop your pupils from achieving . . . Which of these barriers can you overcome?'

Ella, meanwhile, discovering that working all the hours she could was doing nothing to lessen her workload, had decided she wouldn't work beyond eight in the evening. 'Would it be all right by you, Nony, if after eight we didn't discuss anything to do with school?' At 8.30 she'd announce she was off to bed. Getting up at 5.30 was beginning to drain her enthusiasm.

On Saturday morning the sun was shining as I crawled out of bed to attend the training day on striking a work/life balance. The humour of having to use a whole Saturday to learn about this failed to strike me. From 9.30 until five I listened to a panel of superhumans:

FIRST PANELLIST: I think it's really important that after I've put in a solid day trying to save the world I still have time for myself.

SECOND PANELLIST: Yeah, I agree. After I've put in a twelve hour day I always go to the gym on the way home and then make sure I do something fun in the evening.

THIRD PANELLIST: What I do is make sure that I set myself goals for my personal life in the same way that I do for work. I then set myself small, achievable targets. So, for example, I really want to improve my Spanish, so one of my goals at the moment is to book myself some time off in a Spanish-speaking country. All I need to do is spend ten minutes at some point during the day looking for a flight and I know that I'm working towards something that is just for me.

'These people are *crazy*,' I whispered to Lucy, who was sitting beside me. I was looking forward to telling Will about the day, knowing it would confirm his suspicions. I had decided that the most useful way I could make use of the time was in deciding what storage would enable me to not constantly have a mountain of paper on my desk at school.

I raised my hand during question time. 'I was just wondering, how much sleep do you all get a night?'

The response was fairly unanimous. 'Oh,' they looked sympathetic but smug. 'Oh, I'm actually one of those really lucky people . . . ' They were all those androids who can survive on negative amounts of sleep.

I was most looking forward to the final speaker of the day, a therapist from Cambridge. 'Free therapy,' I said to Lucy — 'fantastic.'

'Save yourselves,' he said. 'You can't save your students . . . their own traumas are too great for you to be able to fix them . . . Spend more time talking to your subconscious . . . Learn to breathe . . . Listen to what that small voice inside you is telling you . . . If you've got a headache, maybe your body is trying to tell you something . . . Learn to breathe . . . Save yourself.'

'Is it even possible to 'save yourself' and teach?' I asked Lucy as we left the glass skyscraper where the conference had been held and emerged into the crisp February day. I felt Teach First had administered a plaster. I felt that a person endorsed by Teach First had acknowledged that what we were trying to do — change the prospects of the students we taught — was an impossible job.

Somehow that made the prospect of Monday seem more manageable.

★ ★ ★

With one week to go until half-term, I realized we were officially one down in the Year 10 class. Siobhan had, I believe, run out of second chances. The students are normally a fairly good source of information, but they were rather hazy about what the final offence had been. And, once I knew she wasn't coming back, I sort of missed her. I knew she had sabotaged lessons, and she'd alternated between telling me one week that she really liked me and the next that, to be honest, she hated me. But somehow, in between hiding under tables and short-term exclusions, she'd written a fantastic essay on *Jane Eyre* and I'd thought we were making progress.

Just as I was questioning some students on what exactly had happened to Siobhan, another student arrived at the class looking ashen and faint. Unhelpfully, several dominating girls surrounded her shouting instructions. While I sent Lakeisha to get first aid, it was Coleen who came to Jahanara's rescue.

'Back off everyone, give her some space.' Coleen stayed by Jahanara quietly talking to her.

'Miss, she's diabetic. I think she needs chocolate. She should go in the hall and sit down. I'm going with her.'

'Right. OK, thank you.' I was slightly startled by how assertive Coleen was.

First aid came; Jahanara was taken off; Coleen returned.

In the next lesson that week I asked for a volunteer to read the part of Rita while I read Frank — we were going to eke the next coursework essay out of Willy Russell's play *Educating Rita*. No one put up her hand. I waited. Then Erez offered to read a part. I was surprised — she had barely said a thing in class all year. She read for a bit, and then I offered the part I was reading. Coleen's hand went up.

Two small things in one week seemed to change all my feelings of frustration and desperation about Coleen's months of hostility towards me. I'd felt guilty that recently I'd been doing less and less to try to urge her on. I'd just avoided the issue. Her mother's number was saved in my phone.

'Hello, this is Oenone Crossley-Holland.'

'Oh, what's she done now?'

'I'm actually calling today because I wanted to let you know how pleased I am.'

There was silence on the other end of the phone.

'Oh. She's said she was going to be good. She did say she was really trying.'

'Well, she's made a fantastic start. She was really helpful earlier on in the week with another student who is diabetic and was about to faint.'

'Oh, yeah, she knows what to do. Her cousin has it, and so Coleen knows how to look after someone.'

'And then today she volunteered to read a part in the play we're reading . . . Do tell her that I called you and I'm really pleased.'

'Yeah, I will do.'

'We'll keep in touch.'

★   ★   ★

Valentine's Day fell on a Thursday. I was keen to avoid sitting in a restaurant, across a table from Will, struggling to find conversation and wondering if by the time the food came I'd feel too sick to eat. Perhaps waitressing at a young age had instilled this fear. I'd watched couples sitting reading the labels of bottles, straining to find anything to comment on.

'Perhaps they were just content in each other's company?' my therapist had suggested.

'No. They had nothing to say. I'm going to book theatre tickets for Valentine's.'

'Will, the play starts tomorrow night at 7.30,' I told him. 'Shall we meet before and grab some food [sitting beside each other on a bench]? And I'm really sorry but I haven't got you a present or anything . . . I haven't had time . . . '

Will bounded up the stairs of the flat holding an expensive-looking shopping bag.

'Ooh, no, you shouldn't have . . . I'm a bad girlfriend — I haven't even made you a card yet . . . I had to get a taxi back from school because there weren't any buses . . . I've just got back . . . '

'You can take it back if you don't like it . . . I went shopping with Jerome at lunch. He said that you'd prefer something practical that you can actually wear . . . The woman in the shop said that Hugh Grant had bought the same underwear a few days ago . . . ' Probably not for himself.

The play we saw was an antidote to all things romantic: three actors and a lot of blood and urine and torturous screaming; a man sat by a wall all day listening to the sound of the next-door neighbour peeing. I spied a friend who'd also read English at Oxford. He was there with his girlfriend, and so we broke another Valentine's Day rule and all sat together in the bar afterwards, drinking beer.

'Are you sure it's OK?' I asked. 'If you two want to go off and have a romantic drink together . . . '

The play had rather dampened the romantic mood.

★ ★ ★

The final lessons of the week were fairly uneventful. Coleen seemed set to return to her former self, and relented a small amount only when I asked her if her mother had told her I had rung home. Becky was still making slow but sure progress.

On Friday evening Will and I went off to an exhibition opening before going on to the birthday drinks of Hattie, another friend of mine from university. We made it to midnight before Will looked at me sleepily and asked if we could go home. The dancing was just getting going, but the half-term had taken its toll.

Will had agreed, to meet my mother on Saturday — 'as long as it is on my terms'. His conditions were that it was a coffee, and that my sister was there too to dilute the experience. I reasoned with him that a morning coffee wouldn't work, as I was going to take my mother to the Russian exhibition at the Royal Academy. He agreed to supper, and then endeared himself to my mother by filling her wine glass so that it overflowed when she asked for just a small drop and indicated with her finger where on the glass he should fill it to.

By Tuesday of the half-term holiday I was lying in bed with a temperature. Completely typical — but a thought was niggling me. Was my subconscious trying to tell me something? Whether I wanted to commit to teaching for the next few years had changed from being something I occasionally thought about to a question that ran through my mind more and more frequently.

SPRING TERM
SECOND HALF

I spent half-term snoozing: long lie-ins, and afternoon naps before early nights. After a week of rest I was ready to attack my classes with renewed enthusiasm.

When the lower-set Year 7s arrived to their first English lesson after the week off, they were startled by the change that had taken place in the classroom.

'Miss, why are the chairs . . . ?' Angela was first to enter the room.

'Well,' I started explaining, 'I thought we'd do something different today.'

Genesis entered, looking alarmed.

'Miss, the chairs?'

'Just take a seat and I'll explain.'

A few more came to the door and stopped dead in their tracks.

'Miss, why . . . ?'

'Take a seat.'

'Miss, are we doing drama?'

'Take a seat and all will become clear.'

The last few came in.

'Mi — '

'Just take a seat.'

I'd pushed the heavy desks to the edges of

the room and arranged the chairs into a circle.

'Today we are going to have a philosophical inquiry.' Blank faces. 'Now does anyone have — and I'd be very impressed if they did — any idea what the word 'philosophy' means?' A few hands shot up. 'Oh, well this is fantastic. Um . . . Rose, can you tell us what you think the word 'philosophy' means.'

'Um, well, um, I'm not sure, but is it . . . I think it's when you sit in a circle.'

'Er, no — but we are sitting in a circle so I can see how you might have thought that.'

I turned to another student whose arm was frantically waving in the air — she was a good foot out of her seat, stretching up towards the ceiling. 'Yes, Princess?'

'Finally . . . ' she said, annoyed at having had to wait.

'No, Princess, you wait politely please.' I'm calling your parents, I thought.

'Is it something that when you like, um, no, I don't know, is it . . . No, I don't know.'

'OK, right.' I suspected nobody was going to offer an actual definition, so I didn't call on the remaining few loosely holding up their hands.

'Basically, philosophy is all about asking questions and figuring out what we think about things.'

'Now, I want everyone to stand up,' I said, standing up. Most of the class immediately followed, but a few were suffering from severe laziness. 'Come on, Chantelle — stand up.'

'Ooh, Miss I — '

'Stand up, Chantelle . . . Stand up, Chantelle, please . . . Thank you.'

'OK. There are one, two, three, four . . . twenty-five of us. We are going to count backwards, and as you say a number you can sit down. But if anyone says their number at the same time as anyone else then we have to start from the beginning again. Right, I'm going to start off this round so I'll say 'twenty-five' and sit down, and then someone else should say 'twenty-four' and sit down. Don't speak at the same time as somebody else. OK? Twenty-five.' I sat down.

'Twenty-four!' three people said at once as they sat down.

'No-o,' the students who understood what we were trying to do called out.

'Right, we have to start again. Everyone standing.'

We started again. This time Princess led, starting with twenty-five. We managed to get to twenty-two before Chantelle and Rose sat down together. Everyone laughed. This was the most fun they'd had in English in weeks.

'We'll try this again next time and see if we

can do any better.' I wanted to move on to the next stage in our philosophical inquiry.

On the Wednesday before half-term I'd set cover work for the day and caught a different bus — to Camberwell, for the first of two courses on Philosophy for Children. The idea is simple. A group of students sit in a large circle and are offered a stimulus item: a story, a picture, a short film or an object. Having listened to the story or looked at the picture, the students come up with questions in small groups — not questions with easy answers, but questions that allow for exploration and, I suppose ultimately, encourage you to find boundaries, to discover through dialogue your position in relation to the world around you.

Once the whole class have selected a single question, the group launch an inquiry exploring what the question means and how it might be answered by each individual. What appealed to me about the process was that it seemed to provide an antidote to spoon-feeding students an education.

In a room above a library in Camberwell, Linda, an eastcoast American with masses of dark frizzy hair, guided us through our own philosophical inquiries so that we might see the technique in practice.

Students for the day, twenty teachers sat in

a circle. Linda told the group a Maori story.

Father Sky (whose name was Rangi) and Mother Earth (whose name was Papatua) loved each other so passionately that no light could shine between them, and nothing could grow on earth.

There were no men on the earth then, but Rangi and Papatua had five children. As they grew up, they began to complain about the lack of space and light. They plotted ways they could separate their parents. One suggested they even kill them. In the end it was Tane, god of light and forests, who was successful in drawing them apart.

With his feet firmly planted in the earth, he pushed against the sky and strained to separate them until, with a great tearing sound, the sky broke loose and flew up high away from the earth.

The children, having seen what they had done, and how bereaved their parents were, decided to decorate Rangi and Papatua. They decorated Papatua with flowers and trees, and Rangi with bright stars. Their parents were delighted with all their children had done, but still longed for each other. When Papatua sighs for her husband, her breath is the early-morning mists, and when Rangi weeps for his loss, his tears are the rain.

Having listened like good schoolchildren to

the story, we wrote questions in pairs. We settled into discussion exploring whether, in order to gain independence, something always has to be sacrificed. This is so nice, I thought. So ordered. With her outstretched hands, Linda orchestrated who would speak next. We waited patiently for our turn.

'I think I really value my independence. It is really important to me that I have choices,' one teacher offered.

Someone else put a hand up, and Linda indicated it was their turn.

'But — I'm sorry, I didn't catch your name: — Janet, is it? — I think part of the question, maybe as I understand it, is, How much independence do we need in order to be happy? And does the amount of freedom we require to feel independent vary depending on which culture we are from?'

A few heads lightly nodded, showing their support for the point made. Someone had a hand up for a few moments, and Linda indicated that they would speak next.

'Um . . . ' Before the person who'd been waiting for quite some time could start, another voice interrupted.

'Well, er, the way I see it is . . . '

I stared at the speaker — who had, incidentally, arrived an hour later than everyone else. John, a primary-school teacher from the area, had broken the rules. 'Blah, blah, blah,' he continued. I looked at Linda to see what she was going to do. She listened to his point, then indicated again to the person who had been scheduled to speak.

In between more interruptions from John, the conversation developed. A Bengali woman explained how thankful she was for her liberal parents, and how separate she felt from the friends she has who are in arranged marriages.

'It is difficult. When you teach Asian girls, don't you want to give them the independence you have?' someone asked her.

'No. I accept their culture, and that they might be very happy following the rules of their culture.'

'Yes, I sort of agree,' I added, 'but it is difficult. I'm from a culture where women do have independence — in where they live, in what they choose to do with their lives — and . . . it's not that I don't accept and respect that my students are part of another culture. It's just that I can't help wishing that the girls I teach, some of whom are part of very male-dominated cultures, have the choices that I had.'

The majority of the time the subtle differences in culture go unnoticed: head-scarves stand out only when a student who

215

usually wears one doesn't wear one. But sometimes the differences do bubble to the surface. Muslim students from the strictest backgrounds complain that it is difficult to do homework when your father does not like to see you studying. This is a much better excuse than 'Miss, my dog ate it.' The students from the strictest of homes are also the ones who can't get permission from their parents to go on school trips.

* * *

With the Year 11s, the countdown to their exams had started. I issued calendars which indicated what we would be studying in each lesson up until the exams: the subtext was that there wasn't enough time left to keep on wasting so much of it. If we didn't finish studying a poem or a writing style in one lesson, there would be no time to carry the topic over into the following lesson. For this reason, in our third lesson of the week I asked them to stay behind for a few minutes — they'd easily wasted more time than that at the beginning of the lesson.

'I can see it's break time, but this is the last time we're going to get a chance to go over Jonson's 'On my First Sonne', so I'd like us to just hear the last two groups share their thoughts on the last couplet with the rest of the class.'

Everyone accepted that this was necessary and remained silently in their seats. Everyone except Becky.

'Becky,' I said, 'could you sit down, please? We're just going to finish the poem quickly.' Becky stayed standing.

'Can you sit down, please — you're wasting everyone's break time.'

'That's fucking extra,' she shouted. 'Fucking shit. Fuck you.' She stared at me and then made for the door, swinging her bag on to her shoulder, kicking her chair out of the way, sweeping her exercise book and folder off the desk and on to the floor, and then stamping out, her face burning with anger.

I did nothing.

'Could the remaining two groups finish, please?' I asked, looking more bemused than anything else by Becky's reaction. The rest of the class looked a little weary.

The remaining groups spoke for two minutes and I dismissed the class. I went down to the office and asked for senior management to pick Becky up at the beginning of her next lesson. Swearing at a teacher results in a day's exclusion. I was irritated. What a stupid thing to do with so few lessons in which to prepare for the coming exams — she'd miss a whole day when she, more than anyone in that class, needed the extra time. Why on earth did she do that?

I rang her mum. She apologized. I filled in the forms: the incident report and the record of the phone conversation with her mother. I passed the report to senior management, so that they could record what action they'd taken. The forms were returned to me. I stapled five copies of the phone record to five copies of the incident report and then spent five minutes in the staffroom finding the pigeonholes to post the copies to everyone involved in Becky's care. I had a file two inches thick with incident reports I'd written so far during the year. The section for the Year 10 class was thicker than those for the other three classes combined.

The carbon copies of the reports went into the students' files. Discipline issues are meant to be dealt with by the teacher's department. A student would flare up and, after a series of warnings, usually be sent to another classroom; this was called 'pairing'. If she refused to go, she'd be collected by 'on-call' — a member of senior management with a walkie-talkie. Beyond writing up the incident and contacting home to tell the parents you'd had to evict their child from your room, any more follow-up action would be down to you as a teacher or your head of department. Unless, that is, lots of other teachers who also taught the student were writing up reports on her behaviour. If a head of year was bombarded with reports, they would also meet with the child and a parent. If the other teachers who taught the student weren't having problems, or were too busy to spend time writing reports, the problem was seen to be with the specific teacher.

To try to support us, Steph had decided to run detentions for students on a Friday. However, the students rarely attended, and then what? More phone calls home; more paperwork. I remembered that in my first year I'd tried to hold Becky back on a Friday for a detention. I'd gone down to the school gate to make sure she didn't slip away. She saw me and ran for it. I called home, and then sat down and wrote another report on what had happened.

My frustrations with Becky this year were increased tenfold by the feeling that there were no real consequences at my disposal for her behaviour — I could write up reports till my hands no longer had the strength to press through the carbon copy sheets we wrote on, but nothing ever seemed to really come of all this paperwork. Her head of year might speak to her, a counsellor would work with her, she might occasionally or frequently be taken out of lessons to be put in a room with others who had misbehaved, but nothing was done to truly inconvenience her. No Saturday mornings spent in a detention that made her stop and think before wasting away another lesson. And no feeling that, as a teacher, I was being supported. It made me angry, but there was nothing I could do about it. Naively, in my first year I'd sent an email enquiring if there could be more efficient ways of reporting behaviour — perhaps by email. I was informed that, if I didn't understand the behaviour system, someone could go through it with me.

And now this latest explosion. Why had Becky exploded? Because she does. Because of something outside of class? Because by not engaging in class she was slipping further and further behind and she was smart enough to see that she was losing her grip on the chance to get a decent grade. She was absent the following lesson — owing to the day's exclusion — and then she was absent for a few more lessons.

★ ★ ★

I try to be fair towards all my parents, and so, having met my mother, Will agreed that he would meet my father and stepmother. Each party involved negotiated their terms, and it was finally agreed we would meet at neither my father's club nor Will's, but at a restaurant in Marylebone. My father and stepmother came down from Norfolk and took us out to supper.

Will's mother had been making requests to meet me from an early stage, but had been told by Will that she'd have to wait several months more. Now that he had met three of my four parents, it seemed cruel to keep her hanging on, and so for Mothering Sunday, Will relented and took me home. He didn't tell her I would be arriving with her two sons.

'Don't you think it would be nice for her if we called her to tell her I was coming?' I asked him.

'No, because then she'll spend time trying to get everything ready.'

I was due to be having lunch with my own mother, who had gone to her stepdaughter's who lived, coincidentally, only a short distance from Will's parents.

'You sound like you're trying to be in two places at once,' my mother said. 'I think it's more important today that you just meet Will's mother.' And so I stayed at Will's for a Sunday roast before driving back to London. Will's mother was delighted with the surprise, but dismayed at not having had a chance to get everything ready for my arrival.

* * *

I had started the half-term feeling like I had the energy to get on top of things. After Becky's explosion, things went downhill. The Year 7s in particular seemed to be growing more and more challenging by the day. During the second week back I tried to cut down on all evening activities, to preserve energy. I missed a Teach First evening about Women in Leadership. God, I thought, I can't imagine working where I am and also having children. I know one or two mothers to be who have left school in the knowledge that they'd need to conserve their emotional energy. Others, like Julia, seemed to manage — though Julia, like the panellists at the Teach First day, gets up at 4.30 in the morning to prepare for school, clean her house and have some time for herself. Even the thought of that makes me need a nap.

At the end of the second week, once again I felt rather rundown. In a paranoid and obsessed fashion, I kept prodding the swollen glands in my neck. But a friend with whom I'd read English, who had a voracious appetite for all things cultural, had booked us all tickets for the Royal Court to see a play called *random*, by debbie tucker green. I arrived early and sat penning a *Guardian* column for the following week in the bar downstairs. Dominique arrived completely stoned, and we sat dozily chatting to each other until Will arrived with a present of a bottle of shampoo — he'd seen I'd run out.

We watched the fifty-minute piece performed by one actress with no props, no set, no music. The play presented a day in the life of a black family living in London. The actress switched between monologues by the members of the family: the mother, the father, the daughter and the son. There was a short scene in which we saw the son arriving late for school, to be berated by a teacher:

BROTHER: (*dry*) 'Know you miss me Miss'
TEACHER: 'Siddown'
BROTHER: 's'only juss a ten — '
TEACHER: 'twenty — '
BROTHER: ' — after a ten minutes —'
TEACHER: 'twenty.'
          (Beat.)
BROTHER: See.
          I give ar joke
          even when she try all her —
          harness and teacherness —
          an' teacher-tranin tactics —
          we still gotta little —

TEACHER: 'SIT. DOWN!'
BROTHER: She say I got potential —
           I *know* I got potential —
           but come on now
           bare blastin me out in fronta
              my . . .
           when I was only ten —

The teenage boy is killed in a random act of street violence, and the play ends in the family's bleakness and loss.

This was a play I needed to arrange a school trip for. It seems crass to say that it was a story my students would know, that it in some way presented their lives — but I felt that, whatever their own background, the characters and accents would be recognizable. And for some the story would ring true.

I thought back to the summer term of the previous year. Two of my most difficult year 11s were absent from one lesson. I asked Maria where they were. They were at a friend's funeral. A boy had been stabbed in a gang fight. When they returned, they sat silently, tears rolling down their cheeks. My friend Jo had died only a few months earlier, and so I felt, because of this, that maybe I could say something that would help them. Their GCSEs were only weeks away. I told them to put their mourning on hold.

* ★ ★

The Monday following my evening at the theatre I dropped in to see Tony. Tony is in charge of co-ordinating external mentors — real adults taxied in from the outside world — to come and work for an hour a fortnight with, blissfully, one student. Sometimes I spy them in the library and daydream about how wonderful it must be to only have one student. Tony also has a budget to fund extra-curricular activities. I believe it is substantial, and plan one day to test its depths by asking if I can organize a whole season of theatre trips. I told Tony about the play, and he was thrilled to supply the budget. He handed me forms to fill in, and passed over the number of a coach company — 'Tell them Tony says they're to give you a good price.'

Feeling rather deflated and defeated by the everyday tasks that needed doing and a to-do list which only grew, I was happy to be distracted by something new. I'd always had a vaguely debilitating feeling that the health-and-safety forms and permission slips made the process of taking the students out nearly impossible. I looked at the risk-assessment form. What were the dangers of a trip to the theatre? Humiliation when students talk all

225

the way through the performance. I wrote down, 'Students could run on to the road outside the theatre.' Once you've identified a risk, you have to decide on the level of danger it presents and what precautionary measures to take. Students to be gagged throughout the performance. 'Teachers to supervise students at all times,' I wrote.

I looked at the other forms. Would the students be wearing their own clothes or school uniform? I paused. The non-school-uniform days had been shocking experiences. As a twelve-year-old out in the Midwest, my most pressing fashion dilemma had been whether or not to roll up the bottom of my jeans. In their own clothes, some of my fifteen — and sixteen-year-old students looked easily over eighteen. The girls had, they told me, no problems getting into clubs at the weekend. I could imagine.

I mulled over the best plan of action and decided to organize a trip for twenty-two students and three staff. Easily manageable, a pleasant experience for all involved, not stressful, not chaotic. Emily taught the other top English set in Year 11, and I decided to split the tickets with her.

'I have eleven tickets to offer the first to bring back their reply slips,' I told the Year 11 class of thirty.

'Wot?'

'Wot, Miss? That is not fair.' A chorus of abuse and complaints was shouted out, Abimbola at the head.

'Miss, everyone should be able to go. We've never been on a school trip.'

'Well, if you want to go, you'll just have to get your slip in first.'

School ends at three. At five minutes past, Aysha, who had made her mother come and meet her at the gate, ran back with her reply slip. By nine the following morning I'd had slips thrust into my hands on the bus, and other students had run up to my classroom before school started. Between us, Emily and I had twenty-two students desperate to go. Only a small handful of my thirty students had not been interested in taking home the letter about the performance — Becky was one of them.

Until relatively recently I've always found sitting still for a whole performance a bit of a chore. Perhaps it was a stint at the Old Vic as an usher that cured me. Ella and I, having just come down from Oxford, were desperate to get a flat in London. We wanted the first place we looked at — our tiny flat. Even without any furniture, it still managed to look very shabby. The rooms were all odd sizes, and the layout was completely bizarre, but it had a good feeling.

'Don't you think you're putting the horse before the cart?' my father had asked, concerned that neither of us had the faintest idea what kind of work we wanted. We signed the lease, and I dropped into the theatre at the end of the road to see if there were any jobs going. That's how Ella and I were subjected to watching umpteen performances of Kevin Spacey's Richard II. It's hard to say whether those three-hour performances or the slapstick humour of *Aladdin*, the panto that followed, were more painful to sit through. Two months after moving into the flat, we could perform the whole of *Aladdin* between us for supper guests.

The students showed no sign of being aware that they might be signing themselves up for an evening of torture. Bowled over by their enthusiasm for the evening trip to *random*, I pushed aside all my previous reasoning that the smaller the party the less stressful the experience: I ordered a further batch of tickets, and filled in more forms.

★   ★   ★

The excitement generated by the prospect of a school trip provided a rather stark contrast to the monotony of the teaching weeks. By the third week of the half-term, everyday school life seemed to have lost its appeal. I just couldn't summon up enough energy to get on top of my classes. The students were at the steering wheel, and I felt like I'd been run over at the end of each day. I'd slump down in a chair in Emily's classroom after the students had left. Kitty, Emily and I would look at each other understandingly.

'After teaching that Year 10 class I literally feel like I have been stabbed.' Emily told us.

'I feel like I've been shot in the head on a Tuesday afternoon. I've got my 9s and then my 10s,' Kitty echoed.

We shared the worst incidents of the day. We'd start off wearily, and then become hysterical as the ridiculousness of each situation hit us.

'So today,' Emily told us, 'with the 8s it seemed like we were having quite a good lesson, and then I put them into groups and gave them five minutes to come up with a series of still images. The lesson was so carefully structured and everyone knew exactly what they had to do, and everyone except Lyndsey was keen to start the group work. I went to one table who wanted to check something with me, and when I next looked round the room Lyndsey had emptied a carrier bag full of crisps on to the desk and was trying to sell them to people in the class. 'What are you doing?' I asked her. 'Setting up shop,' she said, and continued with what she was doing.'

'That is so funny. What did you do?'

'Told her to put the crisps away. She wouldn't. It ended up with on-call coming. I've got to write up an incident report.'

We all agreed, altogether, it was too much.

By the evening, the adrenalin from the day had worn off.

'Oh, I don't know whether I can do this,' I whined to Will.

'Leave.'

'I don't know whether I can do another year of teaching like this,' I told my therapist.

'You mean you don't know if you *want* to do another year,' she corrected me.

'Ooh.'

I went round in circles in my head. Leave . . . do what? Would it be harder to move than to stay? Do I want to teach? Yes, and I like the holidays.

It was not a feeling of having reached rock bottom. One of the more amusing presentations we'd been given in our induction at Teach First had been about what we could expect of the coming two years. The CEO, Brett Wigdortz, showed us a graph mapping out what our first year would look like: hills of happiness and valleys of despair. The auditorium of excited graduates laughed, blissfully unaware that in the valleys of despair you cry tears of frustration. In our second year he suggested that things would level out a bit. The lows wouldn't be so low — there would be peaks and troughs, but the peaks would outnumber the troughs. I felt as if I'd worked my way into a trough. There were short term and long-term ways out, but ultimately I wasn't sure I had the energy to keep dragging myself up the mountain.

'Steph . . . ' I poked my head round the door of the head of department's classroom. I don't know how she gets anything done — there is always one of us popping in. 'I just wanted to tell you what I'm thinking at the moment,' I winced. 'I'm not sure I'm definitely going to be here next year . . . '

'Oh no, why?' she asked.

'I just don't know about putting myself through another year of it. I find it so exhausting.'

'Everyone's exhausted — it's just that time of year. They're tired, we're tired,' she offered sympathetically.

'And the behaviour . . . ' I said.

'Well, you've seen my classes . . . ' But Steph seemed to work with the chaos rather than against it. 'And you've got great control . . . I've

231

seen it, and you're brilliant with them . . . '

'I really enjoy it when it's going well, it's just that I've never had so many colds and sore throats, and I just want to make sure I make the right decision about next year. I'm seeing a careers adviser next week' — I'd arranged to make use of Teach First's service — 'and I just wanted to let you know where my thinking was.'

'Err, Miss Crossley-Holland . . . ' The deputy head caught me going up the stairs the following morning.

'Oh, I'm in trouble aren't I?' I waited to hear.

'Now listen, you are *not* leaving,' she said.

'Oh.'

'Now, I've arranged with my mother, and you can go and live with her and then she's going to make sure that you come into school every morning. You'd be absolutely bored to pieces at another school where all the kids did exactly what you wanted all the time.'

I laughed. 'It's not that I don't like it here — I'm just struggling with the behaviour . . . I can't get on top of the classes . . . '

'Now, *why* don't you speak to Julia?'

'Yes . . . ' But I knew all the things I was supposed to be doing. Either they weren't quite working or I didn't have the energy to do them.

'And I'll drop in and see how you're doing with those 7s . . . '

'I know, that lovely class — even they seem to be getting out of control.'

'You'll be fine.' She was decided. I felt less so.

★ ★ ★

At about this time the 2ic duties, which had so far mainly involved sending a few emails to organize some poets to come and perform for the year 7s, seemed to get much more serious. I saw that time I could have previously used to try to make my lessons better prepared, so that they didn't provide opportunities for poor behaviour, was now assigned to departmental tasks. I received a formal letter asking me to attend a meeting with the head and the 2ics from maths and science. We were to present the predicted results for the upcoming SATs, based on the recent mock exams.

Two years before students take their GCSEs, they sit another statutorily required test — their end of Key Stage 3 exams. Across the country, students usually take these tests in Year 9. We'd started putting our top sets in for the exam a year earlier, with a view to all of Year 8 taking the test a year early in future. Year 8 students notoriously go off the rails; it was hoped that making them sit the Key Stage 3 exams then would give them something to be serious about.

The head asked that, as well as presenting the data from the recent mocks, we would share our strategies for reaching our targets. Oh God, how do you figure out percentages? I sat down with the results from the mock exams. How were we going to raise attainment? I talked with Steph. We were going to hold revision sessions after school and during Easter, targeting the borderline students.

'But if a student has been working at a certain level for the last two years, one extra session isn't going to help them get to the next level,' I said to Steph.

'I know, but we'll have tried something.'

On a Thursday afternoon, clutching the wad of papers I'd prepared, I nervously went to the head's office, I was expecting lots of curve-ball questions about figures that I was sure I didn't know the answers to. 'Hello, Oenone,' Cecelia smiled. 'I've laid out some biscuits. Would you like some water or tea?' I breathed a sigh of relief: it was a kind of cookies-and-a-chat meeting rather than a boardroom grilling.

'We've just gathered you here', Cecelia

began addressing the three of us, 'because Harriet thought it would be helpful if you shared with each other what your strategies were for reaching the targets — and also gave me a breakdown of how the mock exams went.' I stuffed my face with biscuits and in between mouthfuls said that we planned to target borderline groups after school and during the holidays. The other departments had planned to do the same.

★ ★ ★

On Saturday night, Rosanna (the red trainer critic) had organized a reel to raise money for a charity mission/holiday she wanted to go on. The rain was falling in sheets as we picked our way along the road having dug out dresses and DJS from the backs of our wardrobes. Will felt his hour had arrived. During our months together, no matter how much he criticized my lack of general knowledge, I always had the ace card.

'God, your general knowledge is so poor . . . ' etc.

'Will . . . remind me, where *did* you go to university? I've forgotten.'

'Ha ha. Just because my father isn't a fellow at the college that accepted you after your twentieth interview.'

'Second interview.'

But now there was, truly, something he was better at.

'Does everybody at Edinburgh have to take a compulsory module in reeling?' I asked as he stomped his feet and clapped his hands in anticipation of the evening's dancing.

★ ★ ★

Only four weeks into the term there was the prospect of a small mini-break. Easter fell early, and so the school had decided we would have just Good Friday and Easter Monday off, then return to school for two more weeks before a full two-week holiday. Though I was still feeling rather Eeyorish about school, and had made no progress in thinking about what I might do, the week ahead looked a doddle. Monday in school, Tuesday out for the second Philosophy for Children training day, Wednesday in, Thursday in school but no students (which doesn't count as a real schoolday because you still feel human at the end of it). The government had decided we all needed a day without the students in, to get to grips with the paperwork they were rolling out, the new National Strategy. Thank you, government. And Good Friday was a bank holiday. Thank you, Jesus.

By Wednesday I felt revitalized as I'd spent Tuesday among adults — especially as John the interrupter hadn't attended the second session — and I was relieved there was only one day of teaching left before a few days off.

The Year 10s were keen to tell me how disastrous things had been in my absence.

'Miss, it was the worst lesson ever.' Mahima screwed up her face in a miserably dissatisfied manner.

'Miss . . . that teacher is bare rude,' Coleen told me.

'Did you have a supply teacher?' I asked — sometimes luckless full-time staff who have a free period find themselves roped in.

'Yeah. He was bare rude.'

I winced thinking about the poor guy.

The remnants of the cover work they were supposed to have done were piled on a desk. Even the blank sheets were unsalvageable: somehow they all had footprints on them. A pile of incident reports sat on my desk — the only real evidence that a lesson had taken place:

Folashade was drinking flavoured fizzy water in class. She had it on her desk and I asked her to put it away. She refused. I asked her again and she refused again . . . I tried to take her drink but I couldn't without touching the student, so I didn't. Later in class her drink was still on the table and I went by and took it off and told her she could have the drink at the end of the lesson. However, she got very angry and charged after her bottle. She had to be restrained by her classmates . . .

Erez came into class and immediately would not follow instructions or do anything co-operatively. She was given two warnings for refusing to take off her coat and take her bag off the desk. 'What? What's my bag doing to you? Is my bag hurting you?' I tried to send her out of the classroom but she refused to go.

Sifting through the five reports, I saw that the offenders were the usual suspects — though not, for some reason, Coleen. I checked the larger cupboards to see if the supply teacher had been gagged and taped to a shelf.

Cecelia stopped me in the hall.

'Oenone, I had to speak to your Year 7 class yesterday.'

'Oh?'

'There was a supply teacher. I was trying to interview a new teacher in the classroom next door, and there was an awful lot of noise . . . Lesson four I think it was.'

'Ah, yes. I'll speak to them.'

When I saw my lower-set 7s, later in the day, I lined them up outside the door before letting them enter the classroom.

'Stand quietly . . . in a straight line . . . stop slouching against the wall.' Rose, who hadn't been touching the wall, stood up so tall she looked like she was ready to march. If only all the class were naughty I wouldn't feel so bad about telling them off. Poor Rose only ever does the right thing, and still she has to listen to me barking at all of them. 'Right girls, I'm very disappointed. Mrs Sharpe came and found me to say that she had to speak to you all yesterday . . . Chantelle, I'm speaking.' Chantelle was whispering in Stella's ear. 'It's very embarrassing to be told that your class is unable to behave appropriately . . . I've noticed that behaviour is getting worse and worse, and I will not have it in my classroom. I want you to walk silently into the room and sit down at your desks. If anyone speaks then we will line up and do it again. No talking . . . Into the classroom please.' I stood my tallest at the door, watching them walk in.

About five students managed to make it into the classroom before Chantelle started talking. 'Right, everyone line up again.'

There was a lot of complaining as they reassembled themselves into the line for the second and then third time and finally made it into the classroom in silence. They sat waiting for me to tell them what to do next, and the lesson that followed ran noticeably smoother than ones in the weeks preceding. I'd forgotten that asserting authority could quash their rebellious nature. Why do I always let it get so bad before I do something about it?

Halfway through the lesson we heard a piercing screaming from Steph's classroom. I ran to her door, imagining a fight had broken out. Instead I saw that Steph was in role as Frankenstein's monster. I went back to my room and told the class; they looked eager to hear that a fight had broken out, or maybe a fire.

'It's all OK — they're just doing drama next door,' I said. Everyone looked miserable.

'Oh!' Princess stamped her foot, 'Why are they always having fun?' Princess is getting out of hand, I thought, but all the spaces for difficult girls in this class are taken already.

After school I called her home. Princess's father answered the phone, and I told him about her recent small digressions.

' . . . I'm so sorry . . . By offending you she has offended me . . . You are her teacher — she must show you respect . . . She will come and apologize . . . I don't know how to say how sorry I am.'

It was a rather unusual experience. There are plenty of supportive parents with children at the school, but I generally spend more time on the phone to the ones who sympathize with me but say that they've also lost control and don't know what to do.

With planning still to be done for the following day, I wrote up a telephone record and then, having run out of time to make preparations for Thursday's inset day, I abandoned work and drifted up to Camden. I was meeting Will for a performance at the Roundhouse.

Lucy and Catherine, two fellow second-year Teach Firsters, had selected a group from each of their schools and developed a dance, drama and performance piece. After pulling a lot of strings, Lucy had arranged for it to be performed in the studio theatre at the Roundhouse. I vaguely remembered her telling me that they'd deliberately selected the most disaffected students in their respective schools — the project was to be a way of giving them something to get excited about.

I'd spoken to Lucy at the beginning of the week, to find out how things were shaping up.

'I honestly don't know if we're going to be ready,' she said. 'I mean, it's *Monday*, we're performing *tomorrow*, and people still don't

241

know their lines . . . We're not ready to perform. We had to kick someone else off at the weekend . . . I'm glad you're coming for the last performance.'

I was also desperate to hear Lucy's impressions of Catherine's school, which I knew she'd visited. Catherine had been placed at a school that made mine sound like Eton. In the first week of her first year the timetables had not been completed. Students roamed the school choosing which lessons they felt like pitching up to — 'Let's go terrorize Miss Crowe now.' She would have forty students she didn't know milling in her room. Hers was the school in the borough that received all the students that other schools permanently excluded.

'Um . . . well,' Lucy began, 'my kids really scared me when I said I was going to visit her school. They were like 'Er, Miss, you're not going on your own are you?' I was genuinely quite concerned. I pitched up at reception and there was a police car and an ambulance parked outside. Catherine met me and she said she'd laid all this on especially for me. And then this boy was wheeled past me on a stretcher. He had a Bic pen sticking out of his chest.'

'Oh my God,' I said. 'Had another kid . . .'
Lucy laughed: 'No, the deputy head.'

'What? Actually the deputy had *really* stabbed him?' I was laughing nervously.

'Yes. The deputy head had *actually* put a Bic pen into the boy's chest. Apparently it was an accident.'

In the Roundhouse, two spotlights shone on a black stage. Over loudspeakers, we heard the sounds of the playground and snippets of interviews with the cast.

At the boarding school I'd attended for my final years of school, there were student productions of *Tess of the D'Urbervilles* and *A Midsummer Night's Dream* performed in an amphitheatre in the forest. Lucy and Catherine's production was of a different genre. The letters of the title, *These Times*, morphed from the newspaper font used for the *Times* newspaper at the edges into chunky graffiti for the middle letters. The performance was the same mix of classical and street.

Describing the events of a school day, the students told their stories — all adapted from their own experiences. There was bullying on the public buses while the adult passengers turned a blind eye, bullying in the playground, experiences of racism, and the frustration of thwarted expectations. The students had ideas about what they'd like for their futures, but spent their lessons not getting anywhere as the teachers dealt with mayhem, fights and disruption. The day was presented through small sketches, monologues, and choreographed dances to music that blended Mozart with hip hop.

The individual stories and incidents rang true for the row of teachers I sat with. My own school had just excluded several students who had attacked a girl on a bus.

In the pub afterwards, I sat with lots of Teach First teachers I hadn't seen for a while. Since being with Will, I'd failed to make it along to the Wednesday pub session they were all religious about attending. It was mid-March, and we were all coming to the end of the Teach First programme; everyone was thinking about their plans for the following year.

'Are you staying on, Leon?'

'No, I'm going to start landscape gardening.'

'Cool.'

'Wes, are you thinking of . . . ?'

'Well surprisingly, Nony, yes I am thinking of tucking into another year . . . '

'I thought you were thinking of switching to private?' Will's ears pricked up, sensing an opportunity to recruit.

'Well, I'm just getting going really . . . '

'That's great.' I imagined Wes, who taught

biology, to be quite special in the classroom, wearing a lab coat and protective glasses. At one of the early pub sessions in our first year of teaching, he'd narrated the details of an experiment he'd recently pulled off.

'Well lads, gather round, gather round,' he told his class. 'Remember I took a swab from the inside of Timmy's cheek yesterday, to get a cell? Well . . . I put the cell in the incubator overnight, and look how it has turned out.' Wes had painstakingly floated a black olive in watery jelly. He'd then wrapped the loose jelly and olive in a delicate layer of clingfilm. He thought the result was remarkably convincing.

'Errgh, Sir! That is bare disgusting. I'm gonna throw up.'

'Right, and if we just take this scalpel . . . ' He cut into the membrane of the cell and, he said, the jelly oozed out perfectly. All around him the students had started to retch. The one who he had taken the cell from looked as if he was going to pass out.

'And you, Nones?' Wes asked.

'Oh, I'm not sure yet.'

'I thought you wanted to be headmistress?' I'd been one of the more zealous converts in my first year, and, while everyone else remained cagey about staying on beyond the two-year programme, I was already sharing my thoughts about trying to get on to some kind of leadership programme that could fast-track me into a headship.

'Yeah, I did. I don't know now, though.' Stay or go? Another school or another career? The questions went around my mind, and I couldn't seem to decide either way. I'd lost the passionate enthusiasm for the day-to-day teaching, and so was looking forward to the session with the careers adviser that Teach First provided.

★ ★ ★

Before we went to sleep on Wednesday, I gave Will a card and told him not to open it until five o'clock on Friday — it had instructions for the evening. I'd stopped breaking into a sweat at the thought of sitting opposite him in a restaurant, and so had booked a table at an expensive and trendy place. I wanted it to be a surprise.

The evening arrived and we sat gazing into each other's eyes. The food was delicious; the wine was exceptional; the restaurant was so beautifully designed; the people closely surrounding us were clearly enjoying their evenings too. After the main course, carried away by the experience, we leaned across the table for a quick snog. The side of my head suddenly felt quite warm, then I saw flames in the corner of my left eye and felt Will slapping my head to try to put them out. My mass of red hair had been set alight by the candle.

A cloud of charred-black tresses sprinkled on to our table. The smell of burning hair filled the restaurant. The people surrounding us looked shocked, and inspected their plates for strands of burnt hair. The French waiters tried unsuccessfully to sweep the table clean with their pristine linen napkins.

'I'm so sorry,' I kept saying between laughter. 'I'm so sorry,' I said to the people sitting less than a yard from us. 'Please could we have the bill?' I went to the bathroom to check the damage and pulled several more handfuls of burnt hair into the bin. The smell was overwhelming, but, despite losing quite a lot, having so much hair on my head meant the overall impact wasn't that great.

* * *

I'd resolved to stay in London over the Easter weekend and write, but at the last moment Will suggested we go to his parents'. I packed a bag, caught a train from Paddington, and met him in Gloucestershire.

On Sunday morning we went along to the

priory down the road. A community of Benedictine monks and nuns live and worked there. We crept in moments before the quiet service began. The small chapel was awash with incense, and the abbot led a hushed liturgy. The welcome note on the pews asked that we respect the quiet, contemplative style of the worship by singing no louder than those who led it. Between the prayers there were gaping acres of silence. I imagined my students attending fervent Pentecostal services, and sank deeper into the solid oak pews.

Will's mother, Lucile, had felt unwell and so had not come down to the place she frequented almost daily. The abbot visited to give her a private service, and one of the nuns called to tell her the gossip from the service she had missed.

'Anne called from the priory. She said she saw you, Nony. She said she was very jealous of how skinny you are.' I thought it was a funny thing for a nun to report.

★   ★   ★

Surgeons often go out with other surgeons because they're the only people who understand the stressful lives they lead. Teachers go out with other teachers because the holidays coincide. Or they're supposed to, but, come the Easter break, Will's holiday did not coincide with mine. Will's school closed from Easter weekend for three weeks. I still had two weeks to teach, and then would get two weeks off.

'So, I was wondering,' Will had said before we compared dates, 'would you like to come out to the Galapagos Islands with me for two weeks?' I thought it was a fairly brave ask considering I'd spent the previous week-long break in Ireland unable to eat much through feeling sick with anxiety. I was initially relieved to find the dates wouldn't work — but when the time came for his departure I felt miserable. I felt miserable that Will was going away, and felt even more miserable that, while he was riding around on tortoises the size of Space Hoppers, I'd be back at school.

Lucy had mooted the idea that Catherine, Milly (another Teach First teacher) and I go somewhere hot for a week during our holidays. Sharm el Sheikh? The south coast of Spain? Morocco?

'There's no point going anywhere unless we have *guaranteed* sunshine. I mean, can you imagine anything worse than turning up to a horrible resort and having to spend the week inside because it's raining?' Lucy tans easily.

'Resort?' I said, surprised to hear the word coming from someone who wore quite so many pearls.

'Yes, Nony. We're poor teachers. It's the only way we can afford it.'

'I can't afford it anyway,' Milly laughed. 'I'm going to put it on my credit card.'

After spending a whole Sunday searching through every page of lastminute.com, we booked a package deal to Gambia. We'd leave the day after Will got back from the Galapagos.

★ ★ ★

With only two weeks to go before the real Easter break, I plodded through the lessons. The Year 7s wavered on the line between being just controllable and completely exhausting. It was as if they hadn't made up their minds how badly they were going to behave — or rather I hadn't made it clear what kind of behaviour they would not get away with.

Becky was increasingly absent from the Year 11 class. Since her explosive exit, she'd only been in again a few times. I worried she was falling impossibly behind. When she was in school, she sat graffitiing her exercise book. I gave her a wider berth than in previous terms. I tentatively tried to draw her into the work we were doing, but she looked as if

250

she'd given up. She wouldn't look at me when I spoke to her, and gave the impression of not listening and definitely not caring. I went and spoke with her head of year, concerned that the chance of a C grade in her English exams was slipping away from her. He was aware this was happening, as was her mentor, a science teacher within the school, who was trying hard to keep her on the right track. But if the energy for her exams was not going to come from her, it seemed there was very little anyone could do. Education was not valued at home, and so it followed that she placed little value on it either.

The rest of the Year 11 class were plodding along. Adalia's relaxed attitude was shared by a large proportion of them. A smaller contingent of students, including Hebba and Maria, were taking their work as seriously as it was possible to in a class where the confident and jovial Adalias ruled.

Coleen and I began a battle over her missing pieces of coursework. Katherine, who works solely on pastorally supporting students in school, started mentoring her. I photocopied the scraps Coleen had written, the reams of advice and notes I'd written, the plans for the essays, and handed them all to Katherine so she could see what Coleen needed to do.

'I think she really wants to get on top of things,' Katherine told me at lunch one day: 'she's just so behind she doesn't even really know where to start.'

'Yeah . . . ' I was lacking in sympathy.

'And she really is such a lovely girl one on one . . . But I can see it must be frustrating in class.' That was an understatement.

'Well, it would be fantastic if you could work with her to complete the coursework.' It would be fewer pieces that I would end up basically writing myself.

I'd helped Becky the year before — held her back after school and typed her missing pieces of coursework when she'd run out of time to do them herself.

'You tell me what to type, Becky, and I'll type it.'

'OK.'

'So, would you say that Rita sees the school system as having failed her?' I asked.

'Um . . . yeah.'

'Right, put that into a sentence for me.'

'Rita sees the school system as having failed her.' Becky had got a B for the piece.

'It's the parents who write coursework in other schools,' teachers had told me. I'd had my dad dictating essays on *Beowulf* down the phone to me while I was at university. I remember sitting in a lecture hall (one of the very few times I did) and being struck that my father had had his translation of *Beowulf* published when he was only a few years older than I was — and I was completely bemused by the lecture, not having even read the translation.

Far from being a model student, he'd failed his prelims (the exams you take at the end of your first year). At the beginning of the summer he'd gone down to the river to revise. He lounged in a punt, Anglo-Saxon grammar in one hand, pork pie in the other, listening to a piece of music written by his father that was being aired on the radio. A passing swan disliked the idyllic picture, and took special offence at the Anglo-Saxon grammar, and so with its 'great wings beating still' it went for my dad. He, remembering only too well the fate of Leda, leaped for the river's bank, tearing the cartilage of his right knee, in the process.

At the Radcliffe Infirmary a visiting professor and three first-year medical students tried unsuccessfully to snap his knee into place. He passed out from the pain, and spent the next two weeks horizontal, with nothing to do but become fluent in Anglo-Saxon.

★ ★ ★

On the last Thursday of March at 6.15 p.m, forty or so students and five staff gathered at the school gate to wait for the coach to take us to the Royal Court. That afternoon I'd managed to recruit a last student to fill a final place.

'Where on earth is the coach? I've left their number in my classroom. Uh-oh.' Having reached the moment we were due to be setting off, it occurred to me that double-checking the details is an essential part of organizing a school trip.

'Don't worry, it'll be fine.' Emily reassured me. Before entering teaching, she'd worked in the City doing some brilliantly organized job. She leaped at tasks like ordering stationery, and was constantly supplying me with schedules of how many lessons remained before the Year 11s had their exams, or resources she'd just knocked up. She spent the whole evening organizing the shepherding of the students, while I ran around searching for lost tickets.

'Ha, ha . . . yes, we'll be fine,' I said nervously. 'As long as none of them die it should be fine . . . Where is that coach?'

My phone rang.

'Hello, Miss . . . it's Adalia,' she laughed, no doubt amused at the idea that she was on the phone to her teacher.

'Oh, how do you have this number?' I asked.

'I got it from my mum's phone.' I always used my own phone to call parents, to save myself the ten-minute round trip to find a school phone to call from.

'Oh.'

'I just want to say, yeah, oh my dayz, Miss, I'm running late. But I am coming.'

'Right, Adalia. Well, you need to hurry up, because we're leaving soon.'

The coach had, of course, gone to a different entrance to the school. We traipsed down the road. Finally there were forty-one students and five teachers sitting on the bus. My approximate calculations indicated that we were missing three students. They were late. We waited for ten long minutes, then told the coach to go. As it rolled off they appeared in the distance, but the wheels were in motion and we sped away without them. Leaving them behind alleviated my concerns about not having booked enough tickets.

Steph, who'd clearly led a few trips in the past, said we needed to call their parents. She searched for the numbers, and told the mothers that their daughters were roaming the streets of south London. But, in contact with their friends who had made it on to the coach, and unbeknown to us, the latecomers made their own way to Sloane Square and joined us minutes before the play started.

On arriving, the girls were using their usual method of communication — shouting rather than talking — and as we entered the theatre I could see a horrified-looking woman watching us. I felt like squaring up to her and asking her what her problem was, but needing my students to drag us apart was perhaps not the best way to model civil behaviour.

As the auditorium lights faded, there were several whoops — I could pick out Adalia's voice the loudest. I closed my eyes and prayed all would be well for the fifty-minute monologue.

. . . And the sun'un in the air —
in the room —
in the day —
like the
shadow of a shadow feelin . . .
off-key — I . . .
look the clock. Eyeball it.
It looks me back.
Stare the shit down —
it stares me right back.

(Beat.)

. . . Till it blinked first — loser.

I heard the first laughs, and began to breathe a little easier.

Some minutes into the production a mobile phone started ringing. *Please don't let it be one of my students.* It wasn't: it was a careless adult. Another few minutes and another went off. Aargh — one of the students. Steph went to speak to her gently at the end of the performance, but the girl went berserk and wouldn't listen to Steph's quiet words of advice. Everyone cringed to see a student treating a teacher out in public the way they treat them in school.

'Did you like it?' I asked Adalia, who was standing with a small group after the lights went up. I had heard my students laughing in mostly the right places.

'Yes, Miss, yes.'

'I cried the first time I saw it,' I told them. They laughed.

'Yeh, Miss, I cried — it was so sad when the brother died,' Adalia gushed.

There was a small amount of commotion before the coach — with all forty-four students — set off from Sloane Square. Two boys were standing on the pavement by the coach throwing small stones at its windows. The girls at the back were angrily standing in their seats and shouting at them.

London lit up at night looked completely

beautiful as we drove back across Westminster Bridge. It felt like the place to be, and that this was the best job to be doing. The girls tumbled off the coach and we waited for them to disperse, a few being picked up by a mother or father.

'Pub, anyone?' Steph suggested.

'Yes,' we said, practically gasping for some cheap lukewarm white wine at the local.

★ ★ ★

The following day a group of Year 11s dropped by for the informal club that had started taking place in my classroom after school. I had not organized this, but somehow word must have spread that Miss Crossley-Holland was not averse to students aimlessly loitering or trying to complete pieces of coursework in her classroom. One of the students, Jumoke, had nothing to do; the others were trying to complete science coursework. I'd never taught Jumoke, but she was friends with several of the girls in my class and had been the student, at the Red Nose Day fund-raiser, who dressed up as me so that the other teachers could guess who she was trying to imitate. Jumoke and Adalia were friends, and the latter had checked with me beforehand that I would be attending.

'Miss, you *are* coming to the tea party.'

'Adalia, I'm so sorry, I'm not in school tomorrow because I've got a training day.'

'No-o-o, Miss, you *have* to come. Miss, you *have* to be there. You *have* to. I can't tell you why, but you *have* to.'

She was clearly up to something, so I told her I'd try to return to school after the training in time for the tea party.

At the fund-raiser, there were lots of suspicious looking cookies and cakes. I did my best to choose bought over handmade while loudly admiring the gloopy-looking stacks of biscuits stuck together with icing. Jumoke stood with the other students who had dressed as teachers. I could pick out Sophie and Julia's doubles, and of course my own. My own had skinny cords and a belted cardigan. She stood mimicking the lines my own students had obviously taught her: 'We're wasting time here. We're not going to get As if we waste time.'

'Did you enjoy the play?' I asked Jumoke as her friends helped each other fill in the missing gaps in their science work.

'Oh, Miss, I thought it was so good.'

'I was very impressed you found the theatre by yourself.' Jumoke had been one of the late three.

'Yeah, Miss, it was really easy. Now that I

know how to get there, I'm going to go again.'
What a result. They should have all missed
the coach. I beamed.

'How did you know where we were?' I
asked. I knew that most of Year 11 rarely
went north of the river.

'Well, we was talking to one of my friends,
yeah, and they said, 'Sloane Square'. Yeah,
Miss, we took the Tube. We couldn't believe
how easy it was to find it.'

'You know, because you're a student you can
get tickets really cheaply,' I said, giving her
the bumper pack the theatre had handed me:
flyers, director's notes and the script of *random*.

I settled back into planning the following
day's lessons, leaving Jumoke intently reading
the director's notes. A couple of times she
quietened her friends to read out a small
passage.

'Oh, did you know she rehearsed with all
the furniture?'

'What?'

'Like on the stage, it was all there — like
when she was in the bedroom there was all
the furniture.'

The others were no closer to understanding.

'So she knew where to look and all.'

'Oh.'

On the bus home I picked up a copy of

London Lite. It reported that two more teenage boys had died after knife attacks in London. I wondered if the students would make the connection between the play and the most recent spate of teenage deaths.

★　★　★

In the last week before the two-week break, it felt like the countdown had really begun. After nearly five terms with my Year 11 set, there were only nineteen teaching hours left before the first of their English exams. But the only one who seemed to be panicking was me.

'It's OK, we can make it,' I panted, gripping on to the interactive whiteboard as if I'd been lost in the desert and had at long last glimpsed an oasis in the distance.

I'd resorted to performances to gain their attention. Most Fridays we had practised writing essays in timed conditions, and yet, though they were intellectually capable of achieving As and Bs, they were still covering only two sides of A4 in fifty minutes. Becky more often than not, during the few lessons she was in, covered many more pages with doodles. I don't know if she was scared: I think maybe she was. I think she was getting more and more panicked about how far behind she'd fallen. Each English teacher in the department was sharing the running of catch-up sessions after school — but Becky didn't stay after school.

The classes' essays so far had been Es and Ds, with a very occasional C. The spring vacation was almost upon us, and I was uncertain whether they were going to do the revision they needed to. Emily was similarly concerned, and so had taken a two-pronged approach. First she asked them all where they were planning to revise. Most admitted they had nowhere quiet to study at home. 'Lock yourself in the toilet for ten-minute bursts,' she advised them. Then on 1 April Emily put into motion her second ingenious plan.

Steph, the head of department, entered mid-lesson.

'Miss Crossley-Holland, I'm really sorry to interrupt, but I've just had this letter through and I think you should know . . . '

She waved some official-looking papers around for the class to see.

'Well, actually,' she continued, 'the news affects this class.'

Fantastic concentration and listening skills displayed by all.

'The English exams have been moved forward to the first Monday back after the holidays.'

The class were furious and worried.

'Wot?'

'They can't do that to us.'

'That's not fair,' etc.

The studious ones, Aysha and Hebba, who had tried very hard from the beginning, simply looked crestfallen.

'Oh no,' I said, and wandered over to the calendar of remaining lessons to count how many we now had left. There were tears in my eyes with the effort of not laughing.

'Settle down, girls . . . shh . . . You are still going to be able to do the exams — we've covered everything we need to [not true]. Now, instead of there being eighteen and a half hours of lessons left before the exams, this will be our last lesson.'

A few students started trying to be positive and suggested we made the most of the remaining twenty minutes. Steph exited, and I started going over again what revision they should do in the next two weeks.

Adalia caught my eye and saw that I was trying to suppress giggles.

'Miss! It's an April fool!'

More pandemonium ensued. A few students didn't hear Adalia, or see my reaction, and so were in a state of confusion until the others, still laughing, explained what was going on.

'Miss, that was *good*. Miss, you really had us,' said Adalia.

The majority were exceptionally pleased with our sense of humour, and a few were simply relieved.

With eighteen teaching hours still to go, they left for the holidays taking their folders and the piles of photocopies I'd handed out. I prepared a pack of photocopies for the two girls who had been absent that lesson, and thought, as I stuffed the papers in envelopes and took them down to the office, that it was unlikely that Becky would even know where to start with them. I felt the balance had tipped: she'd fallen too far behind. She was fairly bright, and I knew that would carry her through parts of the exam, but she'd just missed too much. She wouldn't be able to write essays comparing poems that she simply hadn't studied.

★ ★ ★

I knew that, if I was going to leave the school at the end of the year, the deadline for telling the principal was fast approaching. The prospect of the imminent Easter break and the summer term ahead (always the best term) seemed to make me waver even more in the decision-making.

Finally reaching the holiday, I trotted down the road to the doctor's to pick up a prescription for some malaria pills and get some booster jabs. I mentioned a sore throat — totally to be expected for the end of a term — and the nurse told me it would be best if I returned in a few days to get the jabs, when I was feeling 100 per cent.

I awoke on the first day of the holidays with a hideous bout of tonsillitis. Ella left to spend a week with her parents in a village in Ireland. Will was in the Galapagos, and so I spent five days in bed sending him self-pitying emails. I cancelled all the drinks and lunches I'd put in my diary, and waited for the moment I'd be able to swallow without feeling as if I'd gone at my throat with a cheese-grater. After the noise of the previous term, I seemed to be living in a strangely silent world.

★   ★   ★

One whole week into the holidays and finally better, I had one lovely evening together with Will before I set off for Gambia. The nurse reluctantly gave me all the jabs right at the last minute.

'Most of them take about ten days to start working.'

'Oh, I'll be back in England by then . . . '

After a seven-hour flight, Lucy, Milly, Catherine and I found ourselves in Ocean Bay, a perfectly nice resort on a deserted palm-fringed beach on the edge of Gambia. There were a few hours of tanning left in the day, so we donned bikinis and headed to four sun-loungers. 'Make sure you put suncream everywhere,' I'd patronizingly told Milly in the room we were sharing (later to be renamed the Burns Unit).

'Now, Nony,' Will had told me, 'the African sun is really strong and you will burn. Do not lie out in it, and you need to apply at least factor fifty.'

'Yes, yes, I know. I'm going to be really careful.'

Half an hour after lying out in the sun I had done just about as much damage to my skin as anyone would want to do in a lifetime. It was painfully obvious where I'd missed putting the suncream on — on my nose, on my neck, all across my stomach, and on both knees. Blisters rose from the red-raw patches.

'Really, Nones, it's not *that* bad,' Milly and Lucy tried to reassure me, and every morning Catherine would insist, 'It really is getting much better,' before they all fell about laughing.

Lucy and Catherine had a room with a balcony; the Burns Unit was more of a cave.

After a day in the sun, or under a parasol, we retired to the balcony to drink the duty-free gin we'd bought. Once we'd exhausted all the possible discussions we could have about boyfriends, upcoming dates, previous dates etc., our conversation turned to familiar territory.

'I've told my head of department I'm not entirely sure I'm staying,' I admitted. 'I've been so exhausted this year, and I don't want to be struggling in the same way next year. It's just the behaviour. I want to teach, and not feel completely wiped out at the end of a lesson.'

Milly and Lucy made sympathetic sounds.

'I don't think it will be as hard next year, though,' said Lucy. 'I think your second year still is just quite hard.'

'Yeah, it is hard,' said Catherine. 'I mean, I still struggle with behaviour.'

It was clear from the outset that Catherine was going to be strong at behaviour management. She attended a university in LA, and used to hang out in South Central.

'I had this one girl, right — a new girl — and she turned up in this pink hoodie and scarf. So I told her to take off her hoodie. She didn't. So I told Mohammad, who was next to her, to take off his hoodie. Mohammad took off his hoodie — it's always useful to have someone who you can model your behaviour policy on. I told her, 'We take off hoodies in this classroom,' but she kept it on.'

Catherine does sound hard. I remember in our first year she told me that she'd had a problem with kids keeping their backpacks on in class, and so had delivered a lesson on scoliosis — a back condition she told the students they were likely to develop if they continued to put pressure on their lower spines. When she gave feedback to her Year 11 set on how they'd done in their mock English GCSEs, she simply started the lesson by displaying a large skull and crossbones on the interactive whiteboard and said that she wasn't exactly happy with how the exams had gone. It made a stark contrast to the confusion I'd caused by telling my own students I was heartened.

Catherine took a drag of her cigarette and continued her story.

'So this girl then took off her pink scarf, and I wrestled it off her. I took it to my filing cabinet and locked it in. I told her the scarf had gone into the filing cabinet of death, and she was never going to see it again. Most of the items of clothing that go into the filing cabinet of death end up as board-rubbers. I have a perfectly good board-rubber, but it's useful as a warning to other students

— rather like a severed head on a spike. She *still* refused to take off her hoodie. When the lesson ended, I said to her 'Next time we'll see if we can get along better'. And that's really important. It's important that no matter how much you hate a kid, or how rude they've been to you, they always have to have a clean slate at the beginning of the next lesson.'

We all nodded in agreement. I thought of Coleen and all the times she'd sullied her clean slate within seconds of entering the classroom, and how reluctant I was feeling, even in the lingering heat of a Gambian evening, to keep trying to make progress with her.

'So the next lesson she pitched up not wearing her hoodie. The rest of the class were doing these group drama exercises, and she wasn't getting involved. I went to her and asked her, 'What's going on? Do you not want to get involved in this activity?' And of course she said, 'No.' So I said really enthusiastically, '*Good! I was hoping you'd say that.*' I told her I needed a personal assistant for the lesson. I needed her to check that the other groups were working and tell me who was and who wasn't. I said she could have three powers. One, she could give out green cards — they're like for anyone who's doing really well or something. Two, she could give out red cards to people who were misbehaving. And three, if there were people being really naughty she could steal their stuff to lock away into the filing cabinet of death.

'She didn't give out any red cards or take anyone's stuff, and she was beside me all lesson. So at the end of the lesson I said to her, 'What about I give you back your scarf?' I'd never told her she'd get it back again if she was good, but it seemed like a nice thing to do. But she said, 'No, Miss, you can keep it for a while.' Isn't that strange that she like wanted me to keep it?'

'Yeah,' we nodded.

'She wanted you to keep a hold over her in some way.'

We poured another gin and tonic, and I felt a bit rubbish about the fact that I don't think I'm as good as Catherine at ruling the classroom. Or as funny.

'But I don't have a life during term time,' Catherine added. 'I can't speak to anyone when I get home — I'm too exhausted.'

On our fourth night in Gambia, conversation over the evening's gin and tonics turned more generally to the youth culture of the students we all teach. It's the white working-class kids who get the worst write-up, but each of us had a catalogue of stories about rude and aggressive students of all races.

'How is it that today's youth culture is so different from the youth culture of twenty years ago?' Is it the consequence of Labour's government? The breakdown of communities? Migrant communities displacing those who were there before them?

'Why is there such a lack of pride?'

'And what are the chances for our students? What opportunities are there?'

'How will some of them actually survive when they have to work — when they have to turn up on time and not be rude to their manager?'

'If I were the manager of some of my students, I would have fired them a long time ago,' Catherine quipped.

'But they *do* have opportunities,' Lucy insisted. 'There are so many projects and schemes and — '

'Yes,' I agreed. 'A handful of our Year 11s have gone up to Oxford for a course during this spring vacation. I can't wait to find out what they made of it. I mean, I don't know how you could be in a place like that and not be affected.' I thought of Abimbola, who had thrust over the application form and asked me to fill it in, specifying what areas of English she needed help with, what texts she'd studied. I sort of imagined she was going to come back desperate to learn.

'There should be more incentives for good graduates to go into teaching, not just Teach First.'

'Are you guys going to strike?' Catherine asked.

'Oh, is there going to be a strike?' I had a large pile of unopened mail from the NUT. 'What's the strike over?' I asked, knowing that this was another one of those things I should definitely know.

'The fact that teachers are being paid below inflation,' answered Catherine.

I felt little troubled by this. The fact that I get paid once a month seems very divorced from days spent in school. If I started thinking that the reason I should help Coleen with her coursework, or the reason I should talk Chantelle round from throwing a tantrum, was because I was being paid £15 an hour to do it, I think it would be game over.

'But think about if you had a kid . . . ' Catherine continued.

'Yes,' we all nodded, and Milly and I both added, 'And I'd quite like to send my kids to public school.'

'Really? Why?' Lucy had attended a state school in north London before going up to

Edinburgh. But her parents' decision to send her to a state school had been political rather than financial.

'Well,' I began, using the argument my own parents had used to persuade me to move from a state school in rural East Anglia to a boarding school on the north-Norfolk coast, 'because of the opportunities, the expectations . . . Because it is cool to achieve, and play an instrument, and go on Duke of Edinburgh . . . ' My parents had had a hard job selling public school to me. I was settled: I liked hanging out at the local bus stop and drinking cider. But once I arrived at Gresham's I realized it was a different world: one where boys kissed you on both cheeks when you were introduced to them; where the girls were eccentric and bohemian, and had parents who were like my own parents.

'How many of your staff send their own children to your schools?' I asked.

None.

'And would you?'

'No.'

SUMMER TERM
FIRST HALF

On Monday morning Amber, one of my tutor group, greeted me at the door outside my classroom.

'Miss! You look red.'

'Don't say that, Amber,' I replied very quickly. 'It's not polite.' The top layers of skin had begun to slowly peel.

Will's response had been along the same lines as Amber's: 'You don't tan, Nony. You're not to try to tan any more.'

'Why didn't you warn me properly about the African sun?'

'No more trying to go brown — you just go red. Your skin isn't meant to tan.'

'Fine.'

'I like you pale.'

'Only because it makes you look browner.'

The school year had turned a corner. The light evenings gave the feeling that there was more to the day than just the hours in the classroom. I'd been waiting for the summer term since the beginning of the school year. Last year it had marked a shift in my teaching; this year I hoped it would mark a shift in the way I was feeling about continuing at the school.

It was late April. The decision to be made loomed large. If I was leaving, I needed to let the school know by the end of the half-term. In principle I wanted to stay — I didn't feel as if I'd figured out whether I really could do the job: not just teach, but teach successfully in an inner-city school, and in a way that didn't kill me in the process. I wanted to work for Steph — she was giving twelve hours a day to trying to move the department on, to trying to hold everything and everyone together. But the thought of signing up for another January, February and March seemed like self-flagellation.

What would I do if I left, though? Teach somewhere else? Or find a new career? Journalism? What would I write about if I didn't have my day job? Publishing? I felt the tug of the school holidays — that one summer break is longer than most people get off in their entire year.

'Maybe I want a job where it doesn't matter if I turn up at nine in the morning,' I told Will, mulling it all over.

'You could do that . . . '

'I'm so bored of having to leave parties early, having to be in bed early, having to be responsible.'

'You could go off travelling, do a different job.'

Will had been teaching for only a year

more than I had. His previous career sounded rather appealing: putting together travel magazines, selling advertising space and travelling the world. But, as much as maybe he shouldn't have been, Will was also a tie that kept me in teaching. For a moment it irritated me that I allowed myself to be so attached to him that he was a factor in my decision about my career.

'No, I like my job . . . sometimes.'

'Don't go out so much,' Ella instructed when I ran the argument through with her.

'Yes, you're right.' If I wanted to stay at school but have an easier time, and survive the winter months, very early nights and no alcohol were the only way forward. Ella had given up on going out. She realized she couldn't do school and go out, so she cut her losses.

I'd been due to see the careers adviser during the spring break, but had had to reschedule as I'd been in bed with the lurgy. I'd mentioned to Bella, the Teach First teacher in the maths department at school, that I'd been considering leaving. 'It's the behaviour that drains me most,' I'd told her. 'Can I come and watch you teach? I need to know if it will get better and what your classes are like if you've been here for five years.'

Bella had been in the very first Teach First

cohort. She had signed up when nobody knew what it was. She had short bobbed hair, always dyed purple. She wore bright colours, and I knew the students thought she was a good teacher.

On the first Tuesday back I scurried along to her classroom after teaching my first couple of lessons. She was teaching a Year 9 class. 'I just want a completely standard lesson, nothing special because I'm there,' I'd told her.

The students sat at tables in groups of six or eight. Bella stood at the front while she was setting up an exercise, and then walked around the room while the girls were working. I sat at the back of the room making notes throughout the hour. I saw that the girls were really no differently behaved in Bella's lesson from the way they were in mine — and that seemed rather disappointing. I'd hoped that the longer you taught, the quieter the students. Bella's class grew too loud at points, some achieved less than they should have, Bella gave a handful of warnings and wrote names up on the board. But what was different was Bella. She was like some kind of Zen goddess. She counted down calmly and quietly when she wanted to get their attention. She spoke naturally. The disruptions didn't seem to ruffle her.

I get it, I thought. And so I tried her approach on the Year 10s. I gave up trying to fight them. We'd had two terms of being largely miserable in each other's company, but they knew me now, trusted me, and I knew them. The school rules are that if a student fails to follow your instruction she gets a warning. Three strikes and she's out of the classroom and into someone else's for the rest of the lesson. If she refuses to go, you send another student to call for senior management, who'll come and drag or coax her out. I've never seen a student refuse to leave when someone comes to pick her up — except once.

It had happened with the Year 8 class that Sophie and I shared. Sophie was fantastic with them. It was almost as if she sang lullabies to them rather than giving them instructions. They became sweet and child-like. For half the year I was still learning the ropes, and in a less secure environment they went berserk. One lesson Sharnel, who was particularly troubled, and was frequently sent out, ran out of warnings and then refused to move from her seat. The first member of senior management arrived and asked her to come with her. She refused. Several minutes later the deputy head turned up. Sharnel put her blazer over her head. 'No, I'm not moving

. . . What are they going to do? Call the police?' she said, laughing quietly to the girls she was sitting with. Ten more minutes passed. The rest of the class were far too entertained to engage in any work. Harriet talked quietly to her, and eventually Sharnel stood up, blazer on head, and walked out of the room, arms stretched in front of her as she couldn't see where she was going.

If I stuck to the three-strikes-and-you're-out rule, most of the Year 10 class would be out within the first few minutes of the lesson, if indeed they managed to make it into the classroom.

'Coleen, please would you come into the classroom now,' I often said, standing at the door.

'Coleen, into the classroom, please.' She could hear me, but ignored me.

'Right, into the classroom *now*, please.'

And indeed in some lessons I had evacuated the usual suspects in the first few minutes. It was supposed to make an impact on them, make them behave better the following lesson. But, feeling obstreperous and angry, leaving the classroom often appeared like winning the golden ticket. 'Good, I didn't want to be in this stupid classroom anyway,' many an evicted student has uttered.

And so with the Year 10s I'd given individuals more of a chance, glossing over their first refusals to do what I asked, leaving them for a few minutes and seeing if they were then ready to co-operate. I taught the Year 10s after watching Bella. Mahima shredded her worksheet into small squares, which then fluttered down on to the floor. Clearly she is telling me she doesn't understand, I thought, and remained serene. I picked up another sheet from my desk and took it to her.

If I'm positive and calm, then so are they. I already knew this, but it seems like a miracle every time I pull it off.

★   ★   ★

I met with the careers adviser in the evening. She had pale skin and bobbed red hair, and I liked her immediately because she looked a bit like me. We sat in a bar drinking cranberry juice.

'Do you like organizing and paying attention to the small details?'

'No.' I was sure small details (like numbers on school trips) were not my forte.

'Right, and so the thought of say . . . management consultancy?'

'No interest at all.' I was even more certain about that.

'Right, yes, good.' She posed a series of questions that evidently placed me on some graph in her head, and within a few minutes she seemed to have a fuller portrait than I have of friends after knowing them for years.

'Well, correct me if I'm wrong, but from what you've said it sounds like it's only the behaviour of your students which is making you think that you might want another career.'

'Yes, I suppose it is,' I replied.

'Other than that, it sounds like you really enjoy all the things that teaching offers.'

'Yes.' It's very reassuring to be told that you do actually really like your job.

'So the question really is whether you stay where you are or move to an academically selective state school where it's less about behaviour control?'

'Yes.'

'And from what you've said it sounds like now might not be the time to move: you've got the new role, writing projects planned, you still feel like there is more you want to do at school . . . '

'Yes. Yes.'

'And to allow you to do that you need to think more, perhaps — and as you've already started — about looking after yourself so that you don't get too run-down.'

'Yes.'

I handed over the cash and walked back across Waterloo Bridge feeling relieved. A decision had been made. More than that, it felt like the obvious conclusion was the option I'd wanted all along: I wanted to stay.

Everything sounded so clear and simple when she'd laid it out before me. The option to stay another year was appealing for a number of reasons. I knew the ropes at my school, and as I entered the third year there I should continue to gain more respect from the students. There was also more I wanted to achieve. I wanted to feel as if I deserved my 2ic post; I wanted to be a better teacher for the students I already knew. And my department were fantastic to work with, my head of department happy to spend her free time duping my class into believing their exams had been moved forward. The problem of being too exhausted could perhaps be managed in other ways. Maybe I could do more exercise. Maybe I could go to bed earlier. Maybe I could persuade Will that we both needed larger mattresses.

★ ★ ★

Spurred into action, the following day after school I went to the bike shop on my road

285

and bought a super-light bike. I'm pathetically weak, but was planning on keeping the bike in my flat, which would involve carrying it up a flight of stairs. I'd practised with Will's bike, and almost re-enacted the great fall of New Year's Eve.

It took me fifteen minutes to cycle into school. The journey home took longer for the first week, as I was completely unable to retrace the route I took in the mornings, and always ended up, to my complete bemusement, miles off course. Cycling into school also woke me up, and cycling home allowed me to burn off all my frustrations from the day.

I felt a new determination to try to get things under control. Having so much autonomy in the classroom was one of the best things about the job, but also one of the worst. At the very beginning it had seemed like the most exciting thing. I was in charge; I was the leader. Before starting teaching, I'd spent months at the beck and call of a few magazine editors, trusted with no more than entering meetings into a diary. The exciting shock of teaching was that suddenly every decision was down to me. Well, some guidance was given from above, but by and large during the teaching hours within the day it was really me who decided how a subject — a novel or a poem — was tackled.

More than a year and a half on, I felt aware of the flip side of my autonomy. If there were things to be sorted out within my classroom, there was only one person who could do it.

In my thinking about other careers, I'd wistfully imagined the lack of responsibility — the possibility of arriving to work a few minutes late, having picked up a hot chocolate on the way, and then leaving at six and not taking work home — and that not mattering one iota. The thing that seemed more appealing than even the morning hot chocolate was the prospect of not having deadlines that have to be met hour after hour. If you teach 'challenging' students, you have to prepare lessons and resources. If you don't, you're going to be stuck in a room for an hour with students who will destroy anything you half-heartedly attempt to engage them in.

Ella had struggled to come up with a way to describe what teaching was like to our non-teaching friends as they tried to insist that she really didn't need to get yet another early night. 'It's like' — she hit upon an equivalent situation that a management consultant might understand — 'think about how much effort you put into one presenta-tion at work. Now imagine that you have to give three or four hour long presentations each day — and that you're presenting to a room of colleagues who aren't necessarily interested in what you've got to say.'

'And then imagine', I continued, 'that everyone in the boardroom starts shouting at you and trying to get your attention to help them or to see what notes they've written during your presentation.'

How we laughed.

★　★　★

Having painstakingly extracted a piece of original writing, an essay on *Jane Eyre* and an essay on *Educating Rita* from the Year 10s, I followed Steph's lead and set them the task of writing a review of *How to Look Good Naked* for their piece of media coursework. We spent two blissful lessons watching Gok transform a miserable midwife into a brazen naked goddess. Then we spent two less blissful weeks trying to craft a piece of writing, paragraph by paragraph.

'The trick for this particular piece of coursework is that you successfully write in your chosen style.' I spent two weeks speaking to them in a heavily alliterative chatty magazine jargon: 'Flipping fantastic to see you all. So today we're going to write about how the Gokfather of style turned the mini-midwife into a sizzling sensation.'

It made a nice change to the lessons while we were trying to write an essay on the stage directions in *Educating Rita*.

'Folashade enters the room and stands for a moment at the door. She looks at the room and then struts to her seat . . . We can tell her mood by the way she's walking in. What is her mood?'

'She's happy!' those who were playing along answered.

'Ooh, Miss!' Folashade shrieked. She fancies herself as a diva, and was delighted to be cast as the star of the show entering the room.

'Erez enters the room purposefully. She looks at the teacher confused. She goes to her seat . . . No, Erez doesn't go to the other side of the room, she goes to her seat. We can tell from the way she enters the room that she is . . . ?'

'Angry.'

'Yes, she certainly looks angry.'

'No, Miss, don't even . . . I'm not in the mood today, OK?'

'Right.'

Coleen, though, had unfortunately missed the two key lessons needed to easily complete the piece of media coursework: the ones where we watched the show we were reviewing. I showed her the website. It didn't seem to make sense to her. I asked her to watch the programme in the evenings that it was on telly. She missed them.

I made her a plan different from the one I'd given the rest of the class. I gave her a plan that was so thorough that all she'd have to do was connect the dots. Finally she would be able to catch up with the rest of the class.

She arrived to class agitated. I was standing at the door, and calmly asked her to come and stand with me so that I could show her the differentiated sheet I'd made that would help her complete the work.

'I need to give someone something,' she said, trying to get past me, 'and it's more important than your lesson'.

'Coleen,' I said, calmly pretending I hadn't heard what she'd said, 'can you go and sit down, please, and I'll come over to you instead.'

Coleen went and sat down. I let a minute pass, and then went to her desk to show her the bits of her work I'd marked and the differentiated worksheet. She refused to look either at me or at the paper.

'Coleen, could you look at the sheet please?' This was a farce.

'I'm not interested. Wot? No. And I'm allowed to be rude if you're being rude to me.'

'Coleen, I'm not being rude. I just want to show you how to do this piece of work.'

'I'm not interested.'

'I only want to help you.'

'Yeah? Well I'm not interested.'

'Right. Well, we go through the system then. Verbal warning for refusing to look at the sheets . . . '

'I'm not interested.'

'Written warning for continuing to refuse . . . '

'Fine, send me to pairing — but I'm not going.'

'Fine.'

'Leila, could you go and get on-call, please?'

The deputy head arrived.

'It's Coleen, she's refused to go to pairing.' I took the worksheets to Harriet and gave them to her.

'This is the work she's supposed to be doing. She can do it in the referral base. It's pretty self-explanatory, but if there was any chance you could look at it with her . . . '

'Right, thanks, Miss. Come on, Coleen.'

After school, I found three sides of A4 written in Coleen's large, rounded letters. It was something, but it wouldn't get her a C. I edited it. The following lesson we went through a similar routine. The head of year picked Coleen up, dragging Folashade out of the classroom at the same time — while my back had been turned, Folashade had flopped her head on to the desk. 'All the corrections are on the work — she just needs to write out a second draft,' I instructed the head of year.

Coleen stood against the wall as Folashade was spoken to.

'Right. I'm sending you home. You're obviously too tired to be in school,' the head of Year 10 told her furiously.

'No, I . . . ' Folashade started.

'What? You think you come into school to sleep in Miss Crossley-Holland's lesson? You're wasting her time, and you're wasting mine.'

I sat at my desk at the end of the day writing incident reports. The very process of writing them irritated me. Not only did I have to use more time to recount the details of how a student had wasted aeons, I had to make sure that I pressed the pen hard enough against the top sheet so that the four carbon copies underneath would receive the imprint of the letters.

A woman from reception hovered outside my door for a second, then came in holding a huge bunch of colourful flowers.

'We're all desperate to know who they're from,' she said, giving them to me.

'I have no idea,' I said, and then added, 'though I do have a boyfriend, so maybe . . . '

I opened the card. 'To decorate your new bike with,' it said. 'All my love, W.'

'Yes, they're from him,' I told the receptionist.

'Oh good, I'll go and tell the others . . . He didn't do anything wrong, did he?'

'No, I think they're just a nice surprise.'

I texted Will to say thank you, then remembered I was supposed to be keeping one of Kitty's students behind for detention. She was only eleven, but had severe learning difficulties and I'd seen her plenty of times arguing with teachers in the hallway. I went along to Kitty's classroom and she was sitting at the back, head on the desk.

'Thank you, Miss Crossley-Holland,' Kitty said, seeing me in her doorway. 'Siana, you're going to go to Miss Crossley-Holland's classroom now.'

'No. I want to stay here,' Siana said.

'You need to go to Miss Crossley-Holland's room, because you didn't come to the detention with me.'

'Come on, Siana,' I said, and walked back to my room. I felt a little uneasy, as I knew she was prone to be compliant one moment and obstreperous the next. She followed. She slumped down on a desk. I tidied things at the front of the room.

'Are they real flowers?' she asked, lifting

293

her head from the desk.

'Yes,' I said.

'Can I smell them?' she said, moving towards them.

'Sure.' She bent over them, and was delighted at how pretty they were. 'Which flower is your favourite?' I asked her, and she pointed to the roses.

'You're very lovely,' I told Will on the phone later that night.

'Are they OK?' he asked.

'Yes, they're very bright . . . '

'Yes. I was going to buy you a tasteful bunch and just give them to you, but the girls in the staffroom here told me I had to get them delivered to you at work, that it was much more exciting.'

'Well, it caused much excitement this end too . . . Apparently the women in the office were all wondering who they were from.'

★　★　★

For the two past years I'd run a half marathon on the May bank holiday. This year I'd left training too late — every time I'd planned to go for a run I'd decided against it, feeling coldy. Ella managed to drag herself out for the occasional long run at the weekends and so was ready to go. Charlotte,

294

Kate, and Hattie were also due to run. Charlotte drove us all down to meet Ella at her parents'.

'Nones, you've got to run it,' said Hattie.

'I really would love to, but I just haven't trained.'

'Nones, I haven't trained.'

'Yes, but you ran the New York marathon, what — a month ago?'

'Nones, I haven't trained,' Kate piped up.

'Kate, we go through this every year: you have trained, and you're a very fast runner.'

'No, I'm really unfit this year,' she said. 'I just want to run it with the group.'

'Kate!' It was the same each year. Before the race, Kate flatly denied she was going to run the race competitively, but then somehow, once she'd passed the start line, she couldn't stop herself.

'It's fine. I'll be your supporter,' I declared firmly.

It was miserable. I mean, running the race is miserable, but it feels miserable in an extreme way, and then at the eleventh mile, becoming light-headed from lack of sugar/water/ability of your poor heart to pump blood to your brain, you feel like you've realized some of the great truths about life. And then for the next few days you feel terribly sore, and that feels great. Standing on the sidelines is a more mediocre kind of miserable.

I stuffed my rain-mac with jelly babies, so that I could hand fistfuls to the team as they ran past. One for me, I counted, one for them. By the time we returned to Ella's for the feast her parents had prepared, I felt a little sick from all the sweets.

I was comforted by the fact that, even though I hadn't managed to do any more exercise than the short cycle ride into school, at least I didn't eat as much junk as my students. The staff occasionally drop into the corner shops that abut the school gates to buy newspapers, cigarettes and water. The students — allowed in only in groups of three — sweep through to buy violently flavoured crisps and foamy sweets.

We're meant to send letters home to the parents of students we see gorging themselves on Monster Munch or stuffing liquorice laces into their mouths. 'Dear X, I'm sure you'll be deeply shocked and worried to learn that your daughter survives on a diet of Pringles and chocolate-chip cookies. She was seen this morning digging into a bumper pack of Starbursts washed down with a litre of Red Bull.' I thought of the mothers who handed their children McDonalds through the school gates in the face of Jamie Oliver's school dinners.

* * *

The Sunday after I hadn't managed to run the half-marathon was far more satisfying. I went to school to meet up with a large group of Year 7s and several members of staff, and we then joined two thousand other school-children on a walk crossing ten London bridges. We were all raising money for PEAS — Promoting Equality in African Schools, a charity set up by a Teach First participant to build low-fee secondary schools in Uganda.

Emily had sensibly brought along suncream. I borrowed some, and applied it to my shoulders. Harriet, the deputy head — the only member of senior management on the walk — decided we had best white-out the students with the stuff. Emily watched miserably as her new bottle was used to cover everyone.

Clutching a collection tin, irresistible eleven-year-olds approached every adult along the bridges and riversides.

'Excuse me,' said the cherub-faced Princess, 'Miss, you ask,' she'd then whisper.

'No, you ask — you're better at it,' I said each time.

'Do you have any change? We're raising money for Africa.'

Most of the tourists and elderly couples along the way had already been approached by a thousand expectant schoolchildren asking the same question. I knew Ella was with a group of her students a good twenty minutes ahead of us. Those who were generous had had their pockets stripped bare. Quite a few people feigned not to speak any English, and some ignored the imploring looks and outstretched hands.

'That man was so rude,' Princess would say loudly while the miser remained in earshot.

Vauxhall, Lambeth, Westminster, Hungerford, and then after Waterloo Bridge we paused for lunch and Will joined us to say hello. Princess and Rose, both of whom I taught, watched me closely and gave each other knowing looks.

'They're so small,' Will said. 'They don't look scary at all.'

Princess beckoned me over. I walked to join her on a bench.

'Miss . . . is he your boyfriend?'

'Yes.'

'Oh, I thought so.'

I went back to sit with the teachers feeling a bit sheepish.

When Will left, I walked with him out of sight of my students. Emily and Kitty and Harriet, still sitting with the students, encouraged them to make silly noises as we left.

Though we were out of their view, there were of course two thousand other school-children milling around. As we kissed goodbye, we heard a protest. 'Errgh! Can people not do that in public,' one particularly loud student called after us, much to the amusement of the chaperoning teachers.

After a stretch along the South Bank, we crossed Blackfriars, the Millennium, South-wark and London bridges. Just as we'd begun to flag, the end was in sight. Feeling fairly exhausted but deliciously virtuous for having walked the 10k and not lost any students (though there had been a few moments of mild concern), we crossed Tower Bridge and were awarded badges as they'd run out of halos.

I helped pack the students on the coach, and was then discharged. I called an old schoolfriend, Jen, to see if she wanted to meet for a drink along the river.

'Sure, why don't we meet down by Waterloo Bridge?' she suggested. I set off the way I had come, blisters beginning to ooze beneath rubber flip-flop straps.

★   ★   ★

By mid-May the Year 11s were down from having eighteen hours in hand to having only a few hours left before the first of their English exams — the English literature exam. They would have to write an essay on *Catcher in the Rye* and another in which they compared four poems — one by Simon Armitage, one by Carol Ann Duffy and two from a selection of poems written before 1914. It was a rather contrived exercise, and it felt like a minefield to the students who only had a half-grasp on what was going on. With a couple of lessons to go, I was a little unnerved that those who had only a half-grasp constituted more than half of the class.

'Wot, Miss? Wot poems? Wot? Wot, we haven't done that one . . . Wot? Oh yeah, maybe we have . . .'

It had been decided at some point in the past couple of weeks that Becky would carry out her revision at home. She was no longer within my reach. I'd thought at the beginning of the year that I would target her and make sure she didn't slip though the net, but the hour had passed and all I could hope for now was that her natural ability might just carry her through on the day — with the English language exams if not the literature exam, which relied to a greater extent on prior knowledge of texts.

Emily, steaming ahead with her top-set Year

11s, kept giving me the revision materials she'd come up with. 'I thought, right, they could make a football team out of the characters of *Catcher in the Rye* . . . '

' . . . ?'

'Yeah, like they could name who the defenders would be . . . who the goalkeeper is . . . '

'Oh' I like it.'

I handed my class the sheets Emily had prepared. There was a roughly sketched out pitch, with a circle for each player. The students' knowledge of football was stronger than mine, and without any trouble or too much consideration most of them decided where each of Salinger's characters would play.

'And where would Holden be?' I asked Adalia. She had an advantage over most of the others as she'd been the student who had read great chunks of the novel for the rest of the class. She had a fantastically bored reading voice, which suited Holden Caulfield.

'Oh, Miss, 'ed be in goal.'

'Oh really? Why is that?'

'Because 'e likes to catch the kids, don't 'e? Yer, from falling off the cliff.'

'Oh yer.' The others around her were impressed.

'But doesn't Holden realise he can't play

the role of catching kids before they fall?'

'Oh yer, Miss . . . '

But we didn't get much further: Abimbola wasn't doing the task at all, so I moved to her to explain how simple what she needed to do was.

Adalia had come such a long way from the girl who spent half the lessons with her head on the desk, unable to pry her eyes open. She had stuck the course, chugged along, had occasional moments where she'd come into her own sharing her experience of life in Argentina. She was the strongest and clearest reader in the class, and the two of us had pretty much split the reading of *Catcher in the Rye*. She was not drawn into the subtle intricacies of the poems we studied. I felt she was rather more interested in life than in books. She was quick to be bored and quick to get excited. I'd originally asked her to read a few pages of *Catcher* because I could see she was fast losing interest listening to me read to the class.

Adalia was bright and sparky but, I suppose, not academic. I knew she would not revise at home — that in fact she probably spent very little time out of school actually at home. The anecdotes she occasionally told the class suggested she spent most of her time hanging out on the streets with boys. And because I knew she would not revise, I knew that all preparation for the exams needed to be done in class.

Other Year 11 students from the class (those who took lessons more seriously) had dropped by to talk to me about their subject choices for sixth-form colleges. I had no idea what Adalia's plans were — and I'm not sure she did either.

'That football exercise worked fantastically with my class,' Emily told me at break over a *pain au chocolate*.

'Yeah, I really liked it,' I said, 'but I'm not sure we got as much out of it as we could have.'

'Oh, my class actually came up with some really independent ideas. One person suggested that Holden was the ball being beaten and bashed around, and others thought he was sitting in the crowd watching the game.'

Emily's class were one set above mine. She'd taken them over from Sophie, whom they'd been miserable to lose. It had taken her a lot of hard work, but by the time it came to these last few lessons it sounded as if they were actually ready to sit the exams. I worried that there would be too huge a discrepancy between the two classes in the exam marks when they came out in August.

The first exam fell on a Tuesday. On the

303

Monday a handful of the Year 11s found me during a free period and asked if I'd 'go through' *Catcher in the Rye* with them. Carrying blank A3 sheets, I accompanied them down to the library and we sat round a table.

'Right,' I said, 'has anyone got the list of past questions?'

They scrambled around in their bags, through the piles and piles of dog-eared photocopies, and produced the sheet.

The hour was magic.

'Aysha, why don't you choose a question? Write the question in the middle of your piece of paper.' I did the task as they did. We each created spider diagrams and pinpointed the revealing moments in the book.

'And where do we see this? And what else? . . . Why?' What joy in being able to ask a string of questions without alternating them with requests that food be put away.

The process of planning answers for the essay questions seemed quite magical in itself: taking apart the title, brainstorming, and then — the clever bit — grouping the seemingly isolated events and characters together and spotting the trends, the themes, before finally taking a step even further back and trying to make sense of what Salinger was saying.

'And we're supposed to do all this in five minutes?' Hebba asked.

And then for the greatest trick.

'Let's all take a few minutes to write the opening sentence for this essay — something which grabs the examiner. I quite like starting with quotations.'

They shared the sentences they'd written, and I read mine.

'Miss, that's so good,' they cooed in appreciation. This is heaven, I thought.

In one hour the five of us had covered more ground than I'd been able to in a month of lessons with the whole class. Teaching groups of thirty rowdy, disaffected teenagers doesn't work. In the library, between sharing our ideas, we'd had deep and unbroken concentration. In every lesson with the full class of Year 11s I felt I had to struggle to quell the surge of their energy. I know this is partly because, even in the lessons just before their exams, I couldn't get them all working their hardest. Something about my style, my lack of experience meant I couldn't get enough control. But I also felt it was because the students were not schooled in the work ethic that they needed to make real progress — the kind of progress which might take them out of the bracket of disadvantage. If teachers taught in groups of twelve in inner-city schools, the picture would be rather different.

'When are you going to set up a school?' I asked Sophie over another supper with her and Bella. I handed her a belated birthday card. I'd drawn the front gates of a school and written an imaginary motto on a plaque: 'Actually Educating'.

'Oh, I don't know, Nony! But I have been talking about it more recently.'

'I'll work for you.'

Sophie was almost robotic in the way she ploughed through work. Whereas I flag in the late afternoon and begin to think of cups of tea at home, Sophie, when she was in the classroom next to mine, was always first in and last to leave. She'd got a first from Edinburgh, and applied the same rigour that had achieved that to planning lessons.

'We'd start off with just a small Year 7,' she began, 'and really work with them.'

'I think we should keep the school tiny — twenty-five students in each year group,' I said.

'But then how do you pay the teachers, Nony?' Bella was thinking more practically.

'We just need to find a building — if we build it, they will come!'

We'd all been seduced by stories from Wendy Kopp, the woman who had set up

Teach for America — a programme on which Teach First had to a large extent been modelled. At one conference that she'd visited she told us a story about a teacher in Texas who'd taught at a primary school. He'd made such an impact that the parents, realizing that the available secondary schools would spell an end to their children's successes, went to the district council and demanded the exceptional teacher be given a secondary school — an empty building. Then they went to the teacher and demanded he run a school. When Wendy recounted the story she told us that, statistically, the students in this area of Texas were better off going to this school than to one of the surrounding fee-paying establishments. It was the kind of story that made three Teach First teachers go weak at the knees, their eyes mist up.

★ ★ ★

On Tuesday morning I went to wish the Year 11s a final good luck. They were gathered in the dining hall, jittery and nervous, waiting to be walked across to the exam hall, which smelled slightly of gas and must.

'Good luck, Hebba. Good luck, Nia. Good luck, Adalia . . . '

'Miss, Miss . . .'

'Yes, Adalia?'

'We've got to compare four poems 'aven't we?'

'Yes: one Duffy, one Armitage and — '

'Two of those old ones.'

'Yes. You'll be fine. Read the question carefully. Plan your answer.'

At the end of their exam, at a time when normally I would have been teaching them, I went down to collect them from the exam hall and escort them back to the dining hall. I picked up an exam paper and flipped through to the questions: Holden and relationships with other people — good — and nice poetry questions . . . As they left the hall, a few gave me wobbly thumbs — not thumbs up, and not thumbs down. It was likely to be the exam, out of the two, literature and language, that they would do less well in. The two language exams were easier to pick marks up in, I thought — more common sense, and less crafting of an essay.

★ ★ ★

'Emily,' I said to her after school as we sat eating biscuits in my room, 'Stella is in your tutor group, isn't she?'

'Yes, I know, she's been going a bit off the

rails recently, hasn't she.'

'Yes,' I said. 'I've got an incident report to hand to you from today's lesson.'

'I don't understand it. She was so charming at the beginning, and now . . . '

'I know — I remember watching her helping other Year 7s right at the start. She was the keenest student, and now she keeps ignoring my instructions . . . and she's been talking during class. I don't know what's happened . . . And today I actually had to send her out.' Calling home had not enlightened me: her father had simply said he'd talk to her.

I decided to move her to the front of the room to sit at a desk by herself. There were too many students slightly straining at the reins in the class. Chantelle seemed to have particular influence over several of the girls, and spent much time in each lesson trying to get their attention or to pass them notes, which I intercepted and threw into the bin, trying not to break the flow of the lesson.

The days of 'Suicide in the Trenches' and 'My Last Duchess' seemed a long time ago. Chantelle had made a full transformation from being a student who was easy to deal with to one who was very difficult to deal with. She was increasingly absent, and this seemed to exacerbate problems when she was in. I heard that she'd got in with an unpleasant crowd whom she spent her weekends out with. She wasn't unpleasant towards me, but she was consistently starting to do the opposite to whatever she was asked to do. Phone calls home had no visible impact. Her mother was supportive, but didn't know what she could do. The counsellors in school were working with her. I received a note asking me to drop down and see them. It was about the targets I'd set for Chantelle to concentrate her attention on the behaviour required for English lessons.

'Basically,' Lena carefully explained to me, 'the problem is there is no way that Chantelle could meet any of these targets.'

'Ah, right.' I hadn't really thought that through. I only wanted her to stop wasting large parts of the lessons.

'So you see, this target here' — she pointed to the first one — ' 'No talking while the teacher is talking.' Well, Chantelle can't do that for a whole lesson.'

'Yeah.' Though she had been able to. Only a few months previously she'd been able to sit quietly throughout a class.

'So you need to try and be more specific.'

'For example?'

'Well, perhaps something like 'Listen to the teacher's instructions without talking for at least two thirds of the lesson.''

'Yes, I see.' Of course it made sense. I could see that it was no use writing targets that Chantelle was destined to fail, but at the same time if she spoke over me for a third of the lesson it was like sending an invitation out to all the students to join me in Room 18 for a Mad Hatter's tea party. What about Rose sitting waiting for me to just teach?

'Is there any chance I could get some in-class support with her?' I'd had a few teaching assistants assigned to the lower-ability Year 7 set during the year. They'd made a huge difference: I felt my behaviour improved even if the students' didn't.

'We'll see what we can do,' she promised. 'We really do want to support Chantelle.'

* * *

On Friday evening Kate had invited Ella and me round for supper at the house she rented from her parents in Clapham. At the table I sat next to Owen, whom I'd met a few times before. He'd started Teach First the same year as Alex, Kate's boyfriend, but hadn't finished the programme.

'I didn't even make it to the end of my first year,' he told me.

'And then you joined the army?'

311

'Yes, and went out to Iraq . . . It was easier than teaching.'

'An easier war to win?' I asked, tongue in cheek.

'Yes.'

I'd won a smaller battle with Will — he'd agreed to go home to my mother's for the weekend. We'd both been seeing the same acupuncturist for some time, and each of us complained at length to her about lack of sleep when we were staying with each other. After each session she'd told each of us that we needed to get a bigger mattress. I thought changing mattresses to accommodate us both was akin to picking out a dog together, so felt rather terrified by the idea. But, driven by the desire for a better night's sleep, I hired a white van to drive down to my mother's. She'd offered to swap my measly Ikea bed for a super king-sized one.

My mother taught me from a young age the art of acquiring family furniture. After her father died, we drove up to her family home in Derbyshire and she threaded her small-boned, skinny nine-year-old daughter through a vent in the side of the pantry. We piled the car high with chairs and a table and drove back down to the house we stayed in during the summers, when we weren't in America.

Having been practically trained by my

mother, I felt no guilt in also nabbing two chests of drawers while I had the van. My stepfather, who'd actually bought all the furniture, was rather distraught.

Will and my mother, having discovered they shared a similar sense of humour, settled into being as completely themselves as they could. 'Can the two of you just try to act normally?' I asked, feeling they were both trying to be as bizarre as possible.

Will sat down on a settee, and my mother brought him the books she was currently reading. 'His cock flopped nonchalantly to the side,' Will read out loud as he opened the first page of one of them. I tried to breathe deeply, but knew I was slightly losing my grip on the situation. I retired upstairs and called Lucy.

'I'm freaking out,' I told her. 'They are both freaking me out. They both seem to be catatonically relaxed, and I am not reacting well.'

'Nones, it's fine. Of course it's difficult . . . These are people you care about massively, and you were probably worried about how they'd get on . . . '

'Well I needn't have been — they're doing fine . . . '

Will found me upstairs sitting on the floor of my room concentrating on breathing. As

313

he tried to soothe my worries, I thought I'd throw some really big questions into the mix to properly terrify myself.

'So . . . do you see a future with each other?' I said. He looked a bit shocked.

'Yes . . . of course . . . '

'So do you think we'll live together at some point, then?'

'Yes. Definitely. Do you want to live together?'

'No. Not yet.'

★　★　★

What a relief it was to return to the safe normality of school on Monday. I had a few more 'last' lessons to revise with the Year 11s for the language exams, which they would sit the week after a week's half-term holiday. I was beyond mystified that even at this late stage I had to calm them all into a state in which I could try to teach them. Meanwhile I had also told the Year 10s, after one lesson starting *Romeo and Juliet*, that we would be using this week before the break to prepare for their Year 10 English exams — exams set within the classroom.

Excited about how well the trip to the theatre with the 11s had gone, I organized a last-minute trip for the Year 10s to see

314

Brecht's *The Good Soul of Szechuan* at the Young Vic.

Jane Horrocks was starring, and, as a local school, we were eligible for free tickets.

I told my 10s that I had six tickets. Kitty and Steph also had six tickets for each of their classes. You can imagine the outrage from each class as we announced that not everyone would get to go. Half the class scrambled to snatch permission letters — Coleen being one of the first to grab one.

We'd asked the students to meet us at the theatre on Wednesday, just before seven. I'd bought an extra ticket for Will, and so the two of us met for a glass of wine and a burger before the students were to arrive. Emily, Kitty and Steph turned up early and joined us. Before long the students spied us all sitting together, and one or two of the more confident ones came over.

Folashade, queen bee of my Year 10 class, sat down. She was wearing skinny jeans, a T-shirt and a waistcoat.

'Folashade, we're inside and it's night-time,' I told her — 'you can take off your sunglasses.'

'Oh, Miss,' she replied, rolling her eyes. She watched me for a few seconds, watched the man sitting next to me. 'Miss,' she mouthed, 'is *that* your boyfriend.' I nodded.

'He-ello,' she practically shouted, extending her arm across the table to shake Will's hand. 'I'm Folashade.'

'Hello,' said Will, shaking her hand.

'Ooh, Miss, you go, girl,' she screamed. All the teachers at the table fell about laughing.

We hadn't given the girls instructions about the need to eat supper beforehand. Seeing they had a few minutes, they rushed to the kebab shop across the road and tried surreptitiously to munch their way through the doners and chips during the performance.

In the auditorium, I sat myself next to Coleen. She'd turned up in a grey tracksuit, and seemed to be spending a lot of time juggling various sets of headphones and her mobile, which she was furiously texting away on and occasionally answering. As she furtively mumbled into it, I wondered how anyone on the other end could understand what she was saying.

'You are going to turn it off for the play, aren't you?' I didn't want to sound like a nagging teacher, but I was keen that she remove the temptation of texting through a performance.

At the interval we were brought a box of free ice creams by the theatre. Two old women approached Folashade, believing she was selling the ice creams rather than just doling them out.

'Hello,' one of the old women said. 'Could we buy an ice cream?'

Folashade eye's brightened. 'Miss,' she said in a loud whisper, 'can I sell the ice creams?' I thought it sounded very enterprising, but Steph stepped in.

'No, Folashade.'

During the second half, Coleen's face was occasionally lit up by the light coming from her phone.

'Put it *away!*' I hissed. When she wasn't trying to surreptitiously text, she chatted quietly to the person on the other side of her. '*Shh! Don't talk.*'

At the end of the performance we gathered on the street to dismiss the students. Two parents collected their children, and we waved others off. It was a warm May evening, and I walked with Will back to my flat.

'They're charming,' he said. 'While you were sorting out tickets, Folashade introduced me to the rest of the group.'

'Oh gosh. She's so confident. But in class, when she doesn't want to do what you're asking . . . '

But in class the next day Folashade was more reasonable. I asked her to go to her seat and sit down quietly, and she looked at me for an extra second and then quietened down. 'Aright, Miss . . . ' Our relationship had moved on to a new level.

Things ran a little more smoothly with Coleen too. I'd realized that she didn't talk through just my lessons: she talked through everything. Silence wasn't a mode she did.

★   ★   ★

The Friday was the last day of the half-term. I was exhausted. The Wednesday theatre trip made me rather zonked for the two remaining days of the week. Friday was a day when the Year 7s had the laptops — good for work, even better for mesmerizing the students — and with the Year 11s I decided that, rather than have a tired lesson in which we went over old material, we'd study two poems from the poetry anthology that they hadn't looked at. They had little interest in revision.

At three o'clock the tannoy went. 'Could all members of staff please come down to the hall . . . '

I ran into Steph's classroom. 'Inspection?'

'Yes, I reckon so!'

Everyone had forgotten that one had been promised earlier in the year. I grabbed the list (printed on cream paper) that laid out all the things that would need doing, and walked down to the hall. The list had been reissued, and was waiting on everyone's chair. I looked through it for things I could cross off. Marking up to date — no. Posters with lists of skills needed to be enterprising displayed on the walls — definitely no. Data on students' additional educational needs up to date — no again.

'Thank you all for coming down,' Cecelia began. 'We have been told that HMI are going to visit in the week after the half-term . . . Now I don't want staff to feel that they need to come in over the holidays . . . '

'I'm not coming in,' I whispered to Emily — 'I'm going to Scotland.' Will and I had booked train tickets up to Glasgow and then the West Highlands.

'Me neither,' Emily mouthed back.

' . . . but I did want to let you know, in case you did want to come in, we'll be open all week . . . The inspectors will be coming in on Tuesday, Wednesday and Thursday, and you will need to have lesson plans ready for each of those lessons to hand to the inspectors . . . '

David, the head of the maths department, raised his hand.

'We're due to be having end of Year 10 tests the first week back. Will these need to be moved?'

'I'll check with the inspectors,' Cecelia said, 'but I expect that they are going to need to see teaching. For the week the inspectors are in, we'll have a meeting every morning before school, to keep everyone up to date . . . '

Errgh, I thought. I saw that I really couldn't tick off anything on the cream list. I'd sort it all out on the Monday we returned to school.

★ ★ ★

Will and I spent the weekend at the house of an old friend of his. We went riding again — this time I wasn't put on a lead, and managed to keep control of the horse 90 per cent of the time as we cantered around.

I almost missed the train up to Glasgow on the Tuesday of the half-term. I ran along the platform at Euston with two minutes to spare.

'Don't worry, Nony, I told you the wrong time,' Will said, standing at ease on the platform and seeing the terror on my face. It took me about a day to calm down.

'I feel a bit sick,' I told him.

'Completely to be expected: Will and Nony leave the country; Nony feels sick.'

We arrived in the cold northern city and it was raining.

'Why aren't we in Italy?' I asked as the

320

sheets of rain cut into our jeans and we struggled up a hilly street with our suitcases.

The following day we took another train further north. Will smugly completed bouts of marking, while I avoided finishing a piece for the *Guardian* looking back on my two years as a Teach First teacher. We passed Fort William and continued along the line to Mallaig. Leaving the train at Glenfinnan, we were picked to pieces by midges.

'Why aren't we in Tuscany?' I whimpered.

SUMMER TERM
FINAL HALF

Everyone was buzzing on Monday morning with the prospect that Her Majesty's Inspectors would be arriving on Tuesday.

'I spent all weekend preparing lessons,' Julia told me. She had an unbroken record of receiving the 'outstanding' grade for the observed lessons she taught. The inspectors would be certain to see her.

'We shouldn't get seen,' Emily told me. 'We're still NQTs, so still in training. Apparently all they can do is watch us informally and ask us about the quality of the training we've been receiving.'

'Fine by me.'

At the morning meeting, Cecelia welcomed us back and confirmed that the inspectors would be in the following day.

I gave the Year 11s a lesson preparing for the exam they'd have on Tuesday. It was a remarkably calm lesson. As they were nearing the end of their time at the school they'd been allowed to come in wearing their own clothes rather than uniform, and so all of a sudden they looked grown-up.

I'd decided to make the Year 10s sit the

first half of their exam on the Monday and then pick up *Romeo and Juliet* again on the Tuesday. They'd been told we'd be having the exam in the first lesson back, and I was keen to get it over and done with.

When they turned up to the lesson, they were for some reason shocked to see the desks set up with exam papers and piles of lined paper.

'No! What? We cannot be having a test, no, Miss. We were told we're not going to have them. In maths we're not going to have them. No, no, Miss, no.'

'As I told everyone in our last lesson before half term, we will be having the test . . . '

'No! Miss, you can't do this to us,' Folashade is convinced that being set the test is an infringement of her human rights. I give her a first warning and ask her to settle down.

'Quite frankly,' I tell the class, 'it doesn't make any difference if it's today or tomorrow. If you were going to revise, you would have done it over the holiday.'

'No, Miss, no' — my logic does nothing to quieten Folashade. The torrent of emotion and irrationality continues, and I send her out of the classroom to sit the exam in another classroom.

'Lakeisha, please can you take Folashade into Mr Bolton's classroom?'

'No, Miss,' says Folashade, now even more worked up, 'I can go by myself. I didn't want to be in this classroom anyway.'

Quiet settles after she strides out of the door.

'Right, girls, you have in front of you a paper very similar to the one you will be given almost exactly in one year's time. I want you to chose a question from section A today . . . '

Coleen arrived to class very late. She saw the empty spot (at the front of the classroom) where she had been unhappily sitting for the last few weeks of lessons. She decided that on this day she wouldn't sit there. Two minutes of unsuccessful insistence that she would sit in that seat ended with her too being sent to sit the exam in Mr Bolton's classroom. The better foundations that the trip to the theatre had created had fast eroded.

Another student disposed of, I continued with the instructions 'We will sit this test in exam conditions — that means no talking to each other: if you have a question, raise your hand. Remember to plan your answer, and if you finish early read through what you have written. You have forty-five minutes starting now.'

Erez had been away while we studied the first of the two poems in the exams, Denise

Levertov's 'What Were They Like?'. 'Just write about one poem,' I instructed her in a whisper.

The rest of the class fell into industrious silence. I was impressed. They scribbled away, and I, for one of the few times with this class, went and sat at my desk to watch them. The fact that it was 'exam conditions' had incredibly turned them into worker bees.

After school I marked a batch of Year 10 coursework and then put the coursework essays into folders. I entered marks into my mark book, and wrote letters home for the students that still had pieces due in. Having made a small amount of progress with my to-do list, I cycled home with the Year 10 papers in my bag. Making myself some peanut butter on toast, I slumped down in front of the news, which reported that a teenage girl had been stabbed to death in the area. It unnerved me that it had happened so close to school. I looked on the internet, but couldn't find any more details. I thought of Milly, who had lost three of her students in the last six months — the most recent one an innocent victim in a gang murder.

When I read the Year 10 essays in the evening, I saw that, although most of the girls had written at least two sides, they'd failed to pick up many marks. I'd been trying to teach them a formula for getting a C in one of the essays they had to write — write a paragraph each on imagery, language, structure and feelings, comparing the two poems in each paragraph. I thought it was quite simple: we'd gone over time and time again that they needed to write on the different methods the poets used to help communicate the meaning of the poem. Somehow, however, when it came to writing the essays, they had simply written down a mess of information and quoted lines.

Three essays stood out: Ummi's, Cally's and Lakeisha's. They'd obviously followed through and looked at the work we'd done in class at home. What a difference taking some initiative had made. They each narrowly missed a C, but with a little more work each of them could get there. Ummi had come to me at the end of the exam and asked if she could also hand in the practice essay she'd done at home — with her notes to hand, she had easily cleared the C barrier. League tables are decided on how many A* to Cs a school gains. For an individual student, C is the lowest 'pass' mark.

Pleased with the day's work, I reflected that it had been a day when I thought I could do this job — that I could do it well, and even enjoy it. I hadn't managed to keep Coleen in the class — or Folashade — but their behaviour hadn't stopped the rest of the students.

★ ★ ★

The following morning all the teachers gathered again in the staffroom, waiting to be given any more scraps of information gleaned about where the inspectors might be and when. But Cecelia had some worse news. The facts were unconfirmed, but it was thought that the girl killed the previous day was one of the students from school.

'We'll call the year groups down one by one when the police confirm the girl's identity. We believe it is a girl from Year 10 . . . '

Many of the students knew something had happened, for the press had gathered outside the school by the time the girls were drifting in. We'd been instructed to try and quiet their talking until more was known, and to send a very clear message that no one was to talk to reporters.

I taught a Year 7 class first thing in the morning, and easily and firmly drew their attention away from the rumours flying around. Within a few minutes of the Year 10s arriving for my next class, the tannoy asked the year group to go down to the hall.

'This is the one thing that a principal always dreads,' Cecelia told the whole Year 10 group, before confirming the name of the girl who had been killed the previous afternoon. She asked again that nobody speak to the press, who were at this point being kept at a little distance from the school gates by the police. The school counsellors stood in rows behind the girls, waiting with boxes of tissues.

After the news had sunk in, each teacher took their group back to their classrooms. For forty minutes I stayed in the classroom with the girls in my set, who said nothing but all cried barely making a sound.

The girl had been a close friend of some of them. I had never taught her but I knew who she was, and she had been on the trip to the theatre with us all only two weeks before. She had travelled to England to escape a war-torn country, and had been, two teachers had separately told me quite a long time before her death, one of the most wonderful girls. There was nothing I could come up with to comfort the class. I wanted to make jokes about the awfulness of the situation — when Jo had been killed in Iraq, we'd all spent a lot of time laughing between bouts of tears — but I knew the Year 10s would think I was beyond the pale. I put out paper, and suggested that any who wanted to make cards for her family could use this time to do that.

Coleen asked if she could search the internet for more news. She and Erez sat by the screen looking for information. 'Sometimes,' I warned them, 'it's better not to know all the details.'

The day and the few days following passed with the heavy knowledge of a student's death hanging over everyone. 'It puts the inspection into perspective,' a few staff commented. No one made much of a fuss as the inspectors visited lessons and gave their pronouncements, and the falling rain outside seemed an appropriate accompaniment. The Year 10 students organized a memorial assembly. I felt aware, as I hadn't been before, that I was in an inner-city school. Police surrounded the entrance, and all the staff turned out to help make sure that students got on to buses immediately after school and didn't hang around.

I didn't get seen by the inspectors, but they did loom outside my classroom during registration just as I was being very angry about litter dropped outside the room while students were waiting in the morning before school — ' . . . disgusting eating . . . disgusting just dropping your food on the floor . . . Do you want a disgusting school?'

The Year 10s were knocked sideways by the

news of the death. On Wednesday I tried to teach them.

'Coleen, please could you sit here.' I pointed to her seat at the front of the class. She went to it.

'Do you need a pen?' I asked her, and instead of telling me to get out of her face she nodded.

During the lesson she raised her hand and gave answers about *Romeo and Juliet*. She volunteered to read Juliet's role, and so stood on a desk with Romeo below her for the balcony scene. In the last ten minutes I wanted them to write a paragraph analysing the staging of the scene. Coleen began the moment the task was set.

I rang home. 'Hello, Mrs Randel, I just wanted to tell you about all the things that Coleen did right today . . . '

'Oh good, that is good. She told me that she wanted to make a fresh start.'

I finished the day with a little marking and planning before leaving at 4.30 for a therapy session. Having put in the extra effort to tie up loose ends in preparation for the inspection, I felt that school was very manageable.

★ ★ ★

At the end of the week, as a follow up to the theatre visit, a team came from *The Good Soul of Szechuan* to lead an after-school workshop with the girls who had gone to the performance. I had told the Young Vic that the girl in the news had been one of the students here and so I wasn't sure how many of the girls would come.

Most promised they would, but when it came to it, they slipped away. Only three students turned up. Three students, three members of staff and three adults from the production were present. To compensate for the lack of students, the teachers assumed the roles of students and we sat in a small circle and briefly shared what we'd thought of the production.

Ummi was the only student from my class who was there. She barely spoke in class, but now spent some time telling us all what she had thought while watching Brecht's play — all the little details she'd remembered which I'd not noticed or had forgotten.

'Well, I don't know how much any of you know about Brechtian theatre . . . ' Sarah, who was leading the workshop, began. She looked around the room and saw the blank faces. 'Right, well basically Brecht wanted his audience divorced from what was going on on stage. He wanted them to be emotionally

334

detached, so that they could think about a moral dilemma in a purely rational way — that's why he often set his plays in far-off places . . . ' We all listened intently, the teachers caught up in their favourite activity: learning. 'And there were other techniques he used to try and make the audience aware that they were watching a play and not real life . . . '

She ran through the techniques: reading the stage directions out loud; allowing characters to step out of the action and comment on what they are thinking inside their heads; using exaggerated expressions.

'Right, now I'm going to give you a small script and in pairs I want you to practise using at least two of Brecht's techniques when you read through it . . . It's from *Eastenders* if you are wondering.'

Ummi and I — equally shy about acting — read through the script. We all performed our small sketches. One of Kitty's students seemed to have real talent, and she and the professional actor gave the whole workshop — and the snippets of *Eastenders* — the feel of being something rather sophisticated.

★　★　★

On Saturday I went along to the dentist's. Several years had slipped by since my last check-up. Will recommended I go and visit Kwame in West Hampstead. Kwame recommended I have lots of very expensive treatment including a first filling. But once he'd finished listing all the necessary procedures there was no time to carry any of them out. I paid over a large chunk of my salary and booked an appointment for two week's time.

Will and I headed out to his parents' place. In the year after university, as well as temping I'd also spent some time tutoring for a family in Gloucestershire. The mother was holding a sculpture exhibition in the grounds of her home, only a few miles from Will's mother and father. We drove over to the opening and, walking hand in hand through an orchard, we came across a small boy who was crouched over examining some snails.

'Hello, Jack,' said Will.

'Hello, Mr. Davis,' the lispy boy said, a bit taken aback at seeing his teacher in the middle of the country.

Several sets of parents emerged, with wellingtons and silk printed dresses. They all had children at Will's school, and were buying sculptures and spending the weekend at their country homes.

The following week brought more of the high life. A friend of Will's from his schooldays was having a small birthday party. I met Will near Earl's Court in my most expensive dress. I had justified its purchase the year before by working out that I needed to wear it five times a year for the next twelve years, and that my daughter (when I had one) would then also need to wear it at least ten times in her lifetime. We arrived at the party and, both feeling absolutely boiling, made a dash for a spot beside an open window.

'Excuse me,' I said, pushing past a man in the way. I got to the window and looked back. Will leaned down to my ear and said quietly, 'Do you know who you just pushed out of the way?' I looked over again. Small guy, tanned face, deep-set wrinkles . . .

'Oh, it's Mick Jagger . . . oh!'

Will was determined to speak to the star, and found his opportunity later as Mick was standing in front of the table of puddings.

'Are you protecting the strawberries?' Will asked, grinning.

'No . . . ' said the legend, and moved to the side.

Blown away by the star-studded evening and a butler pouring endless glasses of champagne, we stayed out till twelve o'clock — later than I have ever stayed out on a school night. *So* rock and roll.

'Miss, you look like you just got out of bed,' Amber greeted me at the door to my classroom.

Wednesday was a bit of a struggle, but every time I felt myself flagging I told someone else who I'd been partying with. Mick really helped me get through the day.

Returning to life properly on Thursday, I noticed that the two Year 7 classes had settled again. I wasn't sure whether, through having enough energy, I had quashed their rebellion or whether the warm summer days were helping them to mellow. But Chantelle and Stella, though placed at opposite ends of the room, were still trying to swim against the current. They had chosen each other as close friends, and the choice didn't seem to be benefiting either of them during lesson time.

'Miss, I'm going to try to be good today,' Chantelle would say, coming into the classroom.

'That's excellent news, Chantelle.'

She would sit down, trying to remain serious and resolute, but then Stella would turn her head around and fix her with a naughty stare, and the two of them would fall about giggling. Their attempts at any work were thwarted by the efforts to communicate with each other across the imposed divide.

My responsibilities for the 2ic role were beginning to pick up pace. I'd started organizing a day for the Year 7s in which the whole year group would be off timetable. Eight performance poets were going to come in and lead workshops, and then put on a final show. Endless emails went back and forth between various parties.

Through Will's friend Will, who had helped set up a charity to place writers into schools, I'd also secured a writer in residence for the following year. Aminatta Forna — half Sierra Leonean, half Scottish — came in to meet the English department and take a look at the school after the departmental meeting on Thursday. I met her in the school car park. She looked immaculate: dressed stylishly, hair in perfect curls.

It's impossible to look glamorous after a day's teaching. Often I take make-up in to school and say to myself that I'll put it on before registration. At seven in the evening I get home and look in the mirror. No make-up has made it anywhere near my face, and my ponytail, which was high and tidy, has fallen to my neck and large chunks have come adrift. I look as though

I'm cultivating the mad-woman-teacher look.

I gave Aminatta a short tour of the school. To an outsider's eyes it must look very large and forbidding, even after the £8 million makeover. The walls are thick, the corridors long and polished to a shine each night by the hordes of cleaners who descend and try to scrape gum out from between the grooves of the carpets in the classroom. Apart from the sounds of vacuum cleaners, the school falls into silence at a few minutes past three. I can hear the shrieks of the last few students leaving the site from my classroom four storeys above the playground.

Aminatta and I agreed a timetable for the following year — she'd come after school every Wednesday to work with a group of twelve on creative writing. What a luxury: a class just to write in.

The days had now taken on a different pace. There was still plenty to do — lessons to plan, marking, a forthcoming poetry day for the Year 7s — but things felt good. I was leaving closer to five than to six. It was warm without being hot. Drifting around the school, I was smiling more in the corridors. I think if teaching was always like this I would never even consider what another career might be like. I felt settled.

I was coming towards the end of my second year in the school. I had never imagined when I first signed up for Teach First that, two years down the line, I would enjoy a feeling of quiet satisfaction and contentment teaching in an innercity school. I hadn't thought then beyond the drama and excitement of the first dive into the deep end. I wished there was a way of holding on to this feeling of control and order and taking it into the busy beginning of the autumn term of my third year.

I felt calmer about things more generally. I'd been adamant with the therapist that school wasn't the reason that I'd been feeling such anxiety: that was connected only to Will. But the amount of time we spent talking about school perhaps suggested something different. Once I'd told her the few things on my mind about Will, we'd move on to talking about my work. What were the frustrations? What was I learning? What was within my power to do something about? She'd question me about why my students behaved in the ways they did — and for the more troubled ones it would always come down to the same thing: home life. Parents who were drug addicts, single parents who couldn't cope; parents who didn't know how to keep control of their daughters; parents who were abusive.

341

By the summer, it was more often than not school that I was thinking about when I left her sessions.

★ ★ ★

On Friday after school I didn't need a nap for once. Ella and I headed to Will's for a supper party. Will had invited all his grown-up friends, and I had invited Lucy and Ella.

'How do you do it, Nones?' they whispered to me in the garden while Lucy was smoking a cigarette.

'What? All the adults?' Will's friends were classified as a different generation.

'Yes. I mean, they have *children*.' Lucy made her eyes wide.

'I know. I tend to play with the children — I think I'm closer in age to them.'

By the time food was served I had consumed at least a bottle and a half of champagne. The rest of the evening passed in a blur — but I do remember wisely declining the grappa as Will tucked in.

On Saturday morning we munched on Nurofen for breakfast.

'Oh God, I think I'm still drunk,' said Will.

'I don't feel so good,' I said. 'I think I'm going to be sick.'

It was the worst of days to be hungover.

Will's school was holding its summer fete; his attendance was obligatory. Will performed a shift as goalkeeper while his students pelted him with footballs. Very few of the balls didn't make it to the back of the net. I sat on a step, sipping Coke and watching Will getting battered by the balls.

'Excuse me, do I give my token to you?' the students asked, lining up for the chance to try to assault their teacher. I tried not to breathe on them as I replied.

Fathers milled around sporting tans and chinos; mothers had pulled out yet another brightly coloured printed dress. Someone's pet Mongolian rabbits had been brought in, and groups gathered to pet them. There was a raffle, the prizes mostly weeks in holiday villas abroad.

From his school we went up to King's Cross to catch an afternoon train to my dad's. Hearing that my mother had had a weekend visit, he had extended an invitation, and so we made the journey to north Norfolk for a weekend of pétanque and more wine. I managed a whole weekend with a hangover, Will and my parents without freaking out: what an achievement.

★　★　★

As part of her training, Ella had a week off from her own school to visit other schools and observe how things worked elsewhere.

'Can I come to your school, Nony?' she asked me.

'Yes, brilliant — you can come and teach my 10s.'

On Monday morning we caught the bus in together.

'God, Nony, I can't tell you how nice it is to get up at seven rather than several hours before. I feel human.'

'Poor you . . . Well at least this week you'll have a bit of a break . . . and you can leave at three.'

Ella came along to the Monday-morning meeting in which Cecelia announced the feedback from HMI.

'It's Ofsted who give an overall grade,' she explained to us. 'HMI don't actually give us a grade, so I just want to summarize their main observations. They thought the girls were fantastic, the teaching was by and large fantastic, and overall that the school had an exceptional capacity to improve.'

'Doesn't that just mean we're really bad and have got an exceptionally long way to go?' I whispered to Emily.

Everyone applauded. Having spent only two years at the school, and comparing it to the schools I had gone to, I saw too many of the day-to-day faults and not the bigger picture. There are teachers who had been teaching at the school for more than a decade. I saw that they were part of a very great achievement — one which had taken years.

I'd arranged for Ella to watch a few other teachers teaching, and, keen to get as much out of the experience as possible, she'd agreed to help with the Year 10s.

'He-ello, I'm Folashade,' said Folashade, extending her hand and going into full performance mode when she saw we had a visitor in the class.

'Hello, I'm Miss Miller.'

'Say what?' Folashade shrieked.

'M-ill-er,' Ella said, writing her name on the board.

'Miss, is she a new teacher?' Folashade asked, turning to me.

'No, she's just visiting for the week,' I assured her.

'Everyone, I'd like to introduce you to Miss Miller,' I said once everyone (well, everyone bar the very late arrivals) was sitting down. 'And not only is she a teacher, but she is also my . . . ' I let them guess.

'Sister?'

'No.'

'Girlfriend?'

'No, Miss has a boyfriend, innit?' said Folashade.

'Wot? You don't know,' Erez turned on Folashade.

'Yes, Miss, innit? I met him, Miss innit?' Folashade replied, outraged. I nodded at her.

'Ah, Miss, is she your cousin?'

'Miss Miller is my flatmate. I think I've told you about her before.' She had featured several times in stories for all the classes.

'Oh.'

'And Miss Miller and I are both going to teach you today.' There was a small adjustment in the class, a barely perceptible shift. A newcomer was going to try to teach them, but with Miss Crossley-Holland there too. They were on guard.

I'd been slowly working through the *Romeo and Juliet* balcony scene with the class, daring to do a little performance and then analysing the lines. Coleen had had a whole string of excellent lessons. She'd been studying the play in drama, and so was one step ahead of the game. In class she played Juliet again and again.

Ella and I had devised a series of exceptionally planned lessons. We were going to assault them with activities: freeze-frames, drama, improvisation, matching exercises. It would be like circuit training with two personal trainers checking up on progress. We were going to pick up the pace of the lessons so that there was no time for the girls to start discussing their latest plans for hair extensions. We divided them into groups of four — something I'd avoided since September — and alternated between the two of us to set and lead the short four-minute tasks.

To learn about the iambic rhythm of Shakespeare's lines, Ella told the girls to mount imaginary horses. 'You all need to get on to your horse, take hold of the reins out in front of you, and then we are going to go for a trot around the classroom. Everyone standing up, and behind me.' Ella set off at a fast pace around the room. 'We need to raise our heart rate,' she told the bewildered class. Lakeisha joined in quickly, and Ummi and Mahima rose from their seats. The others took a little time deliberating over whether to get up. Some looked as though they suspected it was a trick: a teacher was asking them to get out of their seats and riotously run around the classroom . . . and yet . . . A few stragglers remained self-consciously in their seats.

Coleen trotted around the classroom laughing, Folashade watched flabbergasted from the sidelines.

'Right,' said a slightly breathless Ella, 'and now,' everyone needs to lie on the floor. Lie on the floor now . . .'

Everyone was laughing. Miss Crossley-Holland's lessons had *never* been this much fun.

'And now I want you to feel your heartbeat — either in your chest or in your neck,' Ella told them. 'Hear the rhythm — ba-bum, ba-bum, ba-bum — and that is the iambic rhythm: the rhythm of the heart.'

They returned to their seats bubbling with excitement, and I took over to ask them why it might seem that the iambic rhythm was particularly appropriate for one of Juliet's monologues.

'Shh, girls, quiet . . . Everyone settle down . . . Yes, Coleen?'

'Because it's the rhythm of her heart, innit?'

'Yes, fantastic . . . Can you explain that more?'

'It's like Juliet's heart is speaking.'

At the end of the three lessons we taught together, Ella and I glowed with satisfaction.

'Give me feedback, Ella,' I told her. 'Don't hold back.'

'Well, there's nothing really . . . you're doing everything . . . except there is one thing which someone taught me and I've found

348

really useful . . . To get a quicker silence, really raise your voice and shout, 'Everyone silent, *thank you*.' You've got to say it in a really definite way. You could try that.'

'Right . . . thank you.'

It did work. The combination of bellowing and certainty in my voice left students faltering mid-sentence — and with such silence in the room that they couldn't pause for a breath and then pick up their conversations again.

Having spent the lessons shared with Ella exploring the language of *Romeo and Juliet*, it was then time for the students to make notes so that they could produce another piece of coursework.

'Miss . . . why are the lessons back like this again?' Folashade asked when, after a quick starter, I had them take out pens and asked the ones who didn't have one to raise their hands.

'Like what?' I asked.

'Boring,' she said.

'I'm sorry you feel that way, Folashade, but we have to do some writing at some point.' I felt no more joy at the prospect of trying to exact coursework than Folashade did at having to produce it. But there was no way of avoiding the fact that at some point we'd need to stop having fun and start measuring ability.

'The 10s really missed you today,' I told Ella back in the flat on Friday. She'd gone to another school for the last two days of the week.

'Oh, Nony, I think it would have been so different if I'd been placed in a school like yours.' Her week away had only made her feel all the more despondent about her own school.

'Is it really so different?' I asked.

'Well . . . yes . . . And the support you receive . . . ' At last, on the home stretch to the summer holidays, Ella didn't seem to be enjoying school any more. 'I was warned it would be difficult seeing other schools.'

'It's not too late, you know,' I told her — 'if you didn't think going back next year was the right thing to do . . . ' The official date had passed for informing schools if you weren't going to be returning the following term, but I was concerned that Ella was slowly having all the life and energy sucked out of her.

'No. I'm going to do the two years, and then I'll do something else.'

'Your second year is easier.' I'd told her this already.

★ ★ ★

The weekend brought a friend's engagement party and a return visit to the dentist's. I sat in the chair bracing myself for the filling.

'That wasn't so bad . . . ' I said afterwards, dribbling a little on one side.

'Yes, and now it's time for the gum treatment said Kwame.' I lay back down. Oh my God, what was he doing? For twenty minutes it felt as if he was using a metal drill to clean below the gum line. I tried to concentrate on the fact that childbirth was sure to be worse.

After the trauma of the morning's appointment, I fell into bed to sleep off the pain. Will brought round supper, and, after eating, the two of us walked to the Tate for a late-night viewing.

'Nony, if you got pregnant would you tell me . . . and would you want to keep it?' he asked, completely out of the blue, as if it were a perfectly normal thing to talk about on a relaxing walk to a gallery.

'Um, yes and yes, definitely,' I answered after taking off a scarf — I'd put on lots of layers for the cold evening. 'Would you want to keep it?' I asked, more tentatively.

'Yes, I think so.' he said. I took off another layer.

'When would you want to have children?' he asked, taking the conversation up a notch

351

from accidental pregnancy to planned.

'Um.' I took off another layer, feeling very hot all of a sudden. 'Well, I suppose before I'm thirty would make sense . . . ' Suddenly thirty, which had always loomed in the far-off distance, seemed very close.

'My dad had two young sons by the time he was my age,' Will went on. 'I mean, if we moved in together I wouldn't want to spend a year pissing around arranging a wedding. I'd want to start having babies.'

'Oh, right.' I was down to a thin T-shirt and feeling a bit panicky. Very panicky.

There was no more to be said, and we arrived at the safety of the Tate's distractions. We went to the Cy Twombly show — I thought his large off-white canvases with etched scribbles looked like school desks before the cleaners have got to them. We went up to the balcony looking over the river, to share a bottle of champagne. I'd calmed down enough to venture that I would quite like to have children with Will. But not yet.

★　★　★

I'd asked my dad to come in and run some workshops with my Year 7 classes in the third-to-last week of term. As a writer for children, he often spends days working in schools. The school library is scattered with his books, and students often take them out and bring them to me to show me they've taken them out.

He was already set up in the classroom when the first class of Year 7s entered the room — the lower-ability set.

'Miss, is that your dad?' twenty-five students asked as they came in.

'Hello, creatures,' he greeted them. They giggled. 'Now, as it's not every day that you get to meet the father of one of your teachers, I thought I'd start by showing you some photographs of Miss Crossley-Holland when she was your age.' He took the well-thumbed pictures of me with gawky hair and wonky teeth out of an envelope and passed them round.

I was sitting next to Chantelle as a precautionary measure.

'Miss! Is that you?' she asked, looking at the picture and laughing.

'Yes,' I said.

'Miss . . . your hair!'

I'd been routinely mortified with embarrassment as a child when my dad had been hauled in by whatever school I was at to talk about his books, read, set writing tasks, and answer questions about his inspiration etc. But by the time he gave a poetry reading at my university I was beginning to be able to

353

listen without wishing I was somebody else's child.

Having gathered the photographs back from pupils keen to hold on to them, he started a riddle by Stuart Henson:

Grab the beast by the horns.
Wrestle it down the narrow streets
'till you break its will
to skitter its own way.
Subdue it. Burden its rib-cage.
Let your children ride.
And then let it stray.
Who cares? They'll send
a herdsman to round it up
at the end of the day.

He held the silence for a moment at the end. 'Now, can anyone guess what I am?'

Most of the class hadn't realized they had been listening to a riddle. 'Tell it again!' I called out.

Stella, engaged and keen to be a top student for this lesson only, shot her hand up.

'A bicycle?'

'Er, no . . . ' said my dad, pressing his fingers together.

'A car?' asked Princess.

'No . . . '

More hands went up. 'Think about what

the horns might be.' Students strained out of their seats.

'A bicycle?' asked Rose.

'No, it's not a bicycle . . . And what could the narrow streets be? Where do you find narrow streets?'

Chantelle roused herself from a daydream and said, 'A bicycle?' My father looked towards me to check that I'd also noticed that, even though he'd clarified that the mystery object wasn't a bicycle, it was still the most popular answer.

He set word games, made them list all the types of blue they could think of, and then told them a story. He drew an old key from his pocket and held it up for them to see. 'Can anyone tell me what is unusual about this key?'

They stared, and Stella threw her hand up gasping, 'It's got letters . . . '

'Ye-es,' Said my dad. 'The teeth of the key actually make out the letters S F. Can you see?'

'Oh'

'What?'

'See'

'yeah, look . . . '

'Does anyone have a name beginning with S?'

'I'm Stella,' Stella said, grinning.

'No! Well, that is strange. There was this woman called Stella' — without faltering, he broke into a story — 'and it was the evening of her wedding. She'd had such a wonderful time, and she just didn't want the party to end . . . She suggested all the guests play a last game — hide and seek! 'I'll go and hide she told the guests.'

'So Stella, in her white wedding gown, went up and up to the top of the house in Scotland they had hired for the reception. She found a small room at the top of the house, and in the room was a large, thick wooden chest. I'll climb in here, she thought, and pulled up the heavy lid of the chest. She nestled down and pulled the lid of the chest closed, and . . . click . . . ' Everyone looked shocked. ' . . . the latch on the lid locked, and she was trapped. 'Help!' she cried. 'Help! Let me out!' But the walls of the chest were thick, and no one heard her or thought to look for her there.

'The guests searched all night, but they couldn't find her. No one could.'

'Was she found?' Princess asked, looking very worried.

'Yes.' Everyone breathed a sigh of relief. 'One hundred years later her bones were found in the trunk — her bones inside her wedding dress.'

'Oh! Is it true?' they chorused.

He started them off writing riddles and stories of their own, and then the session was over. 'Send me your stories or riddles,' he told them, 'and I'll read them all and send a prize to Miss Crossley-Holland for the best. Goodbye, creatures.'

I walked with my dad along the corridors to the staffroom for coffee and pastries.

'Gosh, they're quite a handful that class, aren't they? I can see if you took your eye off the ball for a minute . . . '

'Yes, I know . . . They loved the story.'

The following lesson Angela returned. She had been absent for my father's visit.

'Oh, Miss, I missed him. Can you tell him to come in again?' She was very disappointed. 'I'd been looking forward to it for so long . . . '

'He told us a story,' Rose told her. 'Miss, tell it again.'

'Yeah! Yeah . . . ' A story is always preferable to work.

'Well,' I began, 'it was actually about a girl called Angela . . . '

'No it wasn't,' most of the class called out.

'Yes it *was*,' I said, looking at them seriously.

'No, Miss . . . '

'Yes,' I said, 'it was,' winking in a very

obviously conspiratorial way.

'Oh! Yer, Miss,' they laughed, catching on.

★ ★ ★

By the beginning of July, with just three weeks of school left, the days felt easy and blissful if a little muggy. I cycled in just before registration — sometimes from west London where Will lived, cycling through the parks; sometimes the short ride from my flat. In the afternoons I left with plenty of time to potter around in the evenings. The Year 11s had well and truly disappeared — their attendance at lessons had petered out. Half the class would turn up to do bits of revision for the very last of the GCSE exams, then only a few were in school, and then they were gone. And, fond though I was of each of the 11s in my class, I was glad they were gone.

Adalia had popped by once or twice after school to say hello. Each time she threw herself down on a desk and sat swinging her legs.

'What are your plans for the summer?' I asked her.

'Oh, Miss! I don't know.'

'You should try and get a summer job.'

'Yer, Miss, I know,' she smiled, not taking my advice too seriously.

'Do you know what you're doing in September?'

'Oh, Miss, didn't I tell yer? I got on to a health-and-beauty course.'

'At college?'

'Yer.'

'That's great. You'll have to do my nails one day.'

'Oh yer, Miss.' The idea amused her as much as the idea of speaking to me on the phone had when she'd been running late for the theatre.

'Did I ever tell you my sister trained to be a make-up artist?'

'Is it?'

'Yes. But actually she's going to go and be a teaching assistant now.' My sister Ellie had decided to apply for a position at Will's school.

'Oh, Miss, that's funny. You both work in schools.'

'I know. Weird, eh?'

Even more exciting was the fact that the Year 10s, after a week of calm lessons wrapping up *Romeo and Juliet* with oral rather than written essays, had left for two weeks of work experience. One moment they were there, hot and dopey, complaining only mildly, fairly willing to do what I asked, and the next moment they were dressed in heels and tight black trousers and fitted white shirts and going to work rather than school.

On the noticeboard in the staffroom there were lists of the Year 10 students. We had to select who we'd visit on their placements. I put my initials next to Coleen's name.

*   *   *

I'd run a number of philosophical inquiries with the two Year 7 groups, and for a final session I wanted to try something different.

'Is there anyone,' I asked the lower set, 'who would feel confident in running one of the philosophy sessions themselves?' Much to my delight, Genesis returned after school to volunteer herself for the job. I checked she knew what happened at each stage of the inquiry. She did.

The lesson arrived, we got the chairs into a circle, and I announced that Genesis would be leading the session. She started the warm-up game by asking everyone to stand and close their eyes. I followed the instructions.

A few moments of silence followed, and then Genesis asked us to open our eyes and find the student who had been hidden. Half the class (who'd been much smarter than me and kept peeking at what was going on) rushed out of my room, into the hall. From there, five of them bundled into Steph's lesson to retrieve the student who'd been hiding in her classroom *during* her lesson. This did not give a good impression of how my lesson was going.

'I'm so sorry, Steph,' I said grabbing more of my students by the collar and dragging them back out of her room. '*So* sorry.'

I ushered all the students back into my room.

'Girls, all activities *always* have to be in our classroom . . . ' I brought that on myself, I thought. Perhaps this class weren't ready to manage themselves.

Chantelle and Stella never quite settled after the excitement of breaking free into someone else's lesson, and so the rest of the hour was a bit of a strain. I was relieved when eleven o'clock arrived and it was time to let them go down to break.

'Chantelle, can I speak to you, please?' I asked. She had painted freckles all over her face with a felt-tip pen. She looked at me, snorted like a pig, and walked out of the classroom giggling while I stood trying to figure out if she had actually done what I thought she'd done.

The others rushed out into the corridor, and then I heard lots of shouting. I ran out and saw two of my students — a new girl and another — trying to rip hair from each other's heads.

I bellowed the kind of sound a seal makes, and drew them apart as I shouted, 'What on earth do you two think you are doing? Rose, go and get on-call please . . . Everyone else to break.'

Adrenalin flew through my veins, and I deposited the two by this time hysterically crying girls in different classrooms. I felt a bit responsible. Had the chaotic lesson added to their agitation?

Senior management arrived and hauled the two off to the referral base. I also asked on-call to pick up Chantelle, and explained that she had snorted at me. The two girls who'd fought were suspended from school for the following day. Chantelle delivered a letter:

Dear Ms Crossley=Holland,
    I didn't Oink at you yesterday but I do admitt I did oink it was a private joke between me and Kelly.
    Know I do Admitt I should not of been making noises so I am sorry for making noises but yeah as I said I am only sorry for making noises.
    From Chantelle.

In the last full week of school the weather varied between furiously hot and cooler rainstorms. The Year 7s arrived looking rather wilted and dishevelled from a Portakabin, — still being used while the building works went into their second phase — where, under a tin roof, the temperatures soared. My windows open only an inch, as we are four storeys up and any particularly skinny students might try to squeeze through if the windows opened, say, two inches wide.

In a stretch of time opened up by the Year 11s having departed and the Year 10s being on work experience, I collected my bike from the bike shed and set off to Rotherhithe to visit Coleen at the place where she was working.

I realized I'd left my bike lock at home. Brilliant: I was cycling to Rotherhithe without a lock. The rain started to pour; the piece of paper I'd printed a map on went soggy. I arrived at the address — a small house with a tiny gated driveway. I felt there was a chance my bike might still be there after the meeting.

I signed in on a clipboard hanging on the front door and was let in. There was a narrow, dark corridor, with a dark room to the left and a dark room to the right. Heavy nets were drawn over the windows. Scattered around the rooms were armchairs. In each chair there was an old woman or man staring out into space. One man was shouting quite loudly at a nurse who was trying to help him stand. And in the midst of all this Coleen sat next to an old woman whom she was encouraging to eat the few digestive biscuits laid out on a tray before her.

'Hi, Coleen,' I said.

'Oh hi,' she said shyly.

'I'm just here to see you and see if it's going all right.'

'Oh.'

'And to talk to your supervisor and find out how you've been doing.'

Coleen nodded. She got up and indicated I should go into the room on the other side of the corridor. She was dressed head to toe in grey marl: tracksuit bottoms and a hoodie — a uniform for girls in the area.

In the other room there was only one other woman, looking particularly lost. Coleen and I sat down at a small table. Neither of us really had a clue what to say.

'So, how's it going?' I started.

'Fine.' She smiled an unsure smile. I imagined she might have been thinking, This is hell, get me out of here.

'And, um, what sort of things have you been doing?'

'Er . . . lots of stuff. Helping with breakfast,

helping with lunch, um . . . Everything really.'

'That's great . . . So, do you think you might be interested in working somewhere like this in the future?'

'Er . . . ' Her face said, Are you kidding? 'Maybe.'

Poor Coleen, I thought. The one thing she seems to get excited about is art, and she's ended up in an old people's home for her work experience.

Then conversation dried up completely.

'Coleen, I'll see you in September,' I said, drawing things to a close. 'Can you get your supervisor? I need to ask her a couple of questions'

A woman in her forties came and sat with me at the table. I ran through my questions.

'And just more generally, how would you say Coleen's doing?' I asked her, keen to wrap things up, get back into the light, and check if my bike was still there.

'She's done really well . . . If anything she's quiet, shy . . . She's very quiet . . . But anything we've asked her to do she's done.'

Hm — that was more success than I had had with her for the first eight months.

The bike was waiting for me, and gave me a quick escape from the depressing clutches of poverty and lack of choice. You would not want to take your grandma there. You would not want to work if you thought that what the future held for you was a job there.

The uniforms the students wore at school erased signs of poverty or comparative wealth. Sometimes an unwashed shirt hinted at neglect, but I'd never seen a student show poverty in the way that the lost grandparents sitting in a dark room in Rotherhithe seemed to show poverty.

★ ★ ★

Wednesday was the day of poetry and performance, and all one hundred and eighty Year 7s would be going to a handful of workshops. I'd master-minded the organization. Teachers had been moved out of their classrooms; the English teachers had supply teachers covering their lessons so they could supervise the workshops; students were in groups different from their teaching groups. There is no way this will all run smoothly, I thought, coming into school later than I'd intended. What have I forgotten? The question looped around my vacant brain.

'Miss Crossley-Holland!' Emily emerged from her door. 'Do the English teachers know which classrooms to put their supply work in?' she asked me.

'Shit . . . shit.'

'I can help . . .'

Emily had two student librarians in her tutor group. They have superhuman organizational skills. One of the girls made Emily a homework chart without being asked to — just to make it easier for Emily to keep track of which of her students owed her work. We delegated the task of sticking posters on doors to the two girls — who were in school rather early, and for no reason other than to take on organizational tasks that the teachers had failed to do.

Poets started arriving all over the place. Eight English teachers waited in eight rooms with eight sets of students. Six poets arrived for the start. The poet leading my group's first session was nowhere to be seen. We sat in a large circle playing games. Having learned my lesson, I kept my eyes open at all times.

By 9.30 all eight poets were on site. There was also a male photographer, and an organizer from the charity through which I'd booked the poets. The first session ended and I ushered my group across a hallway into their next session. They spied their next poet through the window in the classroom door.

'Omigod, MISS! He's so tall. Ahhhh!'

'Ahhhh! . . . Ahh!'

Angela ran into the classroom and stood underneath him, pointing her finger up at him.

'You came to my primary school!'

'Nony.' Steph pulled me towards her for a quick conversation. 'Cecelia says we need to wait till the hallways have been cleared and then take the poets to break . . . There's some excitement at having young, beautiful black men on site . . . '

'Oh . . . right. Of course. I hadn't thought that we'd cause mass hysteria by bringing men in.' It's not that there were no male teachers at school — just that the excitement of new blood caused the girls to slam themselves up against windows and doors to get a peek.

The students listened and wrote and spoke, and it was all very exciting and new, and some of the poets were so cool that the girls could hardly stop grinning. The time came for all the students to make their way down to the hall. The girls sat on benches and on the floor in a square; the poets were to perform in the centre. They had each worked with three groups, so had built up fan bases ready to faint when they came on stage.

The Year 7s who had sat in the hall terrified and mute on their first day had morphed into a different kind of crowd. The tallest, most striking young poet stepped into the arena.

'AHHHHH!' The girls screamed and whooped and clapped. It was like being at a pop concert rather than a poetry reading.

Some of the poets rapped rather than spoke, and the audience needed taming between each piece. They were wild with excitement, and the poets, rather than trying to tame them, whipped them up more.

While not performing, the poets sank into crash mats which had been left from PE. The teachers hovered behind their naughtiest students, trying to intimidate them with their presence.

At the end of the hour I stepped into the square, and so did Steph. It took us a few minutes of waving our arms up and down to regain quiet. I thanked the poets on behalf of the students — huge cheers and stamping — and then Rose and Camilla brought me a great bunch of flowers as a thank you.

'You really didn't need to . . . ' I told Steph afterwards.

'Well, it's for the students as well — they need to see that a lot of work goes into something like that.'

The rain was pouring down outside. We tried to control the students leaving the hall, but waves of them crammed through the door, squealing and bustling each other out of the way.

'I hope we'll be allowed to do it again . . . ' I said to Steph, sensing that the school would have a few things to say about the day.

'Yes, well I know they were excited, but I think that's brilliant . . . They were involved; they were learning.' I think the element of chaos had given the day the true mark of creativity for Steph.

★ ★ ★

I had another chance to work on my crowd-management skills on Friday. Along with five other schools, we took over the Crystal Palace stadium to run an inter-school sports day. Only the Year 7s were invited, to trial the day. They screamed for the runners and jumpers in exactly the same way as they had for the poets — though somehow it seemed more appropriate in a stadium.

Cecelia turned up and happened to be standing in front of our section of the stadium just as the staff relay began. The whole crowd tumbled forward to break out of the stands. Cecelia with one sweep of her hand and one 'No!' kept our Year 7s within their section; the rest of the schools flooded on to the track. It was mayhem on an unprecedented scale.

★ ★ ★

I got home after the sports day feeling only a little traumatized. At just after five, however, Ella was already in bed, blinds drawn. She'd been getting into bed as soon as she got home for the past week. The post remained uncollected downstairs; she'd given up trying to cook herself anything in the evening.

'Oh, Ella . . . ' She looked miserable. 'You're almost at the end, of course you're completely exhausted . . . You're almost there . . . '

'But next year . . . ' she said. Her voice was quiet; she looked as if she'd lost the will.

'I'm just so miserable, Nony . . . I don't know what's happened to the old Ella.' The old Ella was so full of energy and enthusiasm I'd thought it was an act for the first month we worked together in India. 'I got a 'Good' today in an observation from the borough, but I was just like 'Oh.' It made me feel better for about a minute. I mean, I'm doing everything. I know I'm doing it all right, and the students are working really hard and we're having such good lessons. But they're not making me happy. I've just stopped feeling anything.'

'Oh, Ella . . . You know you don't have to do this. Maybe it's all just too much . . . ' I'd suggested this more and more frequently.

'Well . . . or I could move up closer to the

school.' Closer to the school was the middle of nowhere.

'Yes, you could . . . But you love living in the centre, and would it make you even unhappier?'

We'd rehearsed all this too. There seemed to be no easy options. She could eliminate the long commute, but she'd still have very little support at school. She could bash on through, but was there any reason why she'd feel completely differently about it?

Along with some other friends, Ella had managed to arrange a fund-raiser on Saturday night. It was for a school in the slums of Nairobi. She'd taken over a club off the King's Road, and masses of tickets had been sold.

'I don't even feel like I want to go to that at the moment,' she said.

After a Saturday madly baking flapjacks to feed the party-goers, she'd perked up. Will and I went along to the fund-raiser. My sister arrived towards midnight, ready for the party to begin; Will and I slipped home to bed.

The money raised by the evening for the school raised Ella's spirits, but by Monday night, after another day at work, she was back on the verge of tears, contemplating another week and a half while I had only two days of the school year left.

* ★ ★

The year ended as it had begun, with a heavy assault on the liver. Late afternoon on Monday the English department retired to a pub a short walk away. By six we'd consumed a small reservoir. We talked about summer plans, future plans, anything but school. John was leaving the department to teach elsewhere.

The Year 10s had come back in for a few hours on Monday — a chance to report back on their experiences. I'd looked out for Coleen, but hadn't seen her. And with the Year 11s gone the school felt only half full. It was funny seeing how much older the students were looking. In only a month and a half they would return to a new year. The 7s would be 8s; new terrified 7s would take their place.

During the last days, Steph and I made the final adjustments to the set lists for September. We decided we'd try to keep the students with the teachers they had had already. With the more difficult students, who take four months to get to know you, it seemed to make sense. But some changes were afoot for the new year. The school would be jettisoning tutor groups and would instead give each teacher a 'family' to look after for forty minutes each day.

'Hello, girls, I'm the head of our family.'
'Where's dad?'

'No, no — we're a broken home.'

In our last lesson together the Year 7s turned up looking their most wilted. It was one of the hottest days so far, and there was a tinge of sweaty polyester in the air. I hadn't planned anything arduous: they wrote small pieces reflecting on the year, with a DVD of *Romeo and Juliet* on in the background. At the end of the lesson I told them they could take their exercise books home.

The most precious of books, the product of hours of their work, was suddenly up for grabs.

'Miss, what will you do with the books if we don't take them?'

'Put them in the bin.'

'Miss, no!'

A few brought little gifts of chocolate and carefully written cards:

Thank you for teaching this year. I have learnt quite a lot (I think), I might not remember all of it, but I'll always remember you!
From your student Amaal

★ ★ ★

Others checked to see if there was anything I'd particularly like.

'Miss . . .'

'Yes, Genesis.'

'Miss, do you like sausage rolls?'

'Um . . . ye-es.'

'Do you like large or small sausage rolls?'

I could see where this was going, and I thought that if I was going to have to eat a sausage roll that had been lovingly squidged and gripped all the way to school I'd prefer it to be small.

'Um . . . I like small sausage rolls.'

'OK. Because I wanted to get you something to say thank you.'

'Genesis, that is really kind of you.'

Ella and I had both got horrendously ill out in India through eating the offerings of our students. We'd look at each other with desperate eyes before digging into a bag of cold noodles that the boarders had specially asked a day student to bring in as a treat for the English teachers.

★ ★ ★

On Tuesday evening I had a last meal of the term with Sophie. I waited outside school, and we caught a bus to a restaurant together. Like Ella, she was not quite at the very end of term. We settled with two beers, and I listened to how her day had been.

'Ergh! For some reason the classrooms are ridiculously hot.'

'I know.'

'So, I say to them, 'I know it's hot. I can see you're hot, and I'm hot too. We're all hot'. I'd booked the laptops for them to be finishing a piece of work, and I try to settle them calmly. It doesn't help that everyone else is already watching DVDs.'

'Yes, I put a DVD on today.' I started smiling, anticipating the events to unfold.

'And just as everyone is calmly working, Dwane enters. 'What? What? We're doing work? This is bullshit, bruv. This is bullshit.' So I say to him, 'Dwane, I don't know who you are calling bruv in here, but that language is not appropriate. I'd like you to come to the office with me.' Dwane is getting more worked up (it *is* very hot), and so we leave the classroom and go to the head of year's office, where there is air conditioning.

'So I step inside the office and explain what has happened and begin to feel far more rational standing in the cool air . . . And so the head of year looks at Dwane and says, 'Now, Dwane, what am I going to do with you? Now, I could send you home, but I'm not going to do that. No, Dwane, I'm not going to do that, because that is where you want to be, isn't it? So instead I could call the police. How about that? I could call and explain that a student has been harassing a teacher and making it impossible for her to teach.' Dwane has spent plenty of time with the head of year, and listens to him watching the floor. He says to Dwane, 'Would that make you change the way you behave? Would it?' and Dwane just purses his lips and says he's not bothered. So then the head of the year picks up the phone and dials 999. I *cannot* believe it. He *actually* does it, and Dwane can't believe he's done it either and looks at me *completely* shocked. And then the head of year turns to me and says, 'Thank you Miss Brigham, I'll take over from here.' So I walk back to my insanely hot classroom.'

We laughed and grumbled about various things at school, before moving on to thinking about the year ahead.

'So, you've decided to stay on?' Sophie said. We hadn't seen each other since I'd made the decision.

'Yeah, it seemed like the right choice . . . I hope it is.'

'Your third year is that step easier,' she told me.

'Really?'

'Yes. Remember how different starting your second year was . . . It's the same moving from your second year to your third — you just know that much more.'

★ ★ ★

On Wednesday the Year 7s, 8s and 9s came in for a few hours in the morning. We all watched a dance performance, and had small parties with our tutor groups.

We had been given express instructions not to allow any food or drinks, but one of my students had brought in a birthday cake. I buckled under the pressure and agreed we could eat pieces if we were extremely careful. The deputy head turned up at the door to dismiss the girls. Everyone was stuffing cake into their mouths. I thought it was important to come clean immediately.

'Um, I'm really sorry, I know we weren't allowed to eat, but . . . it was one girl's birthday . . . '

I expected she might give me a conspiratorial wink. 'No one is allowed to eat in the classrooms,' she said angrily. 'Look, that girl has just dropped a huge piece on to the floor.'

I turned around. The birthday girl's cake was on the carpet. A few of my tutor group were trying to scoop up the icing and soft

378

chocolate sponge, but were only spreading it around more.

'Leave the cake, girls. I'll do it.' I prised them away, furtively encouraging any that still had cake to wrap it in sheets of plain A4 paper. 'Time to go home now.'

We left the classroom and walked down to the gate to say goodbye — 'See you in September . . .'

The staff barbecue awaited: beer and burgers, and speeches for staff who were moving on. At the end of the afternoon I said a few goodbyes and cycled home. It was all over. A summer of lie-ins awaited.

Ella arrived home an hour or so after I did. She climbed into bed.

'Ba . . . ba . . . ba . . . ba,' I said.

'Yes, Nony.'

I sat with her before leaving again to meet Will for supper at a restaurant nearby. Ella and I went through the same conversation we'd been having, on and off, for weeks. But when Will and I got back from supper she had made a decision.

'I'm going to leave, Nony,' she said. She looked happier than she had for ages.

'You wouldn't like to work at a small private school, would you?' Will asked her, hearing the news.

EPILOGUE

On Thursday 21 August the GCSE results came out. I'd texted Emily and Steph to ask them if they were going in. We convened in Steph's classroom at 9.30 in the morning. Emily was incredibly brown from a month in Mexico; Steph had had a few weeks in America and also had a healthy glow.

Will had taken me out to Ireland again. Amazingly, I hadn't felt a tinge of panic. On the one sunny day of the summer we went down to a cove and lay out in the sun. I'd forgotten suncream, and Will had only the expensive cream reserved for faces.

'Please can I put some on my tummy?' I asked, though certain that the Irish sun would be kind to those of a fairer complexion.

'No,' Will said, 'this stuff is only for faces.'

My tummy and legs received their second roasting of the year. The skin is still peeling.

'Ooh, it's strange to be back,' Steph said to us as we surveyed her room. There were delivery boxes of next year's supplies on every table — mountains of exercise books, Pritt Stick, and various other stationery treats that Emily had taken it upon herself to order. My classroom was in a similar state of disarray, with chocolate crumbs still on the desks.

Around our Victorian tower was still a building site. The Portakabins had been taken away, doubling the size of the dirt playing field, but the tower block still had teams of builders milling about. Steph deposited her children in her classroom and searched for anyone who might have results. In a hidden away office, Steph found the sheets we were after, and we took them back to my room to pore over.

'Ooh, we're down overall,' Steph said.

We had the results of the whole year group before us, and Emily and I went through the list writing down the results for each of our students. We gasped as we saw the best and the worst, and each conducted a running monologue as we worked through the sheets.

'Abimbola got two Cs, Nia the same — hm, she could have done better — and Adalia got two Cs ... And then Aysha, Hebba, Maria, all those lovely girls who had tried so hard got a B and an A. I'm so pleased for them ... '

Becky had got two Ds — the lowest results in the class.

'She wasn't there ... what can you do?' Steph reassured me it wasn't my fault, but it felt disappointing.

At eleven we went down to the school gates to meet those who had come in to get their results. They were clutching each other, looking genuinely worried, but dressed to the nines. Some were crying before they even opened their envelopes.

'Miss, I got two Cs,' Adalia said, scrunching up her nose.

'A C is a good grade, Adalia.'

'I know, but I wanted Bs.'

'Oh.' I sounded sympathetic, and I felt it. But though she'd been there and done the work, she'd never pushed herself, never striven, and it was reflected in the grade.

Becky was sitting on a wall beside her. She didn't look at me, but was staring angry and upset at the ground. I should have said something about how it wasn't too late, how she was a bright girl and should redo some of her GCSEs at college. I didn't.

Some girls jumped excitedly up and down, screaming and dancing; others held on to their sealed results and refused to open them.

'Go on, Lisa,' I said to one of them. She was the girl who had joined just for this last year. The coursework from her previous school had been Ds, but we'd reworked and rewritten it. I'd predicted two Bs for her. The head of year had spoken to me — 'She'll be lucky if she gets two Cs.' I stuck to my guns and thought she could do it: She wanted Bs, and worked for them.

'Open your envelope, Lisa,' I told her. She shook her head. She wouldn't do it. 'But what if there are good surprises in there?'

'No.'

When I left she was still standing on the street none the wiser.

★ ★ ★

While I spent the second half of summer writing, Will went off to Malawi to set up a link with a school out there. Ella accepted a job that Will's head offered her, teaching history to Year 4. She also decided it was time to move out of the flat . . . time to shake things up.

I asked Will if he'd like to move in. I sent him cautious text messages making it clear that I was terrified at the prospect but equally couldn't think of anyone I'd rather live with. When he texted back that he also felt rather terrified, but would love to give it a go, I threw my phone halfway across the flat in shock.

I half dreaded the return to school. Actually, way more than half. Emily and I would both have fuller timetables. Having arranged the class lists in the last weeks of term, I knew that there would be an awful lot of terrors in my Year 8 class. The deputy head even flagged this up when she saw the lists — 'Can anything be done to avoid this combination?' Nothing could. Students had to be setted by ability. Because of this and the restraints of the timetable it was often the case that difficult students were setted together.

Preparing to return, I hoped that the 10s, who had become 11s, would continue to mellow and apply themselves, and that Coleen, unlike Becky, would stay the course of the year, turn up to school, and keep trying. At the end of my second year I could see much more clearly than I had before that our school system was not designed for Coleen — nor for most of the students in her class. I wanted them to get Cs — so they could get college places — but I also wanted them to know what it is to be absorbed in work and to feel content. And then I wanted different things for each of them. I wanted Cally to gain more confidence, and Folashade to learn to speak her mind calmly without resorting to impassioned shouting inside the classroom and without resorting to punch-ups outside it.

In September, term started well. The Year 11s were a little more mellow, and the class had shrunk over the summer. Four students didn't return. Two of them had had poor attendance from the beginning, and one girl I was told had been moved out of London by some authority as she was an illegal immigrant. The fourth student missing was Coleen.

'Where is she?' I tentatively asked around.

'Abroad . . . Turkey or Cyprus. Not sure'

'When is she coming back?' The relief of the respite was tempered by the thought that the more school she missed, the more difficult it would be to teach her when she returned.

The weeks passed, but still she didn't return. I found out nothing more, though I did overhear a lunch time conversation which suggested that if she was absent for long enough she would lose her place at the school and then have to reapply — and that she might not necessarily be readmitted. We still don't know if she's coming back.

After two years I felt that I was planning good lessons for all my classes. Emily and I had endless conversations about ways to manage the unfeasible amount of paperwork, but we also put aside precious weekend and holiday hours to plan a few weeks of lessons ahead. After two years, I could actually teach the students effectively enough to be able to see clear results. Even with my off-the-wall Year 8 class we had lots of good days. As ever, there wasn't a spare minute in the day, so I regularly stayed up in the evenings trying to get marking done.

I tried to be of more use to the department, and aligned my thinking more fully with Steph's. We did all need to work together and share planning if we wanted the job to be vaguely manageable. A department full of mavericks doing their own thing is not the way forward.

I was just about holding it all together — the full timetable, an after-school club, the planning, the marking, the meetings and department responsibilities — and then, in the week after the first half-term break, I returned home from school crying three evenings in a row. I was feeling trampled. The end of a lesson didn't feel as though a stampede of elephants had run me down in the way it had in my first year, but the effort was still draining. Though things were easier than in previous years, they weren't easy enough to want to keep going. I longed for classes where the students were more naturally predisposed to listen to each other and work amicably together.

In the hallways, chance encounters with unfamiliar students still left me feeling battered and bruised. In a school of one thousand, even after teaching there for two years there are still a lot of students whom you don't know and who don't know you.

One beautiful October morning I thought I'd take the long way round the outside of the buildings to get as much fresh air as possible before returning to my classroom. The air was fresh and cool, and it seemed so lovely to be spending a few minutes outside. Rounding the last bend, I came across a group of Year 11 students hiding in a corner. I recognized only one of the group, a white girl who had come to a handful of creative-writing workshops.

'Girls, where should you be?' I asked amicably.

'Here,' came the smart reply from the leader of the pack.

'Ah, I don't think so. Back to the playground, please,' I said, not expecting there to be any difficulty.

'Or what?' asked the leader. Oh lord, I thought, why does she want to make this difficult?

'Or . . . ' I said, inwardly rolling my eyes at the ridiculous chore of it, 'or I go inside to the deputy's office and ask her to come out and deal with you.'

The leader sneered at me as I offered the

laborious consequences she could opt for. 'Go on, then.' She said.

Her friends watched silently. I turned to the girl whom I vaguely knew from the writing workshops.

'What's your friend's name?' I asked her.

'Vicky.'

I turned back to the ringleader.

'Vicky, there's no need for me to go and get anyone. Most unfortunately I've come across you all here, and now I'm simply asking you politely to go back to the playground. Just walk round the corner and there's no need for me to do anything.' It was completely beyond me why she wasn't choosing the easy option.

'Or what?' she replied again.

'I really don't like the way you are speaking to me,' I said gently, but beginning to get quite riled.

'What do you mean?'

'I mean I wouldn't speak to anyone the way you are speaking to me.'

'What do you mean?' she repeated. Her tone had been aggressive from the offset, and she certainly wasn't going to back down now.

'I'm finding the way you are speaking to me very rude.'

'What's rude? What's rude?' She was getting more and more worked up.

'Oh no, Miss,' a bystander piped up — 'this isn't rude for Vicky.'

'Come on, girls,' I appealed to the rest of the group — 'back to the playground.'

The girl I vaguely knew gently egged the rest of them on. They mooched away, and I entered the building with all feelings of joy and calm dissipated. I felt irritated that, even if I did take the time to write up the confrontation, nothing would come of it. I felt the school did not demand that students showed respect to the staff, and teachers had to pick and choose their battles.

Pressure from above also seemed to be growing. I don't know whether the demands from senior management for ever better results were genuinely increasing, or whether in my third year I was simply more aware of the school's agenda, but I didn't like it. I dreamed of working in a school where there was a greater emphasis on producing well-rounded individuals. I worried that a large handful of my students would be fired if they ever managed to secure a job, because they wouldn't see any problem in speaking to their employers in the way they addressed their teachers.

In the weeks around autumn half-term I deliberated over the option of leaving in January. I couldn't do it. Leaving halfway through the year felt wrong — too incomplete. I told Steph that this academic year was definitely going to be my last year there. I wanted a school where it was easier to teach, and began looking around for such a place. I still want the energy of an inner-city school, but I'm looking for a school that is academically selective — not somewhere where the battle is a different kind of battle, but somewhere where there isn't a battle.

One Thursday in December I took a short train ride out of London to a top boarding school — I'd been asked to go and speak at a careers evening about teaching.

'Would you ever consider teaching at a school like this?' one of the painfully polite and charming girls asked me.

I'd previously thought that teaching at a very academic boarding school would turn me into an anarchist, but presented with a room of teenagers who seemed to hang on my every word I felt that working in the private sector was not completely out of the question. The one thing I did feel certain of for all of October, November and December was that there was nothing — absolutely nothing — that could be done to make me want to stay where I was.

By the run-up to Christmas, however, my wave of frustration and exasperation at the endless disruptive behaviour and impossible demands from above had waned.

In the few weeks before the end of term, when normally everyone begins to wind down a little, the English department had an internal review — teachers and management from across the school observing two lessons delivered by each member of the department. Much time and energy was put into planning and preparing the lessons to be observed, and there was an expectation you would showcase the best of your teaching.

For the second of the two lessons I taught I was graded as 'outstanding' — the holy grail of the Ofsted criteria.

'Good,' Will said when I told him at home over a celebratory Marks & Spencers chicken tikka. 'Now you can leave.'

'I'm definitely leaving in July,' I reassured him. I was tremendously grateful for the recognition that I was a good teacher, but the accolade didn't change my feelings about wanting to move on to a new school.

★ ★ ★

Will and I had settled very quickly into a homely routine. Whoever got back first put the oven on, and over an early supper we discussed the day's events. Most often Will would smile as he recounted how lovely his day had been. I would furrow my eyebrows as I offloaded, or relate with impassioned excitement something brilliant that had happened. Will remained constant in his counselling that I might be more content in a different school.

For the Christmas holidays we booked tickets to India. A schoolfriend was to be married in Delhi in early January, so we planned a circuit of Rajasthan before the wedding.

It was the first Christmas I'd ever had away from home, and a very memorable one. Will and I arrived in Udaipur, a most beautiful small city surrounding a large lake on which floats the famous Lake Palace Hotel. On one side of the lake there is a jumble of ornate palaces, on the other are smoky hills with pointed peaks for as far as the eye can see. We stayed in a haveli overlooking the lake, and spent Christmas day basking in the warm sun and having massages. School felt a very long way away.

For the late afternoon Will had booked an old white Ambassador taxi to take us up the steep hill to the Monsoon Palace — an abandoned summer residence of the maharana. We watched the sun set, sitting together on the marble floor of an open balcony. Will seemed agitated that hordes of Indian tourists kept squeezing on to the balcony with us.

I knew what was coming. He'd been dropping gentle hints for the past few weeks, and then that morning I'd over-heard his mother ask, as he was on the phone to her, whether anything had happened yet. I'd panicked a little when that had confirmed my suspicions, but by the time we were sitting in the balcony I felt quite calm.

He'd written me a Christmas card in the form of a script — a conversation between the two of us. There was a blank space at the end for me to fill in with my answer. I said yes! It was an answer I'd had planned for the past few months.

So part of my life is much more certain than other bits. The mild Indian days made me entertain the possibility of one more year at my school, but when I returned to icy January I regained my senses. It was lovely going back to school, especially the students' excitement — 'Miss, that ring is blinging! He must respect you!' — but I know it's time to move on.

ACKNOWLEDGEMENTS

I didn't appreciate, before I started, what a very long process writing a book is, and how many people are involved along the way. I first started writing about the chalk face in a series of columns for the *Guardian* education supplement and so, as well as thanking those who have contributed to the book, thanks are due to Claire Phipps and Alice Woolley at the *Guardian* and Brett Wigdortz at Teach First for his guidance. I'd also like to thank my father, Kevin Crossley-Holland, for putting in the missing commas in the first year's worth of columns.

I would like to thank my principal for allowing me to write about my school and all at John Murray, especially Eleanor Birne and Bernard Dive for their guidance and hours of labour. I'd like to thank my students: the ones who behaved for their hard work, and the ones who didn't for providing the more entertaining moments in the book. For making me see the funny side of the poor behaviour, and for their endless support, I'd like to thank my wonderful department and colleagues.

There are a handful of friends and family who have been very involved in the writing of the book and in particular I'd like to thank my father again, my mother Gillian, and my step-mother Linda. Without Caro's support I never would have got through my first two years of teaching, let alone written anything about it, and for that I owe a huge thanks. And finally, I'd like to thank Will for laughing out loud when he read through the manuscript, even if he was only laughing at the bits with him in.

★   ★   ★

The author and publisher would like to thank the following for allowing or not raising objections to the use of copyright material: 'Suicide in the Trenches' copyright © Siegfried Sassoon by kind permission of the Estate of George Sassoon; *random* by debbie tucker green is published by Nick Hern Books, London (www.nickhernbooks.co.uk), reproduced with permission; the shopping trolley riddle by Colin Henson, from *The New Exeter Book of Riddles* ed. by Kevin Crossley-Holland and Lawrence Sail (London: Enitharmon Press, 1999) reproduced by kind permission of Colin Henson and Enitharmon Press (www.enitharmon.co.uk); the extract from 'Education for Leisure' is

We do hope that you have enjoyed reading this large print book.

Did you know that all of our titles are available for purchase?

We publish a wide range of high quality large print books including:
Romances, Mysteries, Classics
General Fiction
Non Fiction and Westerns

Special interest titles available in large print are:
The Little Oxford Dictionary
Music Book
Song Book
Hymn Book
Service Book

Also available from us courtesy of Oxford University Press:
Young Readers' Dictionary
(large print edition)
Young Readers' Thesaurus
(large print edition)

For further information or a free brochure, please contact us at:
Ulverscroft Large Print Books Ltd.,
The Green, Bradgate Road, Anstey,
Leicester, LE7 7FU, England.
Tel: (00 44) **0116 236 4325**
Fax: (00 44) **0116 234 0205**

)